Services, Marketing and Management

Services, Marketing and Management

Audrey Gilmore

SAGE Publications
London • Thousand Oaks • New Delhi

First published 2003

Apart from any fair dealing for the purposes of research or
private study, or criticism or review, as permitted under
the Copyright, Designs and Patents Act, 1988, this publication
may be reproduced, stored or transmitted in any form,
or by any means, only with the prior permission in writing
of the publishers, or in the case of reprographic reproduction,
in accordance with the terms of licences issued by the
Copyright Licensing Agency. Enquiries concerning
reproduction outside those terms should be sent to the
publishers.

 SAGE Publications Ltd
6 Bonhill Street
London EC2A 4PU

SAGE Publications Inc
2455 Teller Road
Thousand Oaks, California 91320

SAGE Publications India Pvt Ltd
B-42, Panchsheel Enclave
Post Box 4109
New Delhi 100 017

British Library Cataloguing in Publication data

A catalogue record for this book is available
from the British Library

ISBN 0 7619 4157 6
ISBN 0 7619 4158 4 (pbk)

Library of Congress Control Number: available

Typeset by C&M Digitals (P) Ltd., Chennai, India
Printed and bound in Great Britain by Athenaeum Press, Gateshead

Contents

PART ONE

UNDERLYING THEMES

1

Underpinning Concepts of Services Marketing Management

Services are all around us – as consumers we use services every day. The growth in the service economy is widely recognized and increasingly contributes to the economic development of many regions. Although the service sector accounts for most of the new job growth in developed countries, the dominance of the service sector is not limited to highly developed nations. Many services such as those in the tourism sector contribute very heavily to developing economies also. By their very nature, services are diverse and therefore have often been difficult to define. However there have been many attempts to describe services and there is an overall recognition of what they are and how they contribute to marketing offerings and the economy.

This chapter considers the underpinning concepts of service management. It briefly outlines the history and origins of services marketing and management and provides some background discussion explaining the debates that have led to the identification of the now widely accepted characteristics of services. Also, the differences between goods and services will be discussed and lead to a description of how the characteristics of services impact on the different elements of the service offering. Then a description of dimensions that form the component parts of conceptual frameworks and models for services marketing is presented. Finally, the most frequently used conceptual frameworks are discussed in some depth, encapsulating the chief characteristics of services in order to provide the underpinnings for the focus of this text on service management issues in the context of service organizations and different sectors.

SCOPE OF SERVICES MARKETING MANAGEMENT

Most frequently, a service has been described as an act, a process and a performance. For example, activities such as accountancy, banking and hairdressing can be recognized as being predominantly service based. Also services can be more widely described as economic activities that create 'added value' and provide benefits for customers (consumers or organizations). Today most products include some element of service.

However, a service 'product' or a service company can be differentiated from customer service that is provided by all types of companies such as manufacturers and IT companies as well as service companies. Customer service usually entails answering questions, handling complaints, dealing with queries, taking orders, the provision of maintenance and repairs and other after sales services. Although customer service is inherent in services marketing it is carried out as an additional function by many industries. There are many products that depend upon service-based activities to give them a competitive advantage. For example, someone buying a new computer may be attracted to the store where s/he will also receive useful information and guidance from a helpful staff member at the store, a hotline service for installing programmes, and other services, in addition to their preferred computer. Recognizing the value of this to potential customers, computer store service managers will aim to offer many additional useful services for customers. This illustrates the value and relevance of understanding and recognizing the importance that service issues have on today's society.

A service business is one where the perceived value of the offering to the buyer is determined more by the service rendered than the product offered. In this way the nature and scope of services pose different challenges for managers in service businesses. Such businesses include those that provide an almost entirely intangible offering, such as legal services, healthcare, and cleaning services and businesses that offer both services and products such as restaurants and retail outlets.

The definition and scope of the service concept is wide and can mean any or all of the following:

Table 1.1 *Scope of services*

Service activities	Service as a concept
Customer service	A service organization
Service-based activities	As a core product
Added value activities	As an augmented product
	As product support
	As an act

- Service as an organization, that is the entire business or not-for-profit structure that resides within the service sector. For example, a restaurant, an insurance company, a charity.

- Service as core product, that is, the commercial outputs of a service organization such as a bank account, an insurance policy or a holiday.

- Service as product augmentation, that is any peripheral activity designed to enhance the delivery of a core product. For example, provision of a courtesy car, complimentary coffee at the hairdressers.

- Service as product support, that is, any product- or customer-oriented activity that takes place after the point of delivery. For example monitoring activities, a repair service, up-dating facilities.

- Service as an act, that is service as a mode of behaviour such as helping out, giving advice.

The scope and concept of services are summarized in Table 1.1.

However from a market or consumer point of view the relative importance of different components of the service offering can range vastly from one customer to another. So a service must be considered from the point of view of many types of customers. For example, two people may pay the same amount for a service but may be paying for different aspects of the service. A business person may dine regularly in an expensive, up-market restaurant because of the convenience to their place of work and the perceived 'status' of entertaining guests there. Other customers of the same restaurant may eat there regularly because of the excellent food, the modern décor and menu choice.

The service sector includes a wide range of industries such as the hospitality industry, the tourism industry, financial services, charities, the arts and public utilities, as shown in Table 1.2. Some service sectors such as charities and the arts operate in non-profit-making operations, other services such as the hospitality and financial services operate in competitive, profit-making environments. Many service industries such as tourism include large

Table 1.2 *Service industries*

Hospitality
Tourism
Financial services
Charities
Arts
Public utility services
Health services
Education services
Professional services

international companies and small independently and locally operated companies. Some examples of larger international service companies include airlines, hotel chains, banking and telecommunications. Smaller operators in the service sector include independent restaurants, business-to-business services, taxis and local tourism services. Therefore we can conclude that the service sector is a very diverse one with many companies operating within the context of very different agendas and sense of purpose.

ORIGINS AND BACKGROUND TO SERVICES MARKETING MANAGEMENT

Services marketing is founded upon the fundamental concepts of marketing. The development of service marketing concepts over the years has evolved in accordance with the philosophy of customer orientation. A marketing orientation puts the customer at the core of an organization's purpose and activity. In many organizations the philosophy is manifested in terms such as 'the customer is king' and 'everything the organization does is with the customer in mind'. For example, British Airways used the slogan 'putting people first' in the 1980s, United Airlines used 'you are the boss' and Burger King invited customers to 'have it your way'. However a more rational and business-oriented approach to service marketing encompasses the philosophy of marketing orientation by concentrating on looking after customers and maximizing their satisfaction in the context of competitive offerings while remaining profitable as an organization.

The philosophy of reaching the customer more precisely has dictated marketing activity throughout its history. In the early part of the twentieth century, trading in 'commodity services' was one form of services marketing. Indeed, this notion is recognized by Regan (1963) as the origin of services marketing when debating the 'service revolution' at that time. In reinforcing that a revolution was taking place in the early 1960s, Regan and others (Judd, 1964; Rathmell, 1966, 1974) set about trying to define services in this new domain. This debate recognized and anticipated the emergence of more

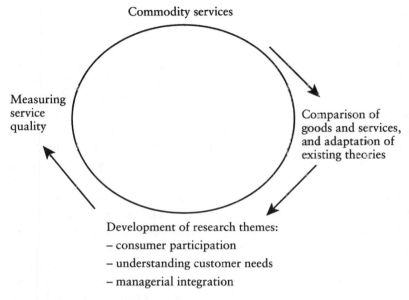

FIGURE 1.1   Early development of services research

formal and autonomous services marketing in areas such as transportation, communication, education and retailing. Attempts were made at this time to redefine services and divisions of service activities in a way that would allow descriptions of services in a wider context. This created the base for future research and discussion. The early development of services literature and research is illustrated in Figure 1.1.

The early service literature focused on defining and refining the specific characteristics of services, the different classifications of the service product and the scope and complexity of services. These definitions and refinements were important in the quest for how services should be marketed and managed. Much of this earlier work emphasized the comparison of services with goods or physical products and how existing marketing theories could be adapted for services. Identifying and clarifying definitions and classifications of services dominated research in services for a considerable time during the 1960s and early 1970s.

By the end of the 1970s research in the services domain had grown and become a body of work in its own right. An international study, commissioned by the Marketing Science Institute of Cambridge, Massachusetts and authored by Languard et al. (1981) represented the most comprehensive analysis and description of services marketing at that time. The study focused on marketing issues that were considered to be central to the management of consumer service business. The findings, based on evidence from several large service companies and surveys of both consumers and managers. linked three separate themes: consumer participation in service production and delivery, management's ability to understand customers' needs and the relationship between operations, marketing and personnel functions in a service organization. These issues became recurrent topics for service researchers over the following decades.

While the services marketing literature has answered many of the issues raised as important research areas in the early 1980s, it has evolved and progressed into new and more integrated services marketing approaches and concepts. However, during the 1980s some of the most referenced and comprehensive empirical confirmation of the main concepts and frameworks occurred. In many instances empirical studies helped to both reinforce concepts and to create new concepts and theories designed to contribute to more effective and efficient services marketing, for example, the work of Parasuraman et al. (1985, 1988) in developing the SERVQUAL measurement technique (discussed in Chapter 2). The research underpinning the SERVQUAL instrument was widely accepted and disseminated in the 1980s. By the mid-1990s, however, the wide and sometimes indiscriminate use of the SERVQUAL mechanism for many contexts was so strong that some service researchers began to argue that many other aspects of services marketing and management had been neglected in its wake. Indeed research in services marketing in the late 1980s and early 1990s was dominated by the adaptation of the SERVQUAL model to almost every service application possible. Eventually studies became more focused on developing more appropriate models for different service situations and management priorities. Many of these conceptual developments are discussed later in the chapter.

SERVICES MARKETING IS DIFFERENT

Central to the debate about marketing tools for services are the characteristics of services, how these characteristics can be refined for different contexts (for example retailing services or not-for-profit services), the tangible and intangible aspects of the service offering and whether there is a difference between services and goods marketing.

In 1963 Regan highlighted that a large and growing market for commodities existed in the development of service systems. In his early work he considered some definitions of services and their characteristics. He recognized that the potential development of the service revolution depended upon the recognition of markets for business expansion, the development of service technologies, consideration of limits and impersonalization of services, the 'massification' of taste and the proliferation of services. In this early work, Regan was forecasting how different market segments might, and indeed did, emerge for different types and levels of service.

Others such as Judd (1968) considered the characteristics of services marketing in a specific context. He studied the similarities and differences in product and service retailing by examining the marketing required in terms of product and service development, sales effort and pricing. He concluded that although there were substantial similarities between product and service retailing, the extent of differences between them could not be dismissed as unimportant.

There was also some development and discussion of how concepts and strategies more relevant to services than goods could be developed. Shostack's (1977) article on breaking free from product marketing illustrated the differences between goods and service products by using a continuum to highlight the predominantly intangible nature of services. Shostack's continuum illustrated the range of tangibility in different types of products and services from a tangible product such as salt, through fast food outlets, with both tangible and intangible components, to predominantly intangible services such as teaching.

In addition, Shostack's work illustrated how some services could be standardized for efficient delivery by breaking down a service into separate tasks. Further development of this work led to the creation of a 'blueprint' to illustrate the different processes in delivering a simple service such as a shoe-shine operation (Shostack, 1981). The blueprint is based on illustrating the different actions and the time involved for each action in delivering a shoe-shine service. Each action in the service delivery has a model execution time allocated to it, with a certain amount of tolerance. For example, the whole shoe-shine operation should take two minutes, but may take up to three minutes longer if the service is not straightforward. There may be some variance in delivering the service in some cases where shoes may need to be scraped clean of soil before brushing or where the wrong colour of polish is used and has to be removed before applying polish again.

Inherent in all these earlier studies was the desire to reach a general agreement on the characteristics and component parts of a service. These characteristics are now widely agreed and cited in most service texts and will be discussed later in this chapter. However there was one final debate about the relevance of service characteristics for all service situations. This was articulated by Middleton in 1983 who rejected the idea of contrasting products and services marketing per se and contended that service characteristics could be applied to both services and goods depending upon their specific classifications. For his argument he outlined the similarities between goods and services marketing in the context of convenience or mass-produced products. He advocated that the mass production of products has many similarities with the mass production of services. That is, fast-moving consumer goods (FMCGs) marketing principles and fast-moving consumer services (FMCSs) marketing principles do not have to be very different. This argument is useful in recognizing that relatively 'simple' products (such as FMCGs) have many similarities and can be marketed in a similar way to relatively 'simple' services (such as FMCSs). Indeed many of the characteristics inherent in marketing FMCGs such as the emphasis on location, easy accessibility and availability for the mass marketing and the importance of standardizing the service process and delivery can be seen in the marketing of FMCSs such as McDonald's. However marketing management and activity need to be very different for more complex services.

UNIQUE SERVICE FEATURES AND RESULTING MARKETING MANAGEMENT ISSUES

The services marketing mix is the set of tools and activities available to an organization to shape the nature of its offer to customers. Goods marketers are familiar with the product, price, promotion and place aspects of the marketing mix. An analysis and description of the marketing mix elements was carried out by Borden (1964) based on a study of manufacturing industry at a time when the importance of services to the economy was considered to be relatively insignificant.

For services marketing, the distinguishing features or characteristics of services are important in the design of an appropriate marketing mix. The identification of these characteristics was the concern of much of the earlier research and conceptual development of services marketing. The core characteristics are now widely recognized as intangibility, inseparability, perishability and heterogeneity. These are defined below.

Intangibility

Even though many services include tangible aspects such as an airline seat, a classroom, a restaurant table and food the service performance leading to a customer's experience is intangible. The benefits of buying a product are based on its physical characteristics whereas the benefits of buying a service are from the nature of the performance. In comparison to physical goods, services cannot be stored or readily displayed. They are difficult to communicate, cannot be protected through patents and prices are difficult to set. The intangible nature of services often means that customers have difficulty in evaluating and comparing services. As a result they may use price as a basis for assessing quality and they may place greater emphasis on personal information sources. This all leads to consumers having higher levels of perceived risk. The intangibility of services makes them very different from the traditional product mix that is frequently analysed in terms of tangible design properties. Similarly, physical distribution management may not be an important element of the 'place' mix decisions because there is no tangible product.

Inseparability

Because services are processes, deeds or acts, customers are involved in the production of a service. Also other consumers may be involved in the production environment and centralized mass production is difficult, particularly if the service is more complex or customized. For most services both the buyer and the seller need to be at the same place at the same time for the service to occur. Because centralized mass production is difficult, consumers often have to travel to the point of service production. For example, it is hard to imagine a haircut without both customer and hairdresser or barber present. Also promotion by the service personnel may take place. For a bank clerk or hairdresser the manner in which the service is produced is an essential element of the total promotion of the service.

Often consumers are co-consumers of a service with a small or large number of others. Thus the behaviour and attitude of other consumers may impact upon the nature and experience of a service. For example, a loud or over-demanding customer can deflect service staff's attention and impact on the quality of service delivery to other consumers. In this circumstance it may be difficult for the service providers to control the quality and consistency of the service, unless staff have been trained to deal with such situations in a precise and effective manner.

Perishability

Given the intangible nature of services, they cannot be inventoried, stored, warehoused or re-used. A lawyer cannot store parts of his or her knowledge for others to use while the lawyer is in court or on holiday. The hairdresser cannot store haircuts so that when a rush occurs on a Saturday morning all customers can have their hair cut at once. Thus the availability of enough opportunities for service delivery at relevant times is important for service managers.

Heterogeneity

Again the intangible nature of services means that standardization and quality are difficult to control. Given that people are involved in providing the actual services in most sectors and that people are unlikely to operate as reliably and constantly as machines it is often difficult to measure and control quality. Therefore it may be difficult for customers to evaluate quality and for employers to measure and control quality. It can be done but is more difficult than measuring and controlling product quality. Also evaluations often depend largely on attitude, opinions and expectations of customers and potential customers.

CONCEPTUALIZING THE SERVICE MARKETING MIX

Given the differentiating characteristics of services, the concept of the marketing mix or overall offering is more complex for services marketing. Some consideration of what might be entailed in the service offering and how it can be designed or conceptualized is outlined here.

The 'product' dimension of a service is predominantly intangible, therefore for marketers and managers to identify, define and illustrate what the service entails it may need tangible surrogates. These surrogates may include different tools to help customers and managers to get to know the product, to distinguish between product features and product benefits and to identify when variations are significant enough to be regarded as having created a different or distinct service. Also the product dimension will be heavily dependent upon the human influence, on how it is delivered and perceived.

The 'pricing' element is very closely associated with perceptions of value. Customers' perceptions of value may be different and the intangible nature of the service product will make it difficult to evaluate. Therefore for managers, costing is difficult and imprecise. Furthermore many services are public services or charities and in such cases there may be no direct price.

The 'promotion' dimension of the marketing mix is very closely related to the product features. Given that there is no physical product to promote, marketers and managers rely heavily on promoting an 'image'. And because service products cannot be stored the promotion message needs to focus on spreading as well as creating demand.

The 'place or distribution' aspect of the marketing mix is, in some ways, a 'virtual' concept. There is no physical distribution system. However because services are performed they need to have a suitable environment for that performance. Therefore the location of premises is vital. If the service has multiple outlets or is delivered in more than one geographical region then the effective management of agents is important. This is always difficult and even more so when the product is intangible.

Closely related to the place and distribution of the marketing mix is the 'physical evidence' aspect of the service experience. This is important in services marketing and management because services have a physical environment or site which may encompass a building, shape, lighting, means of orienting the customer, queues, crowding and methods of stimulating interest and participation. These aspects of physical evidence also provide tangible clues for customers to evaluate the service, and will contribute to the overall 'image' and 'ambience'.

The service 'process' takes account of how the service is delivered, for example, the policies and procedures that ensure an efficient and expert service. Management of the process entails overseeing the pre-, during and post-service delivery experience of the customer, and ensuring managerial and operational 'attention to detail' in all aspects of service delivery.

Inherent in the service marketing mix is 'managing people'. There are many different players or people involved in service delivery. Often people are 'the service'. Customers are also people and other customers and their interactions can have a large impact on the overall service delivery. The different levels of staff and their interactions with customers are important and need to be managed. In order to manage this aspect of the marketing mix some consideration needs to be given to the appropriate selection and training of staff and how to manage and communicate with the different levels of staff and management (often referred to as internal marketing, discussed in Chapter 7). Over time people may need up-to-date training, specialized training programmes and other encouragement for developing job-related skills and competencies (as discussed in Chapter 8).

In considering the services marketing mix it is important to consider where all the interfaces of people management may occur in a service organization. For example, there is the interface between management and customers, the staff–customer interface, various levels of management interface within an organization and the management–staff interface. All of these interfaces require appropriate communication and interaction to ensure effective and efficient service delivery to customers. The nature of these interactions will have implications for service delivery and how services are managed. For example, how can quality be ensured for each service delivery, how can a service 'product' be standardized for each customer and how can services be delivered consistently each time. Such service delivery and customer encounter demands often create dilemmas for managers and service deliverers. These issues have been conceptualized using different frameworks and many researchers and managers have developed ways of operationalizing these frameworks in attempts to improve service management and delivery.

SERVICES MARKETING DIMENSIONS

The multi-dimensional nature of services is a feature of the service literature and the focus of many studies of services. Over the previous decades, many works have aimed to identify and describe some dimensions of service quality for specific and general service contexts (for example, Gilmore and Carson, 1993; Gronroos, 1984; LeBlanc and Nguyen, 1988; Parasuraman et al., 1985, 1988). All of these relate to dimensions inherent in many of the conceptual models that are used to help grasp and understand services better. For example, some frequently used models explicitly recognise and illustrate different aspects of services marketing. These are discussed later in this chapter.

First, some of the most widely recognized dimensions of services marketing inherent in service management, delivery and evaluation are discussed. These dimensions include technical, functional, tangible, intangible, physical facilities and service-scapes, accessibility, reliability, responsiveness, communication, competence, courtesy, credibility, security, empathy, and understanding the customer and image. Many of these dimensions originate from work focusing on managing service quality and were chosen to reflect that consistent conformance to customer expectations and delivering 'fitness for purpose' is important in addition to satisfying the customer.

Technical dimensions are the 'what' or the instrumental dimensions of service delivery. These relate to the more tangible aspects involved in the service package. For example, the hotel customer will expect a comfortable room to sleep in, the restaurant customer will expect a meal and so on. The technical outcome of a service experience is what the customer receives as a result of his or her interactions with a service firm. This is only one aspect of the overall service delivery. Because services are produced through interaction with consumers the quality of technical dimensions alone will not complete the total service experience. Other dimensions such as how the service is delivered will also be important.

Functional dimensions are the 'how' dimensions of service delivery. The accessibility of a service (the availability of a hairdresser or a consultant at a convenient time), the appearance of the service delivery staff, how they behave and what they say will feature very strongly in how the service is delivered. Other consumers experiencing the service at the same time can influence these dimensions. So the service process or the 'how' of service delivery can be different from one experience to the next but is very important in a consumer's overall assessment of a service.

Tangible dimensions relate to the more concrete evidence of a service actually taking place. Tangible dimensions include the physical evidence of the service. For example, the service environment, the appearance of the service personnel, the equipment and facilities used to carry out the service and any other physical representations of the service, such as an airline ticket or a plastic credit card.

Intangible dimensions are usually the core aspects of the service, the actual process, deed, act, performance central to the service delivery. The intangible dimension is the haircut, the advice received from a consultant and other aspects of the service activity. For example, any aspect that contributes to how the customer is treated and processed through the service delivery.

Physical facilities and 'service-scapes' refer to the immediate environment where a service activity takes place. For example, the layout, furniture, facilities and overall quality of the surroundings evident in a doctor's waiting room or the equipment and facilities available in a bank will have an impact on a consumer's overall perception of the service encounter.

Accessibility refers to the approachability, availability and ease of contact with the service company. It will include the ease with which the service company may be reached by telephone or e-mail, the waiting time to receive or experience the service, the opening hours or hours of operation and the location of the service.

Reliability entails the consistency of service performance and dependability. It includes the requirement of a firm to perform the service right first time (often referred to as having 'zero defects') and to live up to its promises to customers. For example, it will include providing accurate bills and performing the service at the designated time.

Responsiveness concerns the willingness and readiness of staff to deliver the service and respond to customers' requirements. It may involve mailing information or transaction details immediately, calling customers back promptly when promised, and giving prompt service.

Communication involves communicating with customers in a language they understand, listening to their requests and responding appropriately. Common areas of customer communication include 'educating' the customer about a service, providing some interpretation of a particular issue or providing guidance with a specific service problem. For example, explaining the service outcome and process and how much it will cost, assuring the customer that their problem will be resolved, explaining different levels of service and different costs.

Competence refers to the ability of the service company to actually deliver the service. It entails ensuring that staff possess the appropriate skills and knowledge to perform the service including the knowledge and skill of the contract personnel, operational support personnel and the overall capability of the service firm.

Courtesy encompasses the politeness, respect, consideration and friendliness of contact personnel and service delivery staff. It includes staff and management having consideration for consumers' property and being properly prepared for customers.

Credibility concerns the trustworthiness, believability and honesty experienced during the service encounter. Wider issues will also have an impact on the overall perception of organizational credibility; these include reputation of the company and its staff, and other businesses or stakeholders associated with the company, in addition to the personal characteristics of the contact personnel.

Security relates to how secure, free from danger, risk or doubt consumers feel during interaction with the service. In a service situation this will impact upon both physical safety and financial confidentiality.

Empathy and understanding the customer is one of the most intangible dimensions in practice. It involves understanding and having empathy with individual customer needs and requirements and responding to these in an appropriate manner.

Image is an important dimension in services marketing. The concept of image is as a mental representation of reality sustained by an individual or group. This dimension entails the combined experience and assessment of many other factors and is inextricably linked with both the whole service experience and previous knowledge of the company. Image is something that signifies customers', managers' and service deliverers' beliefs and understanding of a phenomenon or situation. This mental perception or image held by specific people or groups can be either a good or bad representation of reality but it is always important because it guides behaviour. People act or react because of their own perception of reality whether that perception is fair or not (Normann, 1984). Image can be a very powerful weapon with which to exert influence, but it is a double-edged sword. It has a tendency to reinforce itself and once established, becomes self-fulfilling. In this way it has an enormous impact upon communication and how communication is received. Thus it is easy to see why 'image management' is so important to service organizations. As services are less tangible than physical products and difficult to examine before purchase, customers' perceptions or image of the service and the company are vital.

The image that a company creates will be determined by the nature of the service, how the company is organized, its culture, employees and the users. This means that the management and delivery of the entire service package needs to be carefully co-ordinated and integrated. It is therefore important for a service company to be organized in such a way as to allow efficient and effective service delivery and that all the people involved are competent and willing to carry out their service roles. This emphasizes the importance of excellent services management, the effective use of internal marketing and communication and the development of managerial and staff competence. These managerial topics are discussed further in Part II.

All of the service dimensions outlined above contribute to a variety of conceptual models for services, many of which will be described in the next section. They have been used as fundamental and underpinning frameworks to be included and adapted to facilitate the clearer understanding of services in different contexts. The purpose in being able to define and describe service quality dimensions is to help researchers, managers, and anyone working in service delivery to recognize the complexity of the service and to be able to deliver it and evaluate it in terms of its overall appropriateness, consistency and quality.

CONCEPTUAL MODELS OR FRAMEWORKS FOR SERVICES MARKETING

Conceptual models and frameworks are very useful aids for visualizing service dimensions and helping to illustrate, describe and explain interrelationships, interactions and influences upon service dimensions. Some of the conceptual models or frameworks used in services were originally created to help researchers and practitioners to mentally grasp, understand, develop and explain the complexity of the service situation. The earlier work of classifying and defining services has provided the groundwork and basis for the development of conceptual models. These models have been developed and further refined by focusing on aspects of service delivery, quality, customer satisfaction, and managerial focus and through exploration of services in different contexts.

Many conceptual frameworks address the managerial aspects of services and how services are or should be delivered. Indeed many frameworks operate at a general level and need to be adapted and refined for more specific situations. Essentially the broad concepts are founded upon the characteristics of services and how these impact upon service management and delivery, managing people and the service environment. Much work has focused on determining how service concepts can be different in a variety of circumstances and in measuring the impact on service delivery and services management. Mainly conceptual frameworks feature three broad areas:

1 A focus on the scope and range of service experienced by customers.
2 A focus on the problems facing service managers and how they can be conceptualized at the individual firm or industry and at a general level.
3 A focus on the development of new concepts for use by service marketers or modification of existing concepts and approaches for different service contexts.

In all of these areas service researchers and practitioners have tried to clarify and contribute to management decision processes in order to identify and illuminate 'types' of decisions that all service managers will encounter.

Some of the earlier conceptual models or frameworks were used as a starting point for integrating the complex nature of customer expectations in the context of the processual and varied nature of service delivery. In addition a variety of different service dimensions outlined in the previous section are central to conceptual models and frameworks and can be defined from either a consumer or managerial perspective for different contexts. Some of the key foci of service models are described below.

Conceptualizing the service 'offering'

In traditional marketing texts where most discussion relates to goods marketing, the concept of the augmented product is often used to illustrate the idea of a product package or bundle of benefits included when a customer buys a physical good. Adaptation of this concept for services takes account of the entire service product, process and experience. Given that the basic product concept of a service is its intangibility, it can be difficult for a customer to grasp its meaning and context unless the whole interaction between customer and producer is managed carefully and an integrated service is delivered. The service interaction may involve a distribution system and a form of personal marketing communication. Such aspects are often referred to as the consumer–producer relationship. In services, people are important in both producing and consuming the service product package or bundle of benefits.

A service cannot be easily specified or presented before purchase so a physical product or tangible cue is often used to illustrate exactly what is on offer or what is going to be achieved as a result of receiving the service. Consideration of the service on offer in this way will allow customers to arrive at a description or understanding of the 'service package'. Often one of the aspects or dimensions of the service package will be clearly predominant while others are more peripheral or ancillary to the service. For example, in an airline service, the actual transport of a customer from London to Hong Kong is probably more important than efficient checking-in procedures and the cleanliness of the plane, even though these also contribute to the overall service. Thus in services, we can often distinguish between a core service and other ancillary, augmented or secondary services, although they are all part of the service package.

In some contexts, the distinction between core and secondary services is not always so clear. Services operating in competitive markets may offer a very similar core service but add different secondary aspects in order to be seen to be doing something different from their competitors. For example, airlines may offer a wider range or different business class facilities to attract customers away from their competitors. This focus on secondary aspects of the service package only works if the service package in question includes all the elements, both core and ancillary or secondary, that their customers expect; and the extent to which each of these elements meets the needs of their customers. If it does work, the additional secondary aspects may become integral to the customer's perception of the core service.

Figure 1.2 illustrates the different aspects of the whole service offering for passengers flying from London to Hong Kong. The core aspect of the service is being transported from A to B or London to Hong Kong in this example. The secondary aspect of the service package encompasses a number of services such as regular and fast check-in facilities, cleanliness of plane and departure lounge, airport guidance for customers, helpfulness of airport and airline staff, entertainment/in-flight movies, catering service, drinks on request and games for children.

Concepts of tangible and intangible dimensions

Some of the earlier attempts at conceptualizing the dimensions of services focused on the positioning of tangible and intangible elements within the product/service offering (Bateson, 1979; Shostack, 1977). Indeed many researchers in service marketing have used the tangible/intangible dimensions as a basis for conceptualizing different types of services, simple to complex. For example Shostack (1977) used it to differentiate simple product/service packages from more complex product/service packages. Often these tangible and intangible dimensions will have an impact on how customers perceive a service/product offering and how it will be experienced and measured.

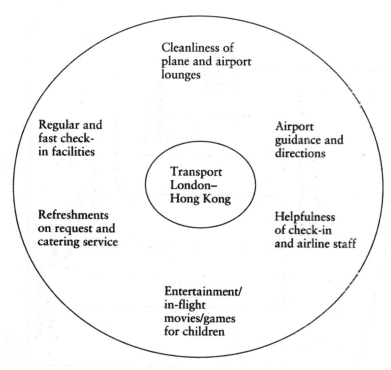

FIGURE 1.2   Core and secondary aspects of an airline service product

Consideration of both tangible and intangible dimensions of services underpins how customers perceive and evaluate services and how service delivery and customer satisfaction can be conceptualized and measured. Much of this work is based on measuring two aspects of customers' requirements. Swan and Combs (1976) argue that customer expectations have two dimensions, as having both instrumental and psychological aspects. Both Gronroos (1984) and Parasuraman et al. (1985) built upon the notion of instrumental and psychological customer requirements as a basis for their studies. The 'instrumental' dimensions can be compared to the 'technical' aspects that Gronroos describes as the 'what' of service delivery. The psychological dimensions of expectations relate to the 'functional' aspects or 'how' of service delivery and include the more intangible aspects such as customer feelings and perceptions about the service performance.

A further development based on the argument that customer expectations have both 'technical' and 'functional' components was that both could be influenced by and contribute to the company image (Gronroos, 1984). This idea recognizes how important it is for service managers to create good 'functional' quality as well as 'technical' quality and so contribute to the overall image of the service package and service company.

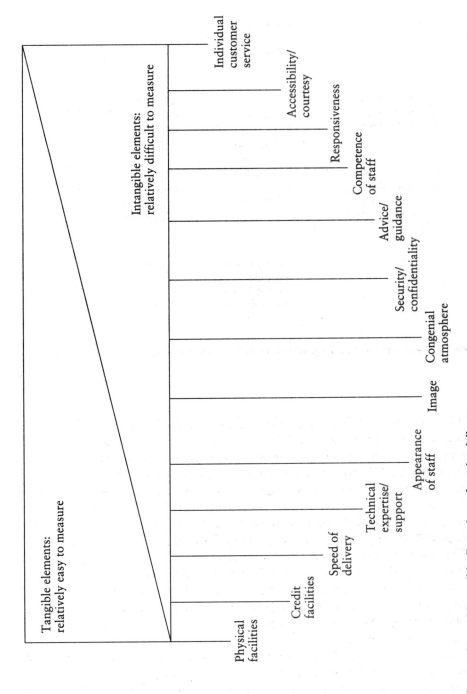

FIGURE 1.3 Tangible and intangible dimensions of service delivery

One outcome of Parasuraman et al.'s study in 1985 recommended that service dimensions should include: access, communication, competence, courtesy, credibility, reliability, responsiveness, security, tangibles and understanding the customer. However their further studies reduced these to five dimensions (Parasuraman et al., 1988): tangibles, reliability, responsiveness, assurance and empathy. Both these frameworks are inextricably based upon the concept of tangible and intangible dimensions of services.

Sometimes in service industries there is a tendency to concentrate on the more tangible aspects of the service delivery because they are easier to measure. In doing so, the intangible dimensions may be neglected. The interrelationships between the tangible and intangible elements of service quality are illustrated in Figure 1.3. The range of dimensions from tangible to intangible highlights the large task that service managers may have in trying to integrate all aspects of the service delivery in order to achieve a more balanced delivery of service quality.

There are many examples of how this theme has been developed in studies of services in different industry or company contexts. For example, a variety of studies in hotel services have identified that important tangible and intangible combinations of service dimensions include physical quality, corporate quality and interactive quality (Lehtinen and Lehtinen, 1982; Lehtinen et al., 1994). Also LeBlanc and Nguyen's (1988) work in financial services conceptualized service quality in terms of the tangible and intangible combinations of a company's corporate image, customer expectations and the perceived quality of the service.

Concept of the performance gap

Because of the heavy involvement of people in planning, delivering and consuming services there are many opportunities for the service delivery to go wrong. Often services have been planned ineffectively, the service deliverers may not be trained properly or are neglectful in delivering the service or consumers may not know what to expect or how to respond to service delivery. All of these scenarios will contribute to a poor service being delivered or complete service failure. All human error in service delivery will result in a performance gap and consumers receiving a poorer service than expected.

A gap model focusing on the identification of the key components of service quality management and delivery based upon customer expectations and perceptions and the service delivery associated with these was created by Parasuraman et al. (1985, 1988). The basic premise of the model was that a gap often exists between customer expectations and perceptions and the actual delivery of the service. This overall gap can be influenced by four different gaps that can occur between customers' and managers' perceptions of service quality.

The gap model provided the basis of the SERVQUAL instrument that was developed to measure service quality performance. The SERVQUAL

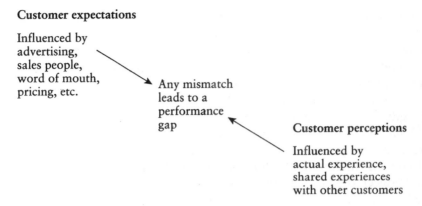

Customer expectations

Influenced by
advertising,
sales people,
word of mouth,
pricing, etc.

Any mismatch
leads to a
performance
gap

Customer perceptions

Influenced by
actual experience,
shared experiences
with other customers

FIGURE 1.4   Performance gap

model was taken up by many researchers and used to replicate the original study in different contexts. Research using the framework can be grouped into two broad areas. Primarily, the framework was used to gather empirical data to measure service quality in a specific industry. Second, research focused on the issue of quality and how to increase customer satisfaction by improving the quality of a service. The SERVQUAL instrument was designed to compare customer expectations with their perceptions of a service. This has been a major focus of attention in the measurement of service quality from the early 1980s until the present day. Indeed the SERVQUAL measurement tool has been adopted by a wide range of industries including hotels, tyre retailers, dental services, car servicing, travel and tourism, higher education and professional services such as accountancy firms and architects (Buttle, 1996).

Concepts relating to customer expectations, perceptions and attitudes

Other researchers focused their service quality management research on the development of different conceptual frameworks and models based on customer expectations, perceptions and attitudes. For example Cronin and Taylor (1992) advocated that service quality be conceptualized as an attitude. Based on overcoming the perceived problems with SERVQUAL, they developed a performance-based conceptualization of service quality and called it SERVPERF. As a result of their research they suggested that service quality is an antecedent of consumer satisfaction and that customer satisfaction exerts a stronger influence on purchase intentions than service quality. Therefore they concluded that service managers might need to emphasize total customer satisfaction programmes, instead of designing strategies to focus solely on service quality, in order to ensure that customers are satisfied. They surmised that perhaps consumers do not necessarily buy the highest quality service and

Table 1.3 *Service quality, customer satisfaction and perceived quality*

Service quality impacts upon customer satisfaction

Customer satisfaction is influenced by presence of other customers

Perceived quality is influenced by contact personnel, environment, tangible dimensions

that convenience, price or availability may enhance satisfaction while not actually affecting consumers' perceptions of service quality. A further outcome of their study suggested that the scale items used to define service quality in one industry might be different in another – a point raised by other researchers in services marketing. Studies of customer expectations, perceptions and attitudes also provided the bedrock for research on service quality and satisfaction, discussed in the next section.

Other conceptualizations recognize that customer *expectations* and the degree of customer satisfaction are influenced by the presence of other customers while *perceived quality* is based upon contact personnel, physical environment and tangible dimensions. Although many models and frameworks for service quality use similar service dimensions they are used with different priorities and emphasis depending upon the focus of the researcher, whether interested in service dimensions, customer expectations, perceptions or attitudes, and the context of where the empirical research is to be carried out.

Service quality and customer satisfaction

There has been considerable debate about the concepts of customer satisfaction and service quality. Each has its own research background and theory development. Service quality is defined in the literature as the ability of an organization to meet or exceed customer expectations. Customer expectations have been defined as the desires or wants of consumers or what they feel a service provider should offer. This definition of expectations differs from the way the term is used in the service quality management and the consumer satisfaction literature. Expectations in the satisfaction literature have been operationalized as predictions of service performance while expectations in the service quality literature are interpreted as what the service provider should offer. Different authors use different meanings for the concept of expectations both between and within satisfaction and service quality studies. Different types of expectations might include ideal, expected, deserved and the minimum tolerable to customers. It is clearly important to know with which type of expectations the customer compares the performance of the particular product or service. Some types of expectations or standards seem to be better than others at explaining satisfaction. In addition relationships between performance and satisfaction may change depending on the standard used and the consumer may also use several standards simultaneously (Bolfing and

Woodruff, 1988; Tse and Wilton, 1988). So this is a very complex area where there are many diverse factors and perspectives within the literature.

In the services domain there is general agreement that consumers may have both desired and adequate service level expectations and that there is a zone of tolerance between these levels (Parasuraman et al., 1991). The service quality literature has, to a large extent, emphasized that the measurement of performance is essentially a measure of perceived performance. The customer's perception of performance counts rather than the 'reality' of performance. In effect, it has been argued that perceptions are reality as far as service quality is concerned (Christopher et al., 1991).

Perceived service quality has been defined as the discrepancy between what the customer feels that a service provider should offer and his or her perception of what the service firm actually offers (Parasuraman et al., 1988). Clearly perceived performance will be a major contributory factor in influencing overall satisfaction and intention to re-buy. However there are some important differences between 'perceived service quality' and 'satisfaction'. Perceived service quality is defined by the customer's attitude or overall judgement of a service over time while satisfaction is considered to be connected to a specific transaction (Bitner, 1990; Parasuraman et al., 1988). Some satisfaction studies have measured expectations at the same time as perceptions. A potential problem with this is that the expectation scales will be affected by the actual offer and will not represent customer expectations before they consume the product.

Customer loyalty

More recently consumer research has considered the construct of customer loyalty. There is general agreement that different stages exist in the development of a customer's loyalty towards a product or service. Recent academic and practical interest in customer loyalty has been fuelled by company loyalty programmes that are often based on repeat buying behaviour (Dick and Basu, 1994; Palmer, 1996).

The most widely accepted definition of loyalty is that customer loyalty is the behavioural outcome of a customer's preference for a particular brand or a selection of similar brands, over a period of time, that is the result of an evaluative decision-making process (based on Jacoby and Kyner, 1973). The customer's attitude towards potential moderators of a repeat patronage relationship are based on social norms and situational factors. More recently Oliver (1997) summarized the work in customer loyalty to include cognition, affect and behavioural intention. This recognizes the key issues of commitment, preference and consistency while acknowledging the dynamic nature of the marketing environment and situational influences. Building on the three-phase model of Jacoby and Kyner (1973) and the later work of Dick and Basu (1994), Oliver has identified a fourth loyalty phase. The first three phases lead to a deeply held commitment predicting that consumers become loyal

Stage 1	Stage 2	Stage 3	Stage 4
Cognitive	Affective	Conative	Action

FIGURE 1.5   Stages in customer loyalty

first in a cognitive (knowing and perceiving) sense, then later an affective (emotional) sense and third a conative (desire to act) manner (Dick and Basu, 1994; Jacoby and Kyner, 1973; Oliver, 1997). These three states may not be in synchrony or linearly related. The fourth phase is related to action loyalty, which Oliver suggests is the missing link. This phase is different to the other stages as it involves commitment to overcome situational constraints that may intervene in a purchase decision. Therefore attempts to conceptualize or measure customer loyalty will depend heavily upon the consideration of both customer attitudes and behaviour.

However in practice customer behaviour is often of more immediate interest to service managers than attitude. Customer attitudes become increasingly important when the marketing environment is volatile and when it is very competitive with many similar service product choices available to customers.

Service episodes and service relationships

Another relevant work in this area puts forward the idea of the need to split the concept of service quality into two different concepts – service episode quality and service relationship quality (Liljander and Strandvik, 1995). Service episodes are defined as an event or interaction that has a clear starting-point and an ending-point. An episode can involve several interactions or acts. For example, a consumer who has travelled with a particular airline on a number of routes can represent an episode. This episode can consist of a number of interactions or acts including check-in, boarding a plane, interacting with in-flight staff and so on. Therefore it is possible to distinguish between different acts within an episode. The importance of each of these acts may vary in explaining episode satisfaction.

In this context, service relationships are defined as consisting of a number of episodes. These will be different for different types of services. If a service is not a continuous one, where the customer signs a contract about service delivery with the service provider, a relationship is established when the contract is signed, for example a telephone service. Instead, if the customer takes a separate decision each time about which service provider to use, some type of relationship is established when the second purchase is made, for example, in visiting a restaurant for the second time the customer may become more familiar to the service staff.

The significance of differentiating between episodes and relationships in service conceptualization is relevant in situations where the service manager may want to encourage suitable customers to become 'relationship'

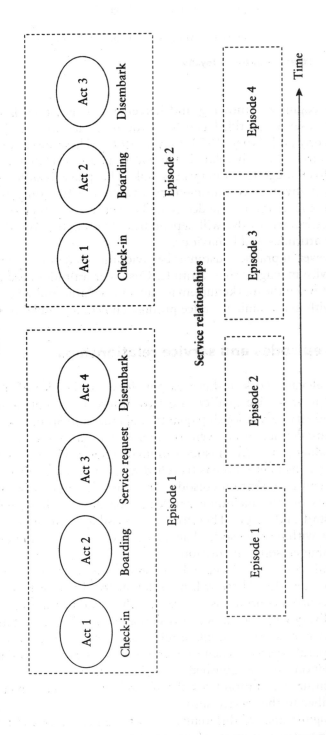

FIGURE 1.6 Service episodes and service relationships

customers as opposed to 'episode' customers or where he/she wants to differentiate marketing activity to these two groups.

All of these conceptual frameworks are used in the service literature to illustrate and demonstrate various characteristics, scope and range of services. Identifying these features contributes to understanding the issues for service delivery and management.

SUMMARY

The development of the services literature has occurred over the latter part of the twentieth century in terms of overall theories and concepts that have been introduced in this chapter. There is considerable agreement about the characteristics and core components of services to include intangibility, inseparability, heterogeneity and perishability. These key characteristics of services have an impact upon the design of the services marketing mix for any service operation. In addition the services marketing mix will also be influenced by the context in which the service is delivered.

All of the dimensions, concepts and frameworks discussed in this chapter illustrate widely recognized and universally acceptable service dimensions. The use of different models for the conceptualization of services marketing and taking account of the characteristics of services and detailed focus required in planning and delivering them has been summarized and illustrated. These are useful frameworks for both academics and practitioners interested in studying, assessing, planning and implementing service marketing activities. Of course, different management styles, structures and competencies will be appropriate for the implementation of service activities in different contexts, and this will be the focus of Part II.

DISCUSSION QUESTIONS

How does the intangible nature of service impact upon the effectiveness of traditional marketing techniques?

What are service dimensions and why is it important for service managers to identify and define them?

Discuss the value of using conceptual models or frameworks for understanding and describing services.

Choose one of the conceptual models described in this chapter and apply it to a service of your choice.

REFERENCES

Bateson, J.E.G. (1979) 'Why we need service marketing', in O.C. Ferrell, S.W. Brown and C.W. Lamb (eds), *Conceptual and Theoretical Developments in Marketing*. Chicago: American Marketing Association. pp. 131–46.

Bitner, M.J. (1990) 'Evaluating service encounters: the effects of physical surroundings and employee responses', *Journal of Marketing*, 54, April: 69–82.

Bolfing, C. and Woodruff, R. (1988) 'Effects of situational involvement on consumers' use of standards in satisfaction/dissatisfaction processes', *Journal of Consumer Satisfaction, Dissatisfaction and Complaining Behaviour*, 1: 16–24.

Borden, N. (1964) 'The concept of the marketing mix', *Journal of Advertising Research*, 4, June: 2–7.

Buttle, F. (1996) 'SERVQUAL: review, critique, research agenda', *European Journal of Marketing*, 30(1): 8–32.

Christopher, M., Payne, A. and Ballantyne, D. (1991) *Relationship Marketing. Bringing Quality, Customer Service and Marketing Together*. Oxford: Butterworth Heinemann.

Cronin, J.J. and Taylor, S.A. (1992) 'Measuring service quality: a reexamination and extension', *Journal of Marketing*, 56, July: 55–68.

Dick, A.S. and Basu, K. (1994) 'Customer loyalty: toward an integrated conceptual framework', *Journal of Academy of Marketing Science*, 22, Winter: 99–113.

Gilmore, A. and Carson. D. (1993) 'Quality improvement in a services marketing context', *The Journal of Services Marketing*, 7(3): 59–71.

Gronroos, C. (1984) 'A service quality model and its marketing implications', *European Journal of Marketing*, 18(4): 36–44.

Jacoby, J. and Kyner, B. (1973) 'Brand loyalty versus repeat purchasing behaviour', *Journal of Marketing Research*, February: 1–9.

Judd, R.C. (1964) 'The case for redefining services', *Journal of Marketing*, 28, January: 58–60.

Judd, R.C. (1968) 'Similarities or difference in product and service retailing', *Journal of Retailing*, 43(4): 1–9.

Languard, E., Bateson, J.E.G., Lovelock, C.H. and Diglier, P. (1981) *Services Marketing: New Insights from Consumers and Managers*. Cambridge, MA: Marketing Science Institute.

LeBlanc, G. and Nguyen, N. (1988) 'Customers' perceptions of service quality in financial institutions', *International Journal of Bank Marketing*, 6(4): 7–18.

Lehtinen, U. and Lehtinen, J. (1982) 'Service quality: a study of quality dimensions', Service Management Institute Research Report, Helsinki, Finland.

Lehtinen, U., Hankimaa, A. and Mittila, T. (1994) 'Measuring the intensity of relationship marketing', in Jagdish N. Sheth and Atul Parvatiyar (eds), *Relationship Marketing: Theory, Methods and Application*. Relationship Marketing Conference Proceedings, Centre for Relationship Marketing, Roberto C. Goizueta Business School, Emory University, Atlanta, GA.

Liljander, V. and Strandvik, T. (1995) 'The nature of customer relationships in services', in T. Swartz, D. Bowen and S. Brown (eds), *Advances in Services Marketing and Management*. London: JAI Press.

Middleton, V.T.C. (1983) 'Product marketing – goods and services compared', *The Quarterly Review of Marketing*, Summer: 1–10.

Normann, R. (1984) *Service Management, Strategy and Leadership in Service Business*, 2nd edn. Chichester: Wiley & Sons.

Oliver, R. (1997) 'Loyalty and profit: long term effects of satisfaction', in R. Oliver, *Satisfaction: A Behavioural Perspective on the Consumer*. London: McGraw-Hill.

Palmer, A. (1996) 'Integrating brand development and relationship marketing', *Journal of Retailing and Consumer Services*, 3(3): 1–6.

Parasuraman, A., Zeithaml, V.A. and Berry, L.L. (1985) 'A conceptual model of service quality and its implications for further research', *Journal of Marketing*, 49, Fall: 41–50.

Parasuraman, A., Zeithaml, V.A. and Berry, L.L. (1988) 'SERVQUAL: A multiple-item scale for measuring consumer perceptions of service quality', *Journal of Retailing*, 64(1): 12–35.

Parasuraman, A., Zeithaml, V.A. and Berry, L.L. (1991) 'Understanding customer expectations of service', *Sloan Management Review*, Spring: 39–48.

Rathmell, J.M. (1966) 'What is meant by services?', *Journal of Marketing*, 30, October: 32–6.

Rathmell, J.M. (1974) *Marketing in the Services Sector*. Cambridge, MA: Winthrop.

Regan, W.J. (1963) 'The service revolution', *Journal of Marketing*, 27, July: 57–62.

Shostack, G.L. (1977) 'Breaking free from product marketing', *Journal of Marketing*, 41, April: 73–80.

Shostack, G.L. (1981) 'How to design a service', in J.H. Donnelly and W.E. George (eds), *Marketing of Services*. Chicago: American Marketing Association. pp. 221–9.

Swan, J.E. and Combs, L.J. (1976) 'Product performance and customer satisfaction: a new concept', *Journal of Marketing*, 40, April: 25–33.

Tse, D. and Wilton, P. (1988) 'Models of consumer satisfaction formation: an extension', *Journal of Marketing Research*, 25, May: 204–12.

2

Evaluation and Measurement of Services

The focus of this chapter is on the most widely used methods for evaluating and measuring different service dimensions in the pursuit of ensuring service quality. Building on the themes introduced and discussed in Chapter 1, the concepts underpinning the measurement of services are considered. The relevance and suitability of measuring customer expectations, customer perceptions, customer satisfaction and service quality is inherent in this discussion. In tandem with these conceptualizations, a variety of methods and approaches have been used to measure service dimensions, processes and outcomes over the years. In covering these topics the debate will relate to the dimensions and concepts surrounding the value and purpose of SERVQUAL, SERVPERF and other means of measuring the key dimensions of service quality and customer satisfaction.

Interest in conceptually developing and testing service theories continues today. Many research studies of recent years have sought to clarify some of the underpinning concepts of earlier models for services marketing and management such as service quality and customer satisfaction and perceptions. Studies of these concepts have tried to build on and further clarify the perceived problems with the SERVQUAL instrument regarding customer expectations and perceptions. Other studies have used different research methods and adapted them for the specific service context in which they were to be used.

There are two different perspectives in relation to service management and delivery – one is the perspective of the consumer and the other is the perspective of the service organization or management. For example, services are often evaluated from the consumers' perspective in terms of their expectations, perceptions and overall satisfaction with a service. From a managerial perspective, however, services are more likely to be assessed in terms of how efficiently customers are served and moved through the service process, how they are managed, and how competently service staff deliver the service. These different perspectives will influence how services are evaluated, what is evaluated, and how and when and by whom the assessment is made.

CONSUMER AND MANAGERIAL PERSPECTIVES ON SERVICES MARKETING

In services marketing there are two main areas of study, one primarily concerned with aspects of service management and one primarily concerned with consumers. As we are all consumers, providing services to consumers most frequently comes to mind but it is worth remembering that business-to-business marketing accounts for approximately 80 per cent of business activities, therefore user or consumer marketing is only part of a much bigger picture. However both business-to-business and consumer marketing are commonly concerned with the importance of the buyer/customer focus.

Concepts and topics concerned with services marketing to consumers cover an array of areas. This research area is strong in its basic and underlying focus, that is, it is research about consumers, perceptions, opinions and satisfaction. However, there are some broad categories of consumer studies research in services, for example:

1 Broad consumer perspectives within the overall context of society's use of services.
2 Consumer perspectives within the context of different service market segments.
3 Specific consumer perspectives within the context of specific consumer services.

Of course, there are many specific research areas both within and beyond these broad categories. For the purpose of this discussion on the scope of services marketing it is enough here to focus briefly on these three categorizations.

Broad consumer perspectives within the overall context of society's use of services

There is a large field of research aimed at gathering statistics on society and its underlying changes and trends. Much of this information relates to service sectors, for example, current and projected use of health services and education services. Most governments seek data on societal structures both for the purpose of historical records or general records, but more importantly for monitoring changes and trends to plan and prepare appropriate societal and governmental infrastructures for the future. In many areas such statistics generate fascinating details of a society's (consumers') preferences, desires, changes, attitudes and perceptions. These statistics are often segmented into mainstream, peripheral and emerging categories. However, the significance of such research data lies in the categorization of the members of society as *consumers* in that, as consumers they are making choices and demonstrating broad preferences for service categories in spending disposable income.

Consumer perspectives within the context of different service market segments

There is a field of research that examines aspects of consumer perspectives, attitudes and behaviours. To know how consumers behave as a homogeneous group within particular environments enables meaningful insights into the range of stimuli, triggers, preferences and dislikes of mainstream collective and extreme perspectives. This type of categorization allows services marketing managers to identify service needs and preferences as well as broad trends and changes in perspectives.

Consumer perspectives within the context of specific consumer services

Another immense field of consumer research lies in researching customers or 'users' of services. This research tends to be much more specific in its desired outcomes. It aims to go further than broad categorizations and investigates more detailed perspectives on needs and wants regarding specific product or service categories. For example, research may examine the usage of services in terms of frequency and regularity of consumption and conformity or non-conformity. In much of this research, the aim for service managers will be to know the perspective of his/her own customers and at the same time to know the perspectives of key competitors and their customers, and to compare variances, differences and similarities of these consumers. This category of consumer service research is closest and indeed may overlap with the service management research areas. This type of research might focus upon consumer decision making in relation to purchasing specific services or a number of services. Studies would seek to quantify consumer purchasing and seek to determine attitudes, perceptions and behaviours or other such aspects of consumer behaviour. Similarly, research in consumer services may be concerned with consumer characteristics as related to service choice, price/value, impact of marketing, competition and many other pertinent issues.

The main focus of this book is from the perspective of service marketing management. However, the outcomes of the consumer research described above will be of major significance to service marketing management decision making, that is, it will enable and inform service managers to plan and implement appropriate service marketing.

Most service marketing managers require much more specific knowledge, indeed, situation-specific knowledge about their own sphere of decision making. In the complex sphere of competitive business activity much decision making in service marketing is not fully understood. Service marketing theories may present specific frameworks, tools and techniques, but how these are applied and used is often not clear, except in the most conceptual and general sense. Just as consumer researchers seek to understand both the broad and intimate perspectives of consumers' attitudes and behaviours, service marketing management researchers seek to understand and evaluate the specific and sometimes complicated perspectives of managers operating within different contexts of decision making.

To date, what is known and understood about service marketing management decision making is often well recognized at a general, theoretical level but understanding how managers operate in practice is poor. Within the service marketing management domain two key (and overlapping) perspectives can be discerned. These are:

1 Service management within organizational structures
2 People management in carrying out service-related tasks.

Service management within organizational structures

Service management involves operating within the structures and procedures of management principles, and organizational structures, processes and hierarchies, and managing people-oriented aspects inherent in the required behaviour and competencies for carrying out service-related tasks. Thus service management focuses on marketing as a function or activity, embracing techniques, approaches and processes of marketing. It depends on the people dimensions and thus involves managing behaviours, skills, relationships, styles and interactions.

Service management occurs within the context of broad organizational management activities and the guiding values of an organization. Management structures may be viewed as the pre-determined arrangements that managers set in motion and that involve flows of information and communication and recurring procedures. Management will have an impact upon the tasks of breaking work up into component and manageable parts and co-ordinating activities on the lines of what to do and how to do it. This will be executed through processes of communication and decision making. How managers interact with others for the purpose of service management and delivery is vital to the long-term success of the company. Researchers in service management focus on these issues, both in terms of organizational barriers to successful management and how to create a suitable organizational structure for services marketing (the focus of Chapter 5).

People management in carrying out service-related tasks

Service marketing management will invariably be concerned with how or the way decisions are made and the implications of those decisions. Thus the managerial processes behind such decisions and the variety and style of the managers taking the decisions are of interest to service marketing and management researchers. The way managers implement decisions is also vital in a service situation. Services are usually carried out by people and these people need to be motivated and capable of doing the job. Services managers continually seek ways to motivate and encourage service deliverers.

Difference styles of management may be relevant in different situations: from extremes of authoritarian to humanistic; where time-scales can be short, medium or long term; where the scope of activities is different in terms of strategic and tactical; and so on.

The two perspectives of marketing management and consumers in service marketing are not necessarily mutually exclusive (this is demonstrated in the third category of consumer service research above). A 'middle ground' incorporating some combination of both domains and perspectives, although with the emphasis on how services can be managed and delivered effectively to create and maintain satisfied customers is a useful focus for service managers.

MEASURING SERVICES

As discussed earlier, services have very specific characteristics and are multi-dimensional and complex. These features need to be considered before trying to measure services. As illustrated in Table 2.1, measurements need to take account of the service process, they need to measure both tangible and intangible aspects of services and they should take account of the specific context in which a service occurs.

Table 2.1 *Measuring services*

Measurements need to:
Take account of the service process
Measure tangible and intangible aspects
Be relevant for different service contexts

Measurements that take account of the service process

Given that services are processes, measurements need to take account of the complete service process. Such measurements need to address all stages in the service experience, the pre-, during and post-service experience of the customer and, where the design of a service is linked to technology, if appropriate. For example, in the case of a financial service, some consideration should be given to alternative service delivery processes involving the customer and the front-line and back office worker in the bank or building society and its multiple branches. These possible points of interaction may include designs that range from minimal to high contact between customer, front office and back office staff.

Technology is now widely used in service delivery and is becoming more and more sophisticated in all service environments. In fact it is a necessary ingredient for service quality in many industries such as the airline and financial services industries. In these cases, technology needs to be seen as integral to the service situations, not only for information processing but also in facilitating the entire service process.

'Blueprinting' the service process

In the 1980s Shostack offered an approach for designing and assessing services on a more scientific, rational basis. It was based on the idea that although the service process could be reduced to steps and sequences, services need to be viewed as interdependent, interactive systems rather than disconnected processes and activities. In an attempt to conceptualize and recognize this Shostack (1981, 1984) devized a series of 'blueprints' covering various consumer circumstances and presented these as illustrative 'maps' of how a service is consumed. Building on this, Kingman-Brundage (1989) proposed a more general framework called the 'ABCs of service system blueprinting'. This was based on the premise that although a service system blueprint is a picture of a service system, there may be different levels of blueprints for service management. For example, a concept blueprint is a macro-level blueprint that demonstrates how each job or department functions in relationship to the service as a whole, whilst a detailed blueprint is a micro-level blueprint which conveys the details of the service system identified but not described on the concept blueprint. Blueprinting can be a simple or more sophisticated means of designing a system to illustrate the aspects inherent in managing and assessing the complete service process, depending on the priorities of each situation.

Methods to measure tangible and intangible aspects

As discussed in Chapter 1 customers have both instrumental and psychological expectations about a product or service performance, where expectations relate to both quantifiable hard dimensions, measured by hard data, and qualitative soft dimensions, measured by soft data. Hard data have been described as relating to performance and reliability standards or any tangible dimensions; whereas soft data are those concerned with descriptions of and knowledge about customers' feelings, perceptions and requirements (Smith, 1987). These are more difficult to measure because they are intangible. Both these elements were brought together in a 'dimensions of service delivery model' in Figure 1.3 (p. 20). The scope of these dimensions ranges from the hard, tangible, relatively easy to measure and evaluate aspects, such as physical surroundings, to the soft, intangible, more difficult to measure and evaluate aspects such as the degree of courtesy and consideration experienced by the customer. A focus on both tangible and intangible service offerings is vital in helping to improve the overall quality of marketing in any given service situation. An example of measuring service quality in a call centre is given below to illustrate the importance of both tangible and intangible aspects of service delivery for customers, service deliverers and managers.

Using appropriate criteria to measure and assess service levels in call centres

In recent years, there has been a vast growth in the use of call centres to deal with customer service queries and requirements. Many call centre studies have found that agents are often required to answer a great number of calls regardless of the quality of the call as they are often judged on how quickly they can deal with the enquiry (Denny, 1998; MacDonald, 1998). However while managers appear to be content to assess performance by the quantity rather than the quality of the calls, employees continue to be frustrated by their situation and become demoralized (MacDonald, 1998). Indeed call centres have become associated with poor employee morale and high staff turnover. Much of this can be attributed to a lack of understanding of the nature of the service and how it can best be measured.

In a recent study of the tangible and intangible aspects of service delivery it was found that managers of a major call centre measured the tangible aspects of the service delivery only. These included the length of calls, how soon calls were answered, how many were answered in an hour, etc. By contrast the call agents felt that completing the service query while the customer was on the phone, and showing empathy with the customer and finding access to relevant help for individual customer problems, were more important in the overall quality of service delivery. There was a high turnover of staff in the call centre under study. Many call centre agents complained that they found the job stressful mainly because they often did not have time to respond completely to the customer's query under the 'three-minute length of call rule'.

(Continued)

(Continued)

To improve the situation, managers eventually recognized that it was imperative to carefully consider the most appropriate way to measure the performance of customer contact staff, taking cognizance of the intangible and psychological dimensions of customers' expectations and staff morale, particularly within the context of an industry where high staff turnover is prevalent.

It is important to identify suitable measures and assessment procedures that take account of all aspects of service delivery, including both tangible and intangible dimensions of services, in the context of adopting an appropriate management style.

The reason why some of the predominantly intangible service elements are more difficult to measure by customers and companies can be traced back to the classification of the properties of goods and services (Darby and Karni, 1973; Nelson, 1974). In particular, services have 'search', 'experience' and 'credence' properties. Therefore they rely on the professional credence of the supplier. Figure 1.3 (p. 20) illustrates that many service dimensions are more tangible (left side of the continuum) and can be categorized as having search qualities; however the majority of the elements towards the intangible (right) side of the continuum contain more experience and credence properties. For example, empathy and courtesy of staff can only be evaluated through experiencing these dimensions. Consequently, this makes the evaluation of these qualities more difficult for consumers and for companies.

It is easier for the producer or manager to determine, offer and standardize 'search' or tangible qualities. In the call centre example, this is manifested in dimensions such as the number of calls successfully completed in a given time period and speed of response. Managers can identify customer expectations by various quantitative methods and can therefore set appropriate specifications, rules or procedures to allow for those requirements. Indeed there is a tendency by managers to concentrate on the tangible or instrumental standards and a corresponding difficulty in defining and measuring psychological standards. In this respect many call centres collect and assess data regarding the time period customers perceive to be reasonable in waiting for a response, or how long they would be prepared to wait in a queue.

However when quantitative measures have been applied to determine less definite dimensions they have been less successful because they fail to take into account the inherent psychological dimensions which relate to the customer's expectation evaluation in terms of experience and credence qualities. For example, call centres have found it more difficult to manage and measure customers' and front-line employees' feelings, perceptions and requirements in relation to the intangible dimensions of the service delivery. Indeed this has led to a high degree of employee dissatisfaction (Denny, 1998) and to high agent turnover (MacDonald, 1998). To summarize, consideration of the tangible elements can be implemented mainly through suitable rules and procedures, whereas the psychological 'soft' dimensions of service quality are determined by an emphasis on perceptions, attitude and behaviour of customer contact staff.

Different measurements relevant for different contexts

This builds on the earlier discussion of the range of service dimensions and how different dimensions will be more relevant in some situations than others. Contextual circumstances will have some bearing upon the suitability and number of dimensions of service quality for any given situation (Buttle, 1996). It is important to recognize and identify the key dimensions in a service situation so that these dimensions are emphasized and measured when looking at service quality. For example, Blois (1987) adapts principles of marketing for not-for-profit organizations and argues that such a marketing approach will improve the organization's effectiveness and efficiency in dealing with its consumers. There is considerable value in carefully adapting concepts in different service contexts given the very different contexts of many services such as the health service, education services, financial services and travel and tourism. These are all services but clearly have little in common with each other apart from their fundamental service characteristics.

Therefore in deliberating upon how to measure service quality, some situation or context specific approach needs to be included in the measurement criteria. For example, the researcher needs to know, who and how many will carry out the service, where the service will be carried out, the overall conditions of the environment such as competitive dimensions and some history of the service encounter.

METHODS OF MEASURING SERVICE QUALITY

Measurements need to take account of different types of concepts and customers. Indeed, different measurement criteria are required for different concepts such as service quality, customer satisfaction, customer perceptions, expectations and loyalty. Assessment of these concepts will also entail the use of different measuring scales, and scope of opinions, attitudes and behaviour. The remainder of this chapter will look at current methods of measuring customer expectations and customer perceptions, SERVQUAL, SERVPERF, Critical Incidents Technique, observation studies, focus group discussions and in-depth interviews and evaluate these methods in terms of their relevance and appropriateness for services marketing in different contexts.

Service companies spend substantial time and resources on measuring and managing customer satisfaction, customer loyalty and service quality.

Indeed many marketing research firms specialize in customer satisfaction measurement alone. Some companies, such as KFC, link employee rewards to customer satisfaction targets and achievements.

At the same time, academic research has focused on the concepts of customer satisfaction, customer loyalty and service quality and the relationship between these. There are some differing opinions about the most appropriate concept, or the need to measure all of these as described earlier. However, the comparison of customer's expectations with their perceptions of a service became a major focus of attention in the measurement of service quality from the early 1980s until the present day. Indeed Buttle (1996) asserts that measuring service quality (using service quality dimensions) has been adopted by many industries. Examples of this are many and varied and typified by the following:

- tyre retailing, in a study by Carmen (1990)
- dental services, studied by Carmen (1990)
- hotels – see, for example, the study by Selah and Ryan (1992)
- travel and tourism (Fick and Ritchie, 1991)
- car servicing (Bouman and van der Wiele, 1992)
- business schools (Rigotti and Pitt, 1992)
- higher education (Ford et al., 1993)
- hospitality (Johns, 1993)
- accounting firms (Freeman and Dart, 1993).

In relation to these concepts many researchers have focused on developing 'scales' to measure service dimensions and customer perceptions and expectations. After the development of the SERVQUAL scale in the 1980s much of the subsequent research in services used this scale. However other scales were developed to focus on different aspects of service quality, customer satisfaction, customer loyalty and customer perceptions during the late 1980s and 1990s.

More recently the growth of interest in relationship marketing has renewed interest in conceptualizing and measuring customer loyalty. As markets become more competitive, companies are more likely to recognize the importance of retaining current customers. Customer retention is considered to be a relatively easy-to-measure and reliable indicator of superior performance. Companies initiate a variety of activities to improve customer retention such as customer satisfaction programmes, complaint management and loyalty schemas. In understanding customer satisfaction researchers have paid particular attention to the management of service quality, developing ways of meeting customer expectations and recognizing the impact that service quality has on profit (Rust et al., 1996). Many of these initiatives build on the earlier work in the realms of customer satisfaction, complaining behaviour and loyalty. The most frequently used methods for measuring and assessing service quality are shown in Table 2.2.

Table 2.2 *Methods of measuring service quality*

SERVQUAL
SERVPERF
Scales for measuring customer satisfaction and loyalty
Critical incidents technique
Observation studies
Focus group discussion
In-depth interviews

SERVQUAL

SERVQUAL was created to measure service quality and is based on the view that the customer's assessment of service quality is paramount. It is operationalized in terms of the relationship between expectations and outcomes. That is, SERVQUAL is based on measuring customer satisfaction in terms of the relationship between expectations (E) and outcomes (O). If the outcome (O) matches expectations (E), then the customer is satisfied. If expectations (E) exceeds the outcome (O), then customer dissatisfaction is indicated. If the outcome (O) exceeds expectations (E), then customer 'delight' may be the result.

Service quality is considered as a multi-dimensional construct and in the early phase of development Parasuraman et al. (1985) identified ten service dimensions. In a further refinement these ten were reduced to five dimensions: tangibles, reliability, responsibility, assurance and empathy (Parasuraman et al., 1988). These formed the core of the SERVQUAL measuring instrument. The five dimensions are measured with an instrument using 22 items. Respondents are required to first give responses about their expectations of service and then their evaluation of the actual service. Satisfaction is calculated as the difference between perceptions and expectations, each item weighted according to its importance. Parasuraman et al. (1988) established that a mismatch between expectations and perceptions of performance causes dissatisfaction or a 'performance gap'. This overall performance gap is made up of five gaps that contribute to the perception of service delivery. These gaps include: any differences in management perceptions and customer expectations (gap 1), any discrepancies between management perceptions and the service specifications enacted (gap 2), differences between service quality specifications and service delivery (gap 3), variations between service delivery and external communications to customers (gap 4) and the overall difference between management perceptions of customer expectations and customers' expected service (gap 5).

Using SERVQUAL to evaluate service quality in a maternity ward

A city hospital sought to evaluate hospital patients' expectations and perceptions of the overall service delivered in a busy maternity ward. The SERVQUAL measurement scale was used to ellicit information about the nursing care, the catering facilities, visiting arrangements and overall family care. During the period of one month new patients were asked to complete a questionnaire on entry to the maternity ward. This focused on their expectations of service regarding the different aspects outlined above. The same patients were then required to complete a questionnaire on their overall perceptions of the quality of these services prior to leaving the hospital. The findings were analysed in terms of the differences between patients' expectations of the service they were about to receive and their perceptions of the service they actually received. The results of the study illustrated the major differences between expectations and perceptions. These were examined by ward managers, ancillary, catering and nursing staff to try to eliminate any gaps in the service delivery.

There are a number of criticisms of SERVQUAL. Fundamentally the problem of measuring expectations is used as a major criticism of the SERVQUAL scale. For example: some researchers think that measuring expectations is unnecessary and that measuring service outcomes or perceptions of outcomes should be enough. The term 'expectations' is deemed to be polysemic. Some suggest that expectations and perceptions should be measured on a single scale, rather than using two scales. Also the item composition uses five generic items and many researchers argue that four or five items cannot capture the variability within each service quality dimension. Some of the more specific issues that have been debated and critiqued by various researchers in service contexts are listed below.

1 The gaps model – some researchers say that there is little evidence that customers assess service quality in terms of performance and expectation gaps (Buttle, 1996).
2 Process orientation – SERVQUAL focuses on the process of service delivery and not on the outcomes of the service encounter, therefore this limits the value of the mechanism.
3 Dimensionality – SERVQUAL's five dimensions are not universal. The number of dimensions comprising SERVQUAL are contextualized and there is a high degree of intercorrelation between the five dimensions.
4 Expectations – some researchers argue that measuring expectations is unnecessary. If they are to be measured, expectations and perceptions should be measured on a single scale.
5 Item composition – four or five items cannot capture the variability within each SERVQUAL dimension.

6 Moments of truth – customers assessments of SERVQUAL may vary from one service encounter (moment-of-truth) to another.

7 There are two administrations of the SERVQUAL scale – two administrations of the instrument causes respondent boredom and frustration amongst respondents.

8 Scale points – the seven-point Likert scale is flawed. The mid-range numbers can only be vaguely related to varying degrees of opinions and many respondents may rate these differently.

9 Polarity – the reversed polarity of items on the scale causes respondent error. In the SERVQUAL instrument some items are reversed to ensure that respondents do not fall into the habit of marking the same scale point for each question; however this can cause confusion.

In the early 1990s the authors made some alterations to the SERVQUAL mechanism. In 1991 a follow-up study changed the wording of all the expectation items (Parasuraman et al., 1991). The purpose of this was to move away from attempting to measure customers' normative expectations and to focus on what customers would expect from *excellent* service companies. For example, 'companies offering ... services should keep their records accurately' was changed to 'excellent companies offering ... services will insist on error-free records'. Details in the wording of many of the items relating to customer perceptions changed also. Two new items, one under the heading of 'tangibles' referring to the appearance of communication materials, and one under the heading 'assurance' relating to the knowledge of employees were substituted for two original items.

The analysis of SERVQUAL could be carried out in a number of ways. It could be analysed item-by-item, dimension-by-dimension; it could represent the perception and expectation statements relating to a single dimension; it could combine to form a single measure of service quality, the so-called SERVQUAL gap.

Some researchers have queried the wide application of the SERVQUAL instrument and signalled caution in some of its uses. For example, many studies have illustrated that the number of service quality dimensions is dependent upon the particular service being offered (Babakus and Boller, 1992; Bouman and van der Wiele, 1992). Contextual circumstances will have some bearing upon the suitability and number of dimensions of service quality for any given situation (Buttle, 1996). Recognition of the shortcomings of previous research has slowly led to the development of new approaches to studying and researching service quality, either by linking the SERVQUAL model with other techniques or by using alternative approaches. For example Rouffaer (1991) developed a GOS model based on the notion that services have three components: Goods, Objectively measured service elements, and Subjectively measured service components. Rouffaer applied his model to the hospitality industry, illustrating its specific relevance to that industry.

Other research has attempted to take a different approach to measuring the concepts of service quality. Major studies have been undertaken, a notable example being the 'customer satisfaction barometer' (CSB) in Sweden by Fornell (1992) which attempts to measure levels of service quality across 30 industries and 100 companies. However none of these models has enjoyed the same degree of use and adaptation as SERVQUAL. In the following sections, SERVPERF and other methods of measuring customer satisfaction and service quality are described.

SERVPERF

Cronin and Taylor's work (1992; Taylor and Cronin, 1994) on measuring service quality attempted to offer an alternative to SERVQUAL. They investigated the conceptualization and measurement of service quality and the relationships between service quality, consumer satisfaction and purchase intentions. Their work focused on trying to overcome the 'perceptions-minus-expectations' measurement focus of SERVQUAL. The development of the SERVPERF model aimed to provide an alternative method of measuring perceived service quality and the significance of the relationships between service quality, customer satisfaction and purchase intentions. In investigating these concepts and the interrelationships between them they argued that:

- a performance-based measure of service quality may be an improved means of measuring the service quality construct
- service quality is an antecedent of customer satisfaction
- consumer satisfaction has a significant effect on purchase intentions and
- service quality has less effect on purchase intentions than consumer satisfaction.

As a result they presented a performance-based measurement, SERVPERF. The SERVPERF scale was created mainly in response to the criticism of the SERVQUAL scale. It particularly sought not to use disconfirmation-based measures as that was perceived to be a flaw in the SERVQUAL scale. It was built upon the premise that the best operationalization of service quality is achieved through measures of services' firm performance. The measures used in this scale were expectations, perceptions of performance, and importance measures. The SERVPERF scale was also simpler to manage as it required only one administration and so avoided the difficulties of measuring both expectations and perceptions.

However after an investigation of the psychometric properties of the SERVPERF scale and results of a multi-industry study, Taylor and Cronin (1994) suggest that SERVPERF appears to suffer from the lack of a consistent and generalizable factor structure. As a consequence of this later study they recommend that:

- practitioners should adapt the factor structure of the service quality data for specific or different settings, and

- academic researchers should revisit the research objective of needing a reliable and valid multi-dimensional scale of service quality that could be generalizable across service settings.

Scales for measuring customer satisfaction and loyalty

There have been many studies aiming to develop attitude scales to gauge the level of customer satisfaction with a company's service. This type of research has developed further into studies of customer loyalty in relation to companies, services and brands and as a means of counting and categorizing customer complaints. In an attempt to measure the complexity of a service or consumer concept scales are used to assess multiple dimensions instead of just one or two. These have been widely used in service situations because of the multi-dimensional nature of most services. Scales focus on covering a range of items and are based on the answers to a number of questions. A score is allocated to particular answers depending on how favourable the answer is to the attitude being measured. The scores for each question are then added together to provide each person with an overall score for that set of questions (scale score). The scale score is taken to indicate a person's position on the abstract dimension the individual question is designed to measure.

Measuring consumers' opinions

Often scales are used to measure positive and negative opinions of service dimensions in a given situation. These may be used at different and frequent time periods in order to compile a picture of any trend in service requirements. They are also used to solicit opinions on various aspects of service delivery to gauge whether some service issues improve or deteriorate over time. Measurement scales can be used to gather information on customers' satisfaction levels with services, negative and positive opinions about services and service levels, and comparisons with other services. More recently measurement scales have been used to identify customers' behavioural intentions and likelihood or willingness to recommend a service to others. Positive behavioural intentions can include:

- saying positive things about a company and/or its service
- spending more money with the company
- remaining loyal
- paying a price premium.

Negative behavioural intentions will include doing the opposite to those listed above and making negative comments about a company to outside companies such as consumer rights bodies, as well as to potential customers.

Critical Incidents Technique (CIT)

The critical incidents technique has also been widely used in service marketing research. The technique was originally developed by Flanagan (1954) to identify critical job requirements. However it has been adapted for use in services situations. In services marketing it is often used to elicit verbatim stories from customers about various service encounters. These can be stories of either good or poor service experiences. The advantage of this technique is that it allows respondents to tell of their experiences in their own words, how they feel about the encounters and any other aspects of the service delivery and management of interest to the researcher.

They can be used as an effective alternative to complaint gathering as they are a useful means of identifying dissatisfied customers and any common service failure issues. Equally they provide an effective means of encouraging customers to describe 'best practice' in any aspect of service delivery or management they may have experienced elsewhere. Detailed descriptions of experiences elsewhere will provide information on customer requirements in different situations and behavioural and attitudinal criteria in relation to service delivery and policies. A critical incidents study should reveal rich data in relation to desirable and undesirable aspects of how service companies deliver various service dimensions in different contexts. This kind of information is very useful to illustrate to employees what customers do and do not like and therefore indicate how to modify aspects of their service delivery behaviour.

> **Perceptions of a Ford dealership**
>
> A critical incident study was carried out to investigate the relationship between front-line employees and customers of a Ford dealership in Ireland. First, front-line employees were asked to provide stories of 'good' and 'bad' service incidents with customers. These stories were categorized in terms of topics and whether they fitted the 'good' or 'bad' category. Secondly a number of customers were asked to provide stories of 'good' and 'bad' service incidents with front-line staff. These were categorized similarly to the previous stories. The stories from both groups were compared. The overall outcome of the study was to illicit key service successes and failures. The detailed information gathered provided rich material to help identify problem areas and develop improvements for the front-line service delivery team in the dealership.

Observation studies

Observation studies are useful for gathering information on how service staff and customers behave. They go beyond what customers and staff may say they do and any opinions they have of service aspects. Instead observation studies will gather information about what customers and staff actually do. This provides information relating to customers' actual responses to marketing activity and the participation and involvement of staff in the service process.

Observation studies form the basis of 'mystery shopping' which is widely used to gather information on customers' service and shopping experiences. They often focus on assessing the quality of service, staff interactions with customers, store layout and appearance, product/service range and merchandising in a services or retailing circumstance. They often include conversing with staff as well as observing behaviour and the service setting. The purpose of such studies is about assessing front-line interactions with customers and everything the customer experiences in a retail, hotel, or other service outlet. They are widely used in the hospitality industry by trade researchers and evaluators such as those who allocate star ratings to hotels, restaurants and restaurant critics.

An example of an observation study of service activities is one carried out on board car ferries in Northern Europe (Gilmore, 1997). The observation protocol was based on what should be observed, where, when, and how these observations should take place. In this study the research protocol was based on carrying out observations of all elements of marketing activity in service settings, taking account of both tangible and intangible marketing dimensions in a relatively complex service delivery. The service dimensions deemed to be very relevant to this service context were physical facilities, choice and range of product/service, information available, staff accessibility to customers, communication and interaction with customers and customer response to products/services.

The purpose of the observation study was to carry out a comparison of each major ferry company's marketing activity in relation to the facilities and service quality on the major Irish, UK, Northern European and Scandinavian routes. The Northern European ferry companies studied included operators of Irish, UK, Dutch, French, German, Swedish, and Finnish origin.

Observations of on-board service delivery

Observations of the facilities on board and customer/staff interactions were carried out at the beginning, during and end of each sailing time. These were carried out by researchers and immediately followed by extensive data recording. The similarities and differences in the level of service on board each of these company's ferries was observed in relation to physical facilities, choice and range of product/service, information available, staff accessibility to customers, communication and interaction with customers and customer response to products/services.

Physical facilities
This included observations of the layout and spaciousness of the ferry and how these contributed to the freedom or otherwise of passengers' movement. The number and size of service outlets was also taken into account.

(Continued)

(Continued)

Choice and range of products/services

Observations focused on the range of food offered in the restaurants and cafeterias, the range of products in the on-board shops, the range of drinks in cafeterias and bars and the range and scope of entertainment for each age group observed on board.

Information and advice available

Visual and verbal communication and promotion to customers, tannoy announcements, guidance signs and information leaflets were all aspects of the information and advice observed on board.

Staff accessibility to customers

This involved observing the presence of staff when they were required for delivering a service to customers in the various outlets on board such as the restaurants, cafeterias, bars, entertainment facilities and shops.

Staff communication and interaction with customers

This included observing the courtesy and politeness shown, whether staff helped customers, and the competency of staff in carrying out their jobs.

Customer behaviour/response to the product and services

Customer responses were observed in relation to all the on-board product and services offered such as the extent of use of the restaurants, bars, entertainment facilities and shops.

To take account of service consistency observations were made in relation to aspects of on-board service delivery and recorded with descriptions and examples of occurrences at the beginning, during and the end of each sailing. The levels of these offerings and activities were measured on a five-point schematic scale where a rating of 1 denoted a non-existent or a very low level of that element in evidence whereas a rating of 5 denoted a high level of such a circumstance. However these ratings were used as guidelines only and were justified and explained by the descriptions and comments of what was observed and how this resulted in such a comparative rating.

Observation studies can be used in a variety of ways and for a variety of purposes. In services contexts observation studies can be an integral means of reaching deep and insightful understanding of *real* phenomena that provide meaningful and usable data for service marketing managers.

Focus group discussions

Focus groups of homogeneous or heterogeneous respondents such as consumers, front-line service deliverers, supervisors and managers can be a very useful means of assessing service quality and delivery. Focus group discussions may be conducted in a non-directive and unstructured fashion to aid in the generation of the researcher's understanding and analysis of the service delivery process and activities of service staff. For example broad open-ended questions may be used and discussion may focus on the experiences and expectations of customers, and the experience and opinions of staff. This type of data collection will provide information about the reasons behind specific opinions, attitudes, behaviour and perceptions of staff and customers.

The main characteristic of focus group research is the simultaneous involvement of a number of respondents in the research process. It explicitly uses group interaction to 'produce data and insights that would be less accessible without the interaction found in a group' (Morgan, 1988: 12). Indeed, focus groups are one of the few research techniques in which participants are encouraged to interact with each other. Focus group research also incorporates the active role of the researcher in addressing the research problem. So it is primarily a 'research technique that collects data through group interaction on a topic determined by the researcher' (Morgan, 1988: 130).

Customer perceptions of a high street restaurant

Focus groups were used to illicit the opinions and attitudes of customers of a high street restaurant regarding choice and range of menu, price ranges in relation to value for money, service and food presentation and how staff communicate with customers. The discussions were carried out during a time of increasing competition and when the restaurant was losing business. As a result of the focus group discussion the managers gleaned some in-depth insights about:

- how customers thought the menu could be more varied with the addition of some 'lighter' and healthier options
- how price ranges could include some special offers at specific times of the day and suggestions that maybe a 'family meal' offer could be introduced at weekends
- including more snack items during off-peak times of the day
- improving the menu cards and wall displays
- improving staff communication with customers, encouraging staff to give customers information about daily and weekly specials and any other variations and offers available.

In-depth interview

Interview data is a major source of information gathering particularly for carrying out research with busy practitioners and service managers. In-depth interviews vary in scope from very unstructured interviews designed to discover insights and understanding, and more structured interviewing focusing on a more structured questioning approach. Whatever an interview's form, its purpose is to get inside someone's head and enter into the other person's perspective (Patton, 1990) to find out things like feelings, memories and interpretations that researchers cannot observe or discover in other ways. Thus the researcher should always be careful of imposing his or her own perspective onto the respondent, even though researcher comments and contributions, based on prior experiential knowledge and learning, will undoubtedly enhance the overall data collection. Interview data are very useful for assessing the thinking behind services managers' decision making and approaches to service quality, managing service personnel and delivery.

In-depth interviews range in form. At one extreme, they can be almost like an informal conversation with an individual that explores a person's perceptions of a chosen phenomenon such as what they think of a company's service delivery policy. Such interviews have virtually no structure or direction placed on them by the interviewer since their main aim is to explore the internal reality of the respondent. At the other extreme, interviews can be more structured and directed where perceptions are interesting not for themselves but for the picture that they present of an external reality. Interviews seeking knowledge and managerial perspectives from individual service marketing managers are examples of this form of interview.

Investigation of managerial decision making regarding call centre service delivery

Call centre managers were all interviewed individually to gather their opinions, perceptions and attitudes regarding the overall service delivery in the call centres, the specific scope and nature of service delivery and the appropriateness of the measurement approaches used. This resulted in some in-depth insights about the management process, particularly the differing perspectives of managers and supervisors at different organizational levels regarding service delivery.

SUMMARY

This chapter began with an overview on both consumer and managerial perspectives of services marketing. This was followed by a discussion of current thinking on the relevance and importance of measuring service quality and customer satisfaction. The key issues and debates arising from such a challenge were discussed. Then the chapter focused on some of the most widely used methods of measuring service quality to date. This included a discussion of the advantages and disadvantages of using SERVQUAL and the development of SERVPERF to overcome some of the perceived problems of SERVQUAL. The chapter then focused on other methods of researching and assessing the service dimensions inherent in delivering excellent service quality and customer satisfaction.

This chapter completes the review of the underpinning, core concepts in service marketing delivery and management. It also sets the scene for Part II which attempts to build upon and develop the issues covered in Part I by focusing on the management issues that impact on the quality of service delivery.

DISCUSSION QUESTIONS

What issues contribute to the difficulties in measuring service quality in different contexts?

Describe the SERVQUAL method of measuring service quality and outline the recognized advantages and criticisms of SERVQUAL.

Can you describe at least two other approaches that could be used to measure service quality?

What research approach would be most appropriate for gathering detailed information from service marketing managers and why?

NOTE

Some of the section entitled 'Consumer and managerial perspectives on services marketing' is adapted from Carson, D., Gilmore, A., Gronhaug, C. and Perry, K. *Qualitative Marketing Research*, Sage Publications, London (2001), Chapter 2.

REFERENCES

Babakus, E. and Boller, G.W. (1992) 'An empirical assessment of the SERVQUAL scale', *Journal of Business Research*, 24: 253–68.

Blois, K. (1987) 'Marketing for non-profit organizations', in M.J. Baker (ed.), *The Marketing Book*. London: Heinemann, pp. 404–12.

Bouman, M. and van de Wiele, T. (1992) 'Measuring service quality in the car service industry: building and testing an instrument', *International Journal of Service Industry Management*, 3(4): 4–16.

Buttle, F. (1996) 'SERVQUAL: review, critique, research agenda', *European Journal of Marketing*, 30(1): 8–32.

Carmen, J.M. (1990) 'Consumer perceptions of service quality: an assessment of the SERVQUAL dimensions', *Journal of Retailing*, 66(1), Spring: 33–5.

Cronin, J.J. and Taylor, S.A. (1992) 'Measuring service quality: a reexamination and extension', *Journal of Marketing*, 56, July: 55–68.

Darby, M.R. and Karni, E. (1973) 'Free competition and the optimal amount of fraud', *Journal of Law and Economics*, 16, April: 67–86.

Denny, C. (1998) 'Remote control of the high street', *The Guardian*, June 2.

Fick, G.R. and Ritchie, J.R.B. (1991) 'Measuring service quality in the travel and tourism industry', *Journal of Travel Research*, 30(2), Autumn: 2–9.

Flanagan, J.C. (1954) 'The critical incidents technique', *Psychological Bulletin*, July, 51(4): 327–58.

Ford, J.W., Joseph, M. and Joseph, B. (1993) 'Service quality in higher education: a comparison of universities in the United States and New Zealand using SERVQUAL', unpublished manuscript, Old Dominion University, Norfolk, VA.

Fornell, C. (1992) 'A national customer satisfaction barometer: The Swedish experience', *Journal of Marketing*, 56, January: 6–21.

Freeman, K.D. and Dart, J. (1993) 'Measuring the perceived quality of professional business services', *Journal of Professional Services Marketing*, 9(1): 27–47.

Gilmore, A. (1997) 'Marketing in the northern European ferry industry: an overview of on-board activity', *Journal of Vacation Marketing*, 3(3): 207–20.

Johns, N. (1993) 'Quality management in the hospitality industry, part 3: recent developments', *International Journal of Contemporary Hospitality Management*, 5(1): 10–15.

Kingman-Brundage, J. (1989) 'The ABCs of service system blueprinting', in M. Bitner and L. Crosby (eds), *Designing a Winning Service Strategy*. Chicago, IL: American Marketing Association, pp. 30–33.

MacDonald, A. (1998) 'Special report: call centres', *Precision Marketing*, 27 April: 28–30.

Morgan, D.L. (1988) 'Focus groups as qualitative research', *Qualitative Research Methods*, Newbury Park, CA: Sage.

Nelson, P. (1974) 'Advertising as information', *Journal of Political Economy*, 91, July-August: 29–54.

Parasuraman, A., Zeithaml, V. and Berry, L.L. (1985) 'A conceptual model of service quality and its implications for further research', *Journal of Marketing*, 49, Fall: 41–50.

Parasuraman, A., Zeithaml, V. and Berry, L.L. (1988) 'SERVQUAL: a multiple-item scale for measuring consumer perceptions of service quality', *Journal of Retailing*, 64(1), Spring: 12–40.

Parasuraman, A., Zeithaml, V. and Berry, L.L. (1991) 'Understanding customer expectations of service', *Sloan Management Review*, Spring: 39–48.

Patton, M.Q. (1990) *Qualitative Evaluations and Research Methods*. Newbury, CA: Sage.

Rigotti, S. and Pitt, L. (1992) 'SERVQUAL as a measuring instrument for service provider gaps in business schools', *Management Research News*, 15(3): 9–17.

Rouffaer, B. (1991) 'In search of service: the GOS model', *International Journal of Hospitality Management*, 10(4): 313–21.

Rust, R.T., Keiningham, T.L. and Zahorik, A.J. (1996) *Service Marketing*. New York: Harper Collins College Publishers.

Selah, F. and Ryan, C. (1992) 'Analysing service quality in the hospitality industry using the SERVQUAL model', *Service Industries Journal*, 11(3): 324–43.

Shostack, G.L. (1981) 'How to design a service', in J. Donnelly and W.R. George (eds), *Marketing of Services*. Chicago, IL: American Marketing Association, pp. 221–9.

Shostack, G.L. (1984) 'Designing services that deliver', *Harvard Business Review*, Jan/Feb: 133–9.

Smith, S. (1987) 'How to quantify quality', *Management Today*, October: 86–8.

Taylor, S.A. and Cronin, J. (1994) 'An empirical assessment of the Servperf scale', *Journal of Marketing Theory and Practice*, 2, Fall: 52–69.

PART TWO

MANAGING SERVICES

3

Services Marketing in Specific Contexts – the For-Profit Sector

In this second part of the book the focus of discussion is on the management of services. The earlier chapters have focused on the theories and concepts based upon the unique characteristics of services and services marketing. While these theories and concepts may hold true at a general level of definition and description, how well do they translate to an industry or individual firm situation? This is an issue that has concerned many scholars and practitioners from the earliest stage of research in this area. Blois (1974) was one of the first to conceptualize the translation of general concepts and theories to individual products in the market. Focusing on buyer behaviour, Blois attempted to relate theories of services to different 'levels of abstraction'. This perspective differentiates the techniques of services marketing from consumer and industrial marketing and considers how these in turn apply to individual service or product marketing and at individual industry level. Levels of abstraction can be considered as different levels of generalization for buyer behaviour theories. The general marketing concepts, approaches and theories occur at the most abstract level. These can be distilled and refined by taking account of the techniques and concepts that are specific to services marketing. Further refinements and distillation are brought about by consideration of industry-specific characteristics, for example, the characteristics of industrial and consumer markets. Eventually, complete refinement of a service marketing circumstance is achieved by consideration of a single firm's situation-specific marketing circumstances (Rushton and Carson, 1985). This conceptual framework can be applied to any marketing situation. Indeed any studies which have looked at specific industries and firms within an industry implicitly apply this framework, for example Bateson's (1977) consideration of airlines, Gummesson's (1979) study of professional services, Lewis' (1991) study of banking services, and Lewis' (1987) and Lehtinen et al.s' (1994) studies of hotel services. In particular many of these specific industry studies have focused on defining the nature of service and service dimensions in a useful way. Different service contexts in both for-profit and not-for-profit businesses are considered here. First, in this chapter, financial services, tourism and hotel services are described in terms of the specific context characteristics and the service dimensions most relevant in that context. In the following chapter the examples of charities and museums are used to illustrate service marketing in not-for-profit contexts.

CONTEXT 1 – SERVICE MARKETING FOR RETAIL BANKING CONTEXTS

What concepts of services marketing apply to retail banking financial services and how can these be managed? Some of the relevant concepts of service marketing discussed in Chapters 1 and 2 are used as underpinnings in the development of a conceptual framework for retail banking services in this chapter. The conceptual framework is used as a base to highlight and evaluate the services marketing dimensions for financial service management and marketing.

A key issue for financial services today is to recognize the relevant service marketing dimensions required for reaching both new and existing customers, many of whom are changing the way they use financial services. Carrying out both transaction marketing, aimed at new customers and the mass market, and relationship marketing, aimed at maintaining profitable customers, has major implications for management particularly if they are to do this in a cost-effective and integrative way. Such integrative activity needs to be combined with the availability and opportunity to use sophisticated technology as part of the service delivery.

In the past, financial services were principally concerned with operational, risk and financial issues. In marketing terms they were product-led (Knights et al., 1994). Historically retail banks were established to handle money transmission and transaction processing activities and not to manage customer relationships or to sell products and services (Axson, 1992). Retail bank marketing activity has altered considerably over the last number of decades and most significantly in the final decades of the twentieth century. Regulatory, technological and changing consumer dynamics in the marketplace have had an impact on both the nature and extent of marketing activity in retail banking and have created considerable uncertainty for banks. At the same time, the requirements and expectations of customers have changed and technological developments have made huge differences in the scope and modes of financial service delivery.

Like many businesses today, financial services take place in an everchanging context. This has manifested itself in a number of ways. First, because of the increased dynamism in the external environment such as growth in competition, retail banks now need to focus on new customer recruitment. In an increasingly competitive marketplace, customer recruitment can contribute to reducing costs, maintaining and enhancing profitability and increasing market share. Secondly, as the financial marketplace becomes more dynamic and competitive, banks also need to focus on retaining existing clients through effective relationship marketing. In this context the benefits of long-term retention of existing customers, such as increased profitability, reduced costs in relation to the individual customer and word of mouth referrals from satisfied customers, become important (Gronroos, 1992, 1994; Heskett, 1987; Reichheld, 1993; Reichheld and Sasser, 1990). However the overall implication for retail bank marketing and management is that they need to have the expertise and resources to simultaneously recruit and retain customers.

Traditionally retail banks operated within a bureaucratic, conventional, slow-to-change industry within an environment of limited competition and acceptable profitability. While operating within this context, there was little need for overt or aggressive marketing (Devlin and Wright, 1995; Hughes, 1994). Traditional characteristics of retail bank marketing are summarized below.

1   There was little emphasis or resource allocated to managing supply and demand, for example customers were offered little choice in products and pricing was standardized.
2   Few resources were directed at controlling quality and productivity, or managing the customer's interaction with the retail bank; traditionally distribution occurred through one all encompassing channel, the branch network.
3   Few resources were directed at managing customers' expectations; for example, many traditional activities were driven by the transaction and processing needs of the bank as opposed to the needs of customers.

However in recent years this position has altered because of regulatory, technological and changing consumer dynamics. Today the characteristics of this sector are different in the following ways.

1   Deregulation has had an impact upon credit restrictions and pricing controls and lowered the barriers that traditionally protected the banking sector. This has led to increased competition between the banks and other financial service providers.

Table 3.1 *Context characteristics for retail banking services*

Characteristics	Impacts upon	Leads to
Deregulation	Credit restrictions, pricing controls, protective barriers	Increased competition
Technology advancement	Bank/customer interactions	Cost reductions, increased competition
Change in nature of demand	Competitive activity, customer dynamics	Increasing customer requirements and expectations

2   Technological advancements have altered the nature of the bank/customer interaction (Howcroft and Kiely, 1995; Trethowan and Scullion, 1997). Costs have been reduced (Devlin and Wright, 1995) and increased competition has occurred because non-traditional players have considerable access to the financial service marketplace from which they had previously been excluded (Howcroft and Lavis, 1986; Thwaites, 1989).
3   A change in the nature and extent of demand in the sector (McKechnie and Harrison, 1995; Trethowan and Scullion, 1997). This includes augmented competitive activity and changing consumer dynamics such as increased education levels and higher incomes, increasing what the customer expects and requires from the financial service provider (Devlin and Wright, 1995; Hughes, 1994; Knights et al., 1994; Walsh, 2001).

All of these changes have major implications for financial service providers, as seen in Table 3.1. The overall effect of these changes is that the marketing environment is now much more open and attractive for competitive financial service provision. There is increased competition as many companies traditionally not involved in banking (such as Marks and Spencer, Sainsburys) offer financial service products previously offered only by banks, and there has been a reduction in the profitability of traditional areas of bank business. High cost structures and the prevalence of unprofitable customers (for example, customers who use current accounts purely to process wages) have forced contemporary retail banks to focus on supply and demand management. So today retail banks recognize that they need to become more adept at marketing services to customers. For example, customers require different modes of service such as contact face-to-face or by electronic means, so banks need to offer appropriate modes for customers.

Therefore for retail banks where the focus of service is on retaining existing, more traditional customers *and* attracting new, longer-term and increasingly profitable customers, the key issues for management are marketing to both transaction-type and relationship-type customers. This is often a difficult challenge for banks with experience in traditional practices and limited expertise in current competitive, hi-tech and dynamic environments.

Service dimensions for retail banking services

Retail bank marketing activity is usually aimed at a mass audience with little differentiation of products evident in relation to the activities described below. The retail services product activities revolve around the provision of mortgages, personal loans, payment services and specific products such as children's accounts and student packages. Traditionally retail bank distribution was based upon the branch network and automatic teller machines (ATMs). Today the service can be delivered through telesales and web-based banking. Pricing aspects of retail services include fees and service charges for processing transactions. In order to reach a mass audience retail banks use mass communication to reach customers, sending the same advertising message to everyone, emphasizing the current package of financial products with the same logo and promotional details. Sales promotions are usually price-based or product-based, featuring generic products and using branch promotional literature. Publicity and sponsorship activities revolve around local and national events and sporting associations. Personal communication and sales activities often use a similar message, a message for the mass audience but sent to customers via the branch outlet with a specific local manager's name attached.

Also for retail bank services the physical evidence dimension of the branch network – space, management of queues and ATMs – is important in the overall marketing activity. Some banks have attempted to separate this dimension of service delivery for relationship and transaction customers. The service process is inherently linked with the physical evidence and the whole management of the service delivery will require careful integration of all the dimensions of marketing which are often encapsulated in the interactions with front-line staff. Therefore the people dimension in terms of managing staff and giving customers an effective and efficient service is vital. The scope of service dimensions for retail banks is illustrated in Figure 3.1.

However the relevance and relative importance of these dimensions will be different for transaction-type and relationship-type customers. The dimensions most appropriate to transaction marketing activity and relationship marketing activity are described in the following sections.

Most relevant service dimensions for transaction marketing

For discrete transactions (where both parties receive and give benefit or value), the most important service dimensions are product activities, distribution activities and pricing activities and achieving competitiveness by managing costs efficiently.

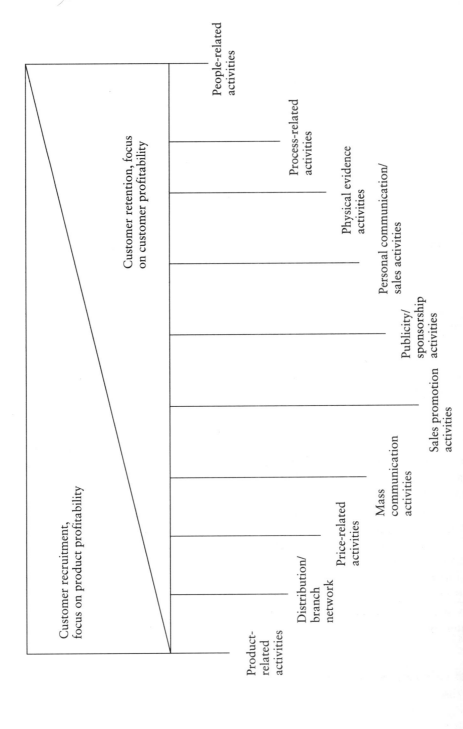

FIGURE 3.1 The scope and range of service dimensions for retail banks

In repeated transactions, while the price is still important, other activities that facilitate demand stimulation such as brand loyalty, differentiation and preference may also be significant. Thus transaction marketing incorporates mass marketing but may also include more personalized, direct interaction between the two parties to an exchange, such as the personalized interaction that may happen between the buyer and the firm's salesperson. For repeat purchases, brand loyalty, satisfaction with the product and repeated personal interactions mean that relationships may or may not be established.

Therefore while transaction marketing is wide in scope, some activities are of more importance than others and as such require more resources. Clearly product, distribution and pricing activities are of key importance in transaction-based marketing and some aspects of communication and personal selling may become more important in repeated transactions. This indicates that retail banks engaging in effective transaction marketing need to invest resources in delivering these most relevant service dimensions to reach this market segment.

While retail banks need to engage in effective transaction marketing activity to ensure ongoing recruitment they also have to deliver appropriate service dimensions to retain profitable customers. Strengthening relationships with existing customers leads to greater profitability than equivalent efforts aimed at attracting new customers. In seeking to identify the customers with most potential for becoming relationship customers, organizations should not focus on the entire customer base but on those customers that are profitable (Berry, 1995). Some long-lasting customer relationships, where the customers are obviously satisfied with what they get, are not profitable in the long run (Storbacka, 1993). This is particularly true in retail banking where implicit pricing, high money transmission usage and low balances may result in some customers being unprofitable. Consequently, as the environment becomes increasingly competitive, retail banks are making retention and segmentation decisions based on customer relationship profitability analysis. Many retail banks appear to be applying the Pareto principle, assuming that 20 per cent of customers contribute 80 per cent of the profits (as shown in Figure 3.2), to their existing customer base in an attempt to identify profitable customers and segment them from those that contribute less profitability (Neenar, 1993).

Most relevant service dimensions for relationship marketing

Relationship marketing activity focuses primarily on the interactive relationship between the buyer and seller (Gronroos, 1994) and is deemed to be effective in achieving customer retention objectives (Berry, 1995; Webster, 1992). The objective of relationship marketing focuses on creating continuous value for both parties who invest resources to develop a mutually beneficial, adaptive relationship (Coviello et al., 1997; Gummesson, 1998). In the relationship situation the customer evaluates ongoing value creation and the quality of the relationship ties that exist (Gronroos, 1994). Similarly, the seller focuses on the extent to which the relationship facilitates the achievement of

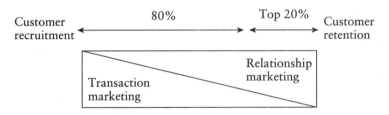

FIGURE 3.2 **The Pareto principle applied to transaction- and relationship-style customers**

objectives that may or may not centre on profitability. Consequently, in relational exchange the relationship itself and its economic and non-economic elements become important aspects of the service delivery. While activities such as the product and price are not unimportant, they require less emphasis than those activities that support interactive marketing at the individual customer level.

Thus while relationship marketing is wide in scope, some activities are of more importance than others and therefore require more resources. Consequently to engage in successful relationship marketing retail banks have to apportion resources to service dimensions on the basis of the importance to this customer segment. Managing customers' interactions and expectations in relation to physical evidence, process and people are the service dimensions of key importance in relationship marketing which indicates that these activities require more resource investment than other dimensions.

CONTEXT 2 – SERVICE MARKETING FOR TOURISM CONTEXTS

Tourism is a complex phenomenon. It encapsulates a varying number of services and processes. It is not an industry or a sector in the traditional sense, rather it is an economic activity that runs through all of society, involving many different and varied sectors, pushed forward by market forces, controlled by regulatory frameworks and governed by general economic conditions (Doswell, 1997).

The tourist industry is one of the largest, most dynamic industries in the world. It is one of the largest employers of all industries and continues to grow from year to year and is recognized as one of the world's largest and fastest growing industries. Indeed this sector has become the biggest source of job creation in many developed and developing countries. In many countries and regions tourism is vital to the economy because it attracts visitors who bring spending power. In many of these areas tourism businesses such as hotels and unique attractions are a vital part of foreign earnings and a focal point for tourism development.

However in many smaller regions, tourism as an economic activity suffers from a lack of impact on the world market. Often this is because of a relatively small promotional voice, promoting different elements to different markets. To exacerbate this any promotional activity may have its impact reduced by the various and many other market noises coming from other regions, countries and continents.

Tourism has many benefits. It can encourage civic involvement and thus help create pride within the community. Tourism money helps support the community infrastructure and services such as recreational facilities that an area may not otherwise have been able to afford. Due to its labour intensity it can also help improve educational standards, as demand increases the need for trained, educated and skilled tourism employees in many localities. Environmentally tourism can encourage community beautification and revitalization. It also helps encourage the conservation and protection of an area's historical, cultural and natural resources (Archer and Cooper, 1994).

Many definitions of tourism have been put forward. At an international conference on travel and tourism organized by the Canadian Government and the World Tourism Organization (WTO) held in Ottawa in June 1991, new definitions were laid down aimed at standardizing the measurement of tourism. These differentiated between the different types of tourist, traveller and visitor.

Tourism describes the activities of persons travelling to and staying in places outside their usual environment for not more than one continuous year for leisure, business and other purposes. A traveller describes any person on a trip between two or more locations. A visitor is any person travelling to a place other than that of his/her usual environment for fewer than 12 consecutive months and whose main purpose of travel is not to work for pay in the place visited. A tourist (or overnight visitor) is a person staying at least one night in collective or private accommodation in the place visited. A same-day visitor (or excursionist) is a visitor who does not spend the night in collective or private accommodation in the place visited.

Given the unique characteristics and the complex nature of the tourist service, there are many different demands for tourist services. There are many varying combinations that travellers can choose from in terms of destinations, accommodation, types of transport, services and activities that have led to the creation of a wide range of differentiated products. Over time and experience different types of tourism have been developed to include:

1 Domestic and international travel, according to whether the destination chosen is inside or outside the frontiers of the tourist's own country.
2 Sun and sea holiday, with the chosen destination on the coast in an area where the climate is usually good.
3 Cultural tourism that is focused on arts events, monuments, museums, exhibitions, visits to historical and archaeological sites and festivals.

Table 3.2 *Context characteristics for tourism services*

Characteristics	Impacts upon	Leads to
Involvement of both public and private companies	Planning co-ordination, different levels of management efficiency and effectiveness	Lack of overall coherent directions
Many companies are Small – medium sized enterprises	Limited resources and expertise available	Lack of involvement in wider industry networks and planning
Variety of service products	Markets for different services, type of message to be communicated to market	Potential for mismatch between advertising message and market
Fragmentation of industry and infrastructure	All marketing planning and activity	Inefficiencies, duplication of marketing activities, market confusion

4 Sports tourism, where the motivation is to participate in or attend a sports event.
5 Health tourism where the aim is to undergo some form of health treatment, normally involving specially trained qualified staff. For example, health farm, spas and thermal baths.
6 Rural tourism, which entails the use of resources in a rural area in order to increase the general welfare of the community and the visitor.
7 Leisure and business travel, depending on the main reason for the trip. Business travel may include meetings, conferences, conventions, training and sales missions, general promotional and professional contact work. It is usually concentrated in economic centres. Leisure travel will be independently organized or through a travel agent and is likely to include more regional spread with more diverse destinations.

In addition to these, there are other types of tourism, many relating to specific interests of groups of visitors. However many of these types of tourism are not mutually exclusive and often visitors seek a number of the different experiences listed above from one holiday.

Tourism marketing is directed to a mass market. It is aimed at both local and global customers. In recent years, more affluent lifestyles have led to higher demands for quality in both tangible and intangible aspects of tourism services. Overall this has occurred in the context of increased competition and better standards of service quality in the industry in general. The tourism sector has some very specific characteristics that impact upon any marketing activity. These are illustrated in Table 3.2 and discussed briefly below.

Involvement of public and private companies

Tourism is 'managed' by a number of private and public organizations. Usually within a geographical region, there is a national tourism organization. This organization's role is to guide the development of the sector through planning, marketing, supporting, directing, promoting and co-ordinating various endeavours and activities. However in practice, this is a complex and difficult role given the number of other public and private businesses involved and the different agendas that each of these organizations may have.

Traditionally the public sector in the form of national and regional tourism organizations has had a key role in the successful development of tourism. It has been argued that for the long-term interest of the tourism service/product, public sector intervention is necessary to ensure that the associated benefits of tourism are maximized and any potential problems are minimized for the benefit of the economy, society and environment (Witt and Moutinho, 1994). On the other hand, although many public sector organizations exist to plan and manage the sector and work in close collaboration with all other interests, the public sector has been accused of being indirect, inefficient and ineffective.

However, because tourism contributes to local and national economic regeneration, local authorities become involved in the management of tourism destination areas. Activities are limited because local authorities often have small promotional budgets at their disposal and they are dependent on the activities of other firms in the industry for success. They are also not known for their culture of entrepreneurship, a characteristic currently needed within the increasingly competitive market for attracting tourists.

Public and private companies have different ways of working and different priorities in how they do business. Because of this and the number of different private and public companies involved, tourism suffers from a lack of a strong and focused co-ordinating role in many regions. This impacts upon the success or otherwise of attempts to market the product in its entirety, deal with fragmentation within the industry, strive to create a national competitive advantage and develop the overall tourist product necessary in every tourist country or region.

The tourism product is compiled from a combination of elements from both the private and public sectors. The private sector is responsible for tourist attractions operating to narrow commercial criteria, while the public sector has responsibility for infrastructure and planning policies that affect tourism. Local authorities play a large part in promoting the benefits of their areas. For example it falls upon local authorities to provide ancillary facilities, and services such as car parking and clean physical facilities and locations, that will impact on a tourist's visit. They are also responsible for many local planning and conservation policies. However local authorities are often constrained by a bureaucratic culture and political pressure to meet the needs of their own residents as well as those of potential visitors. Also local councils may often be competing with those from other areas for a limited number of visitors.

More recently, local collaborative marketing ventures have become common in this field (Palmer, 2001). For example, in some regions, tourism development action programmes have been created to overcome some of the problems discussed above. These involve partnership between public and private sector organizations such as district and county councils, urban development organizations, local landowners, hotel owners and operators of tourism attractions. These action programmes aim to support tourism and promote inward tourism and result in more tourist spending across the area as a whole.

Private companies involved in tourism are often providers of very specific services such as food, accommodation or leisure activities. Many of these companies are small- to medium-sized enterprises.

Involvement of SMEs

Small- to medium-sized enterprises by their very nature have limitations of resources in terms of finance and expertize. In this sector, as in any other, SMEs are restrained by the limitations of resources, from financial to human, and the impact this has on their marketing activities and specialist expertise (Go et al., 1992; Witt and Moutinho, 1994). For example limitations include lack of staff to carry out marketing duties, limited promotional budgets, limited marketing knowledge and background, limited expertise and limited time.

Often SMEs in this sector perceive that they work within an under-developed industry, where the region's marketing activity has little impact on the wider market. SMEs in this sector often suffer from an overall lack of competitiveness and may have very limited offerings for the tourist. Indeed, many SMEs in the tourist industry have a lack of involvement in local or regional tourism structure and networks and do not explicitly recognize themselves as part of the wider industry.

Variety of service products and marketing the destination in its entirety

Within any region there will be a wide variety of offerings. It is more effective to offer a service product package that can be 'sold' as a whole offering, including a desirable area with different options for visitors, for example, where visitors can choose to experience any combination of attractions including areas of natural beauty, unique features and specific facilities such as golfing, cinemas and museums. Managers involved in tourism services now recognize that potential tourist trade will come from people wanting to visit the regional or national geographic area as well as experience specific facilities, so that the destination needs to be promoted and sold as an integrated and complete offering.

Fragmentation

The industry is recognized as being fragmented because of the scope and dimensions that make up the various parts. The involvement of both public and private companies and the diverse nature of the private companies, many of them SMEs, contribute to this fragmentation. Fragmentation makes it difficult for a national tourism organization in any region to brand or market a national destination because of geographical and socio-cultural diversities.

Equally the nature of some of the organizations involved in the tourism sector contributes to the fragmentation. Public and private companies have different agendas and each will have different ways of operating and doing business. Also the large and small companies involved will do business in different ways.

In addition to these characteristics there are changes occurring in the overall market environment that will have an impact on the tourism sector. Recently the impact of the Internet upon the whole tourism industry is being welcomed. It is anticipated that it will have an overall positive effect in relation to benefits for both the customer and the tourist region. It allows the tourism sector to expand its marketing and reach a larger market. It also creates an easy-to-access and wider level of choice for the customer and exposes them to various choices of service product and different levels of service quality and so should have a positive effect on service quality within the industry. However because of its ability to reach customers without any contact with other players in the industry it could also be argued that it contributes to further fragmentation of the industry.

A number of environmental and socio-economic factors will inevitably influence the development of the tourism industry during the next decades. These include enhanced consumer sophistication, demographic changes, and a growing awareness of 'green', ecological and sustainable tourism issues. All will have an impact upon the perception, management and significance of tourism marketing.

Services marketing dimensions for the tourism sector

Services marketing dimensions for the tourism sector reflect the range and multi-dimensional nature of tourism service products, managing the tourism product, the importance of effective and consistent service delivery and the communication message and region's image. These dimensions are illustrated in Figure 3.3 and described below.

Range and multi-dimensional nature of tourism service products

The scope and range of tourism service products are vast. They can range from very tangible products such as geographical areas, unique sites, and man-made facilities to more intangible specific attractions, destination facilities and amenities, accessibility, images and price. All aspects of the tourism service product must be recognized, explicitly provided in relevant places and in adequate numbers. Deficiencies need to be identified so that they can be met both in terms of the infrastructure and tangible elements and the intangible aspects of service. Large investments are required for the tangible aspects of

Range and nature of service	Managing the tourism product	Effective and consistent service delivery	Communication message and region's image
Geographical area	Differentiation and positioning destination image	Physical infrastructure, facilities and service	Public and press messages
Unique site		People involved in service delivery	Branding
Man-made facilities	Developing and marketing tourism brand		Image building
Destination facilities			
Accessibility	Looking for new markets		
Image			
Price range			

FIGURE 3.3   Service dimensions for tourism marketing

tourism services and therefore financial support often needs to be provided from public bodies for aspects of service development. The overall development of the tourism product needs to focus on meeting market deficiencies and delivering tangibles and intangibles. Given the scope and range of tourism service products there is a considerable managerial role implied in co-ordinating this service delivery.

Marketing the tourism product

Today consumers have an expanding choice of destinations. Consequently tourism marketers need to persuade customers in an increasingly competitive global market to achieve competitive advantage. Marketing the tourism product involves differentiating and positioning a strong destination image, developing and marketing a tourism brand and looking for new or niche markets. To achieve this the companies involved in the tourism sector need to come together to integrate their market focus and offerings. A strongly integrated and recognizable tourism service needs to evolve and strengthen over time before an appropriate brand can be developed based on the overall market positioning of the tourism service product for any area.

The entire tourist service process consists of many services and different groups of service employees. For example, a typical 'fully extended product' experience for a tourist will include a long and often sequential path. First, a potential tourist will choose a location from a wide range of locations within a specific region. Each location will offer a wide range of services and price ranges. Promotional and communication activities will be most successful if there is a joint investment in marketing by all parties involved in the delivery of the tourism product. Often a varied range of promotional material is used for different aspects of tourism marketing.

Tourism service providers need to be familiar with the area and be able and willing to respond to detailed queries about the local area. In addition a referral network needs to be developed between the area attractions, hotels and other service facilities. For example leaflets about a hotel's facilities and services should be available at the local tourism centre and at public centres such as museums and cinemas, and vice versa.

Effective and consistent service delivery

Tourism is widely recognized as being a people business. The full range of features and characteristics that make up any tourism experience is extremely wide and will vary from customer to customer. Each experience will be different due to the characteristics of services, both tangible and intangible.

As discussed earlier, the technical or instrumental aspects of a service product delivery need to be satisfied before the functional or psychological aspects of service delivery can be delivered. In a tourism context this translates into the need for a physical infrastructure, facilities and security before attracting visitors to an area. This creates a challenge for smaller or poorer countries and regions as continued success requires careful marketing planning and financial resources to ensure that competitive international tourism benefits and facilities can be offered. The large number of companies, groups and organizations involved in any region's tourism activity result in a complicated and diverse industry to be managed, marketed, improved and co-ordinated.

Often people will carry out the more intangible aspects of the service delivery. This highlights the importance of staff training for this sector and competence in delivering a wide choice and range of services in a flexible way. In addition, as tourism is aimed at a mass market, there is an inherent need to deliver a wide range of service products that satisfy the needs of different groups within that mass market in terms of price ranges and product variability.

The communication message and the region's image

Communicating to the general public and press within a region or internationally is a large challenge. What is written about a country, whether the country appears positively or negatively in the press, news releases or general word-of-mouth can have a large influence on the country's future as a tourist attraction. Often such communication can occur without any direct intention of reaching the media.

A universal brand name is often used to send a range of messages to the market and public. A successful brand name can be very useful in a competitive marketplace as this will help differentiate a region from many local or national competitors. In recent years, many regions have focused on developing a brand for their region in order to attract tourists in a competitive arena.

Often a country is influenced by its history. Building an image involves clarity in identifying key country values, aims and objectives and may be based upon the country's historical values and purpose. Well-designed and appropriate communication messages, combined with the successful branding of a region can create and maintain a suitable image for a region over time.

CONTEXT 3 – SERVICE MARKETING FOR HOTEL CONTEXTS

Hospitality has been defined as the friendly reception and entertainment of guests or strangers. The hospitality industry consists of all those businesses that give their customers any combination of the three core requirements of food, drink and accommodation, at an appropriate service level, within a physical and social environment that caters for their physiological, psychological and social needs (Littlejohn, 1990). Any establishment that caters for any of these needs and offers food, drink or accommodation falls within the hospitality industry. These include hotels, motels, small businesses such as bed and breakfast establishments, hostels, restaurants, bars and canteens. This example focuses on the hotel sector.

The hotel industry is one of the largest, most dynamic industries in the world. It is one of the largest employers of all industries and continues to increase along with any increase in the local economy, tourism and business travel.

Hotels play many important roles within an economy. First, they provide facilities for the transaction of business, for meetings and conferences, for recreation and entertainment. In doing this hotels contribute to the overall output of goods and services at community, national and international level. In addition hotels are important outlets for the products of other industries such as construction, food, drink and other consumable services and a wide range of manufacturers. They are also a local source of amenities for local residents, and so many hotels have become social centres of their communities.

In many areas hotels are important attractions for visitors who bring spending power that, in turn, contributes to the local economy. Many regions that attract foreign visitors depend upon the existence of a suitable number and quality of hotels to create the infrastructure for a vital part of foreign currency earnings and to act as a focal point for tourism development.

The hospitality business has been identified as being a people business. The full range of features and characteristics that make up any hospitality experience are extremely wide and the use of the variety of services will vary from customer to customer. Each experience will be different due to the characteristics of services, both tangible and intangible.

The most relevant context characteristics impacting upon the service marketing requirements for a hotel service are marketing the destination in addition to the hotel, marketing to new customers *and* those who make repeat visits to same hotel, and consistency among services offered and among similar chain hotels. These are illustrated in Table 3.3 and described below.

Marketing the destination in addition to the hotel
In marketing a hotel's offerings to the national or international market, a hotel needs to provide information about the local region and geographic area as well as the hotel services. This will be part of the reason why visitors

Table 3.3   *Context characteristics for hotel services*

Characteristics	Impacts upon	Leads to
Marketing the destination and the hotel	Hotel advertising, publicity activities, range of hotel facilities	Need for integrated and competitive marketing effort
Attracting new visitors and repeat visitors	Marketing activity, range of hotel facilities	Need for variety and regular updating of facilities/premises
Consistency among hotel chains	Operational standards and procedures	Need for competitive edge, strong branding

will come to the hotel and region. Such information should be included in the hotel's overall promotional materials. For example, attracting international conferences will be easier if the location of the hotel can be 'sold' as a desirable area to visit where delegates can have the option of visiting some local attractions such as golfing, cinemas, museums, areas of natural beauty. Such material should be included in the hotel's advertising and promotional material.

The local knowledge of the hotel staff is also important so employees can successfully sell the destination as a whole. Indeed many hotels provide area familiarization information and seminars to educate employees about the most frequent questions asked regarding the local area. This type of effort helps to market the hotel in the long term. In addition a referral network could be developed between the area attractions and the hotel's management and staff. For example leaflets of the hotel's facilities and services can be made available at the local tourism centre, at public centres such as museums, cinemas, and so on, to help raise the hotel's profile.

The use of the Internet by the hotel industry has had an overall positive effect in relation to service quality for both the customer and the hotelier. It allows hotels to expand their marketing and reach a larger market. It also creates easy access and a wider level of choice for the customer and creates awareness of the various levels of service quality available in the sector.

Attracting new visitors and repeat visits to the same hotel
Much of a hotel's marketing effort is focused on attracting new customers or new markets, such as conference business or weddings. However, because hotels are associated with hospitality and home-from-home experiences by many customers, they often recognize the importance of developing a database of regular customers, their preferences and characteristics. Indeed, customers using the same hotel over and over again expect to be recognized by staff, to be called by name and have some acknowledgement given about their service preferences. Such additional intangible benefits are often sought and expected by repeat customers.

Consistency among hotel chains

Consistency is a key factor in running a service business. It means that a customer will receive the expected product and service without unwanted surprises. Within the hospitality sector many hotel chains have worked extremely hard at developing a set of standards and procedures to ensure that each hotel within the chain operates to a specific level of performance. Indeed many chains have built strong brands in relation to the different levels of hotel facilities and performance within their larger network of hotels. For international visitors, brands create an immediate recognition of the standards of service a hotel is likely to offer.

A number of environmental and socio-economic factors will inevitably influence the development of the hotel industry during the next decade. These include increasing competition, a greater demand for productivity, enhanced technological sophistication, demographic change, and a growing awareness of 'green', ecological issues. All will have an impact upon the perception, management and significance of service quality in hotels in the future.

Recognition of the existence of the 'global customer' and more affluent lifestyles has led to higher demands for quality of both tangible and intangible aspects of service, leading to an increase in competition and better overall standards of service quality.

Services marketing dimensions for hotels

The entire hotel service process consists of many services and different groups of service employees. For example, a typical 'fully extended product' experience for a hotel guest will involve a long path through many processes and experiences of different types of service. Initially a potential hotel guest will choose a hotel from a range of hotels within a specific location that offer relatively similar services and price ranges. When a hotel has been chosen the potential guest will then make a reservation and receive directions to the hotel if necessary. When the time comes, the guest will then travel to the hotel, park the car or arrive by taxi, walk into the hotel and enter the service environment. This is where they will experience first impressions of the environment after all the pre-purchase effort of selecting and travelling to the hotel. The during-purchase experience now begins with entering the lobby and being greeted by reception and/or porter staff. Then the guest will check in, have luggage taken to the room and will go to the room. At this point the first impressions of the room are important. The guest will look around the room in order to find everything he/she will possibly need during the stay. Often at this stage the guest may seek information from the brochure and promotional material in the room and may need some assistance from a hotel employee in room service, laundry service or information on how to use business or leisure facilities. Other services the guest may want to use include using the telephone system to call home, the hotel's business equipment or its work-out facilities; or he/she may want to have a shower and/or get advice

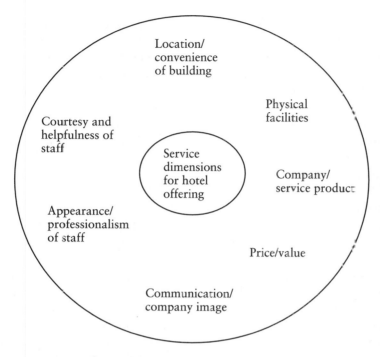

FIGURE 3.4   Service marketing dimensions for hotels

on restaurants. At the end of the stay the guest will have breakfast, check out, retrieve the car from the car park or order a taxi, and travel home or to the airport. However, this should not be the end of the contact between hotel and guest. If sufficiently proactive, a hotel will provide some follow-up initiative to ensure the guest will consider staying in the same hotel again. The specific dimensions of the service marketing 'package' for the hotel industry are illustrated in Figure 3.4 and considered below.

Location/convenience of building

The general location of the hotel is important in the first place in attracting visitors to that region or part of town. The convenience of finding the hotel is important when the guest is actually travelling to the hotel. For example, the ease of finding the hotel, the convenience of parking facilities, the effectiveness and visibility of signage to the hotel, security, the range of types of transport links and ease of access to the building are all important aspects of this service dimension. Also the close proximity to tourist attractions and/or business locations are vital for different visitor markets.

Physical facilities

Hotels need to maintain an up-to-date internal and external appearance and image. The overall appearance and detail of the physical facilities are very important in how the hotel is perceived. A hotel's appearance should be in keeping with the type of service provided. Facilities need to include both hygiene factors and motivators. In the context of a hotel service hygiene factors include standard requirements like the cleanliness of toilets. Customers will expect these to be adequate otherwise they will be dissatisfied. Motivators are those characteristics of service that customers value highly – for example, the range of facilities available. Often motivators are intangibles; for example, customers expect hotel staff to make them feel valued and important and it is this treatment that will motivate customers to use the service again. Hotel staff are ultimately expected to be honest, polite and courteous to all guests.

Company/service product

The hospitality service product consists of a wide variety of services such as restaurants, bars, entertainment and leisure facilities. Clearly hotels need to offer a range of food, drinks and other facilities to suit different needs of guests. Food services using different styles of operation such as à la carte, buffet and cafeteria may also be offered to suit the time available and usage required by guests. The range of entertainment should also take the needs and preferences of hotel guests into account and be suitable for different events, times of the year or week and the requirements of guests staying in the hotel at the time. The location of the hotel will also impact upon the range and scope of services offered. A remote country hotel may offer comprehensive in-house leisure facilities and entertainment whereas a city centre hotel may not need to offer such a range of facilities as guests will be more likely to go out of the hotel to experience the city.

Price/value

The pricing aspect of the hotel service needs to take account of a combination of tangible and intangible aspects of service delivery. It will include convenience, hotel location, the quality of the room, availability, choice of facilities and overall image of the hotel. Pricing tends to capture the value of the product in the customer's mind – it directs their attention to the value of the product and service. To hoteliers setting the appropriate price is important so that they can cover costs and make a profit. To customers value for money and what they get for different prices is more important. However the overall aim is to provide the tangible and intangible dimensions expected from the service at a price that reflects the image of the hotel and is competitive in that context.

The communication/company image

Communicating the company and/or individual hotel image incorporates both an external and internal element. The external element includes the promotion of the hotel to the market. This will involve communicating to the general public and press within a region or indeed, if the hotel is part of a chain, nationally and internationally. What is written about the company, whether the hotel appears positively or negatively in the press, news releases or general word-of-mouth communication can have a large influence on the hotel's future. Often such communication can occur without the hotel's direct intention of reaching the media. A company or hotel brand name is often used in the hospitality industry and the brand name sends a lot of messages to the market and public. A successful brand name can be very useful for a competitive hotel or hotels as this will help it differentiate itself from many local or national competitors.

However, company image is much more than a general idea that consumers get from externally created communication. It will also be influenced by the management's choice of promotional mix activity and messages about the different hotel services aimed at different target markets. The messages these promotions carry and the way these are executed will also contribute to the company image. In addition the price will provide an indicator in relation to the overall level of service and image to be expected from the hotel. Often a company is influenced by its history and sometimes by a previous management ethos that may be difficult to shed. Although this can be controlled by new management it may be difficult to change in the short term.

Building a company image involves clarity in identifying company values, aims and objectives, based upon the company's historical values and purpose. This needs to be instilled in the whole organizational ethos.

The values or meaning of a hotel brand are conveyed in the way the company does business and so the communication of values is vital throughout the organization. An advertising campaign or promotional activity alone cannot communicate company image. It also depends on everyone in the company, from the top down and especially the front-line service staff. Therefore staff training should be built around the delivery of service consistent with the overall image the company seeks to exude.

Appearance and professionalism of staff

Hotel guests' perception of staff will be determined by how the staff appear and the level of professionalism demonstrated. This will entail both tangible and intangible qualities. For example the physical appearance of staff in terms of being clean and tidy and identifiable as staff is important. Also the more intangible aspects of appearing to be professional depend on staff attitudes, actions and ability to carry out the service role in relation to all aspects of service delivery. Thus hotel staff need to be provided with an appropriate uniform or something to identify them with the hotel, such as a name badge. They also need to be suitably trained in both the technical aspects of service such as food service, but also in relation to interacting with customers and other aspects of customer care.

Courtesy and helpfulness of staff

Because of the highly people-dependent services in hotels, the quality of face-to-face interactions and front-line company staff can have a major influence on the perceived service quality and customer care in general. Human performance plays a central role in customers' perceptions of service quality.

Carlzon (1987) has famously called these interactions 'moments of truth'. These interactions can be interpreted as moments of opportunity where the hotel's reputation is under scrutiny. Other studies have illustrated that companies can create differential advantage through developing the courtesy and helpfulness of staff in delivering the service. For example, Judd (1987) argues that the role of people should be defined as the fifth 'P' in the marketing mix of some organizations. The importance of staff courtesy and helpfulness is vital and any staff training or on-the-job development should instil the notion that every individual within an organization needs to know it is important and understand how they and other members of staff can put it into practice.

To improve perceptions of staff in relation to serving and helping customers, many companies have tried schemes which involved treating employees as customers, that is internal marketing training. Berry describes this as 'viewing employees as internal customers, viewing jobs as internal products and then endeavouring to offer internal products that satisfy the need and wants of these internal customers while addressing the objectives of the organization' (1981: 34). Internal marketing (discussed in Chapter 7) is useful in emphasizing that customer service is not just the responsibility of front-line staff. Indeed it is the responsibility of all hotel employees service to customers to provide excellent, be they front-line or back office/support staff; this demands a commitment from all levels of management.

SUMMARY

This chapter has discussed the contextual issues impacting upon marketing and management in retail banking, tourism and hotel services. The most relevant service dimensions in each context were discussed. These included the range and nature of the multi-dimensional service product, marketing to the relevant target markets and the key issues affecting consistent service delivery in each context.

In the context of retail banking services, the different service dimensions for transaction and relationship services marketing were considered and the relatively diverse concepts underpinning transaction and relationship marketing were discussed. In increasingly competitive and dynamic environments retail banks need to identify the range of issues involved in integrating these two perspectives and effectively allocate resources to achieve both customer recruitment and retention or penetration objectives. Many retail banks may not fully recognize the situations where discrepancies can exist between trying to deliver both transactional and relationship marketing in practice.

Secondly the most relevant service dimensions in the context of tourism were discussed. These included the range and nature of the multi-dimensional service product, the difficulty in managing the tourism product, the effective and consistent service delivery and the communication message and the region's image.

Finally, the service context and relevant service dimensions for the hospitality industry were discussed. These highlighted the wide range of service dimensions included in a hotel service. Also the discussion recognized the high reliance on people and the implications this has for the management of hotel staff.

DISCUSSION QUESTIONS

In what ways do the different contexts of services have an impact upon the nature and scope of service dimensions to be delivered?

What is the difference between transaction- and relationship-type customers? Why are these differences important to the financial service manager?

What contextual issues impact upon marketing tourism services?

What service dimensions are most relevant to tourism marketing and how can the overall tourism service be managed effectively?

What service dimensions are most relevant to hotel service marketing and why?

NOTE

Some of the retail banking section of this chapter is based on the following article: Carson, D., Gilmore, A. and Walsh, S. (2003) 'Integrating transaction and relationship marketing activity in retail banking', under review for the *Journal of Marketing Management*.

REFERENCES

Archer, B. and Cooper, C. (1994) 'The positive and negative impacts of tourism', in W. Theobold, *Global Tourism. The Next Decade.* Oxford: Butterworth.

Axson, D. (1992) 'A return to managing customer relationships', *International Journal of Bank Marketing*, 10(1): 30–35.

Bateson, J. (1977) 'Do we need services marketing?', in P. Eiglier (ed.), *Marketing Consumer Services: New Insights*. Cambridge, MA: Marketing Science Institute, report no. 77–115, pp. 1–30.

Berry, L.L. (1981) 'The employee as customer', *Journal of Retail Banking*, 11(1), March: 34.

Berry, L.L. (1995) 'Relationship marketing of services – growing interest, emerging perspectives', *Journal of the Academy of Marketing Science*, 23(4): 236–45.

Blois, K.J. (1974) 'The marketing of services: an approach', *European Journal of Marketing*, 8(2): 137–45.

Carlzon, J. (1987) *Moments of Truth*. New York: Bellinger.

Coviello, N., Brodie, R.J. and Munro, H. (1997) 'Understanding contemporary marketing: development of a classification scheme', *Journal of Marketing Management*, 13(6): 501–52.

Devlin, J. and Wright, M. (1995) 'The changing environment of financial services', in C. Ennew, T. Watkins and M. Wright (eds), *Marketing Financial Services*, 2nd edn. Oxford: Butterworth-Heinemann.

Doswell, R. (1997) *Tourism. How Effective Management Makes the Difference*. Oxford: Butterworth-Heinemann.

Go, F.M., Milne, D. and Whittles, L. (1992) 'Communications as destinations: a marketing taxonomy for the effective implementation of the tourism action plan', *Journal of Travel Research*, 30(4): 4–13.

Gronroos, C. (1992) 'Facing the challenge of service competition: the economies of service', in P. Kunst and J. Lemmink (eds), *Quality Management in Services*. Maastricht: Van Gorcum, Assen, pp. 129–40.

Gronroos, C. (1994) 'From marketing mix to relationship marketing: towards a paradigm shift in marketing', *Asia-Australia Marketing Journal*, 2(1): 9–29.

Gummesson, E. (1979) 'The marketing of professional services – an organizational dilemma', *European Journal of Marketing*, 13(5): 308–18.

Gummesson, E. (1998) 'Implementation requires a relationship marketing paradigm', *Academy of Marketing Science*, 26(3), Summer: 242–9.

Heskett, J. (1987) 'Lessons in the service sector', *Harvard Business Review*, 65, March–April: 36–42.

Howcroft, B. and Kiely, J. (1995) 'Distribution channels', in C. Ennew, T. Watkins and M. Wright (eds), *Marketing Financial Services*, 2nd edn. Oxford: Butterworth-Heinemann.

Howcroft, B. and Lavis, J. (1986) 'A strategic perspective on delivery systems in UK retail banking', *Service Industries Journal*, 6(2): 144–58.

Hughes, J. (1994) 'The financial environment', in P. McGoldrick and S. Greenland (eds), *Retailing of Financial Services*. London: McGraw-Hill.

Judd, V.C. (1987) 'Differentiate with the 5th P: People', *Industrial Marketing Management*, 16(4): 241–7.

Knights, D., Sturdy, A. and Morgan, G. (1994) 'The consumer rules: an examination of the rhetoric and "reality" of marketing in financial services', *European Journal of Marketing*, 28(3): 42–54.

Lehtinen, U., Ojasalo, J. and Ojasalo, K. (1994) 'Consumers perceptions of service quality dimensions', *Quality in Service Management Proceedings*, European Institute of Advanced Studies in Management, Paris, May.

Lewis, B. (1991) 'Service quality: an international comparison of bank customers' expectations and perceptions', *Journal of Marketing Management*, 7: 47–62.

Lewis, R.C. (1987) 'The measurement gaps in the quality of hotel service', *International Journal of Hospitality Management*, 6(2): 83–8.

Littlejohn, D. (1990) 'Hospitality research: philosophies and progress', in R. Teare, L. Moutinho and N. Morgan (eds), *Managing and Marketing Services in the 1990s*. London: Cassell.

McKechnie, S. and Harrison, T. (1995) 'Understanding consumers and markets' in C. Ennew, T. Watkins and M. Wright (eds), *Marketing Financial Services*, 2nd edn. Oxford: Butterworth-Heinemann.

Neenan, D. (1993) *Added Value Banking*. Dublin: Lafferty Publications.

Palmer, A. (2001) *Principles of Services Marketing*. London: McGraw-Hill.

Reichheld, E.E. (1993) 'Loyalty-based management', *Harvard Business Review*, 71, March–April: 64–73.

Reichheld, E.E. and Sasser, W.E. Jr. (1990) 'Zero defections: quality comes to service', *Harvard Business Review*, 68, Sept.–Oct.: 105–11.

Rushton, A. and Carson, D. (1985) 'The marketing of services: managing the intangibles', *European Journal of Marketing*, 19(3): 19–40.

Storbacka, K. (1993) *Customer Relationship Profitability*. Helsinki: Swedish School of Economics and Business Administration.

Thwaites, D. (1989) 'The impact of environmental change on the evolution of the UK building society industry', *The Service Industries Journal*, 9(1): 40–60.

Trethowan, J. and Scullion, G. (1997) 'Strategic responses to change in retail banking in the UK and Irish Republic', *International Journal of Bank Marketing*, 15(2): 60–8.

Walsh, S. (2001) 'The adoption and integration of transaction and relationship marketing activity, marketing management decision making/ implementation and marketing management competencies in a retail bank circumstance', unpublished DPhil thesis, Faculty of Business and Management, University of Ulster.

Webster, F. (1992) 'The changing role of marketing in the corporation', *Journal of Marketing*, 56, October: 1–17.

Witt, S.F. and Moutinho, L. (1994) *Tourism Marketing and Management Handbook*, 2nd edn. Harlow, England: Prentice-Hall International.

ADDITIONAL USEFUL REFERENCES

Augustyn, M. and Ho, S.K. (1998) 'Service quality and tourism', *Journal of Travel Research*, 37(1), August: 71–5.

Begg, H.M. (1996) 'The impact of improved ferry services on an island economy: the case of Mull', *World Transport Policy & Practice*, 2(4): 8–12.

Bramwell, B. and Lane, B. (1993) 'Interpretation and sustainable tourism: the potential and the practice', *Journal of Sustainable Tourism*, 1(2): 71–80.

Brotherton, B. (1999) 'Towards a definitive view of the nature of hospitality and hospitality management', *International Journal of Contemporary Hospitality Management*, 11(4): 165–73.

Calantone, R.J. and Mazanec, J.A. (1991) 'Marketing management and tourism', *Annals of Tourism Research*, 18(1): 101–19.

Danaher, P.J. and Mattsson, J. (1998) 'A comparison of service delivery processes of different complexity', *International Journal of Service Industry Management*, 9(1): 48–63.

Eccles, G. (1995) 'Marketing, sustainable development and international tourism', *International Journal of Contemporary Hospitality Management*, 7(7): 20–6.

Grimwade, G. and Carter, B. (2000) 'Managing small heritage sites with interpretation and community involvement', *International Journal of Heritage Studies*, 6(1): 33–48.

Henry, I.P. and Jackson, G.A.M. (1996) 'Sustainability of management processes and tourism products and contexts', *Journal of Sustainable Tourism*, 4(1): 17–28.

Ingram, H. (1999) 'Hospitality: a framework for a millennial review', *International Journal of Contemporary Hospitality Management*, 11(4): 140–8.

Jones, P. (1999) 'Multi-unit management in the hospitality industry: a late twentieth century phenomenon', *International Journal of Contemporary Hospitality Management*, 11(4): 155–64.

Morrison, A. and Thomas, R. (1999) 'The future of small firms in the hospitality industry', *International Journal of Contemporary Hospitality Management*, 11(4): 148–54.

WTO (1993) *Tourism at World Heritage Sites: The Site Manager's Handbook*. Madrid: World Tourism Organization.

WTO (1993) *Tourism to the Year 2000*. A WTO tourism forecasting publication, Madrid.

WTO (1996) *What Tourism Managers Need to Know: A Practical Guide to the Development and Use of Indicators of Sustainable Tourism.* Madrid: World Tourism Organization.

WTO (2000) *Sustainable Development of Tourism: A Compilation of Good Practices.* Madrid: World Tourism Organization.

4

Services Marketing in Specific Contexts – the Not-for-Profit Sector

In addition to having different service industry characteristics to those of the for-profit sector, the not-for-profit sector has very different service issues to address. In particular, companies in the not-for-profit sector often have very different goals to pursue, they have different organizational agendas, have a strong sense of purpose and may have many different clients or groups of people to please simultaneously. In trying to deliver their service, not-for-profit organizations often have to rely on voluntary, short-term or part-time labour forces. Demand for the service may exceed their ability to supply the service. A flexible approach in delivering the service may be called for and many aspects or dimensions of service may be required. Managers often find themselves working in environments where different groups of people have different cultural values and ethics.

This chapter uses two quite different examples of not-for-profit services to illustrate service marketing in specific contexts. First, the context characteristics and services marketing dimensions of museums are discussed. In this not-for-profit example the services marketing challenges relate to the changing role and purpose of museums against a context of declining government or state funding.

Secondly, charitable services are discussed, illustrating how the service dimensions are different for different markets, particularly in relation to donors and users of the charitable service. The marketing dimensions identified

Table 4.1   *Context characteristics for museum services*

Characteristics	Impacts upon	Leads to
Traditional custodial role	How collections are cared for and managed	Focus on quality of collections and less focus on service delivery to customers
Requires public/private funding	Collections, scope of services available	Need for accountability, efficiency

are central to the specific challenge for charities to develop and maintain support and donations in the long term.

CONTEXT 1 – SERVICE MARKETING IN MUSEUMS

Recent changes in museum management have seen a move from a historical position of the museum being almost superior to its public to an era in which the museum's role is one of service to the public. Combining an aesthetic mission with the achievement of marketing goals is the aim of many museums seeking long-term success. Meeting the aesthetic mission and delivering a service to the marketplace are two distinct aspects of the management agenda. To this end museums need to balance the artistic needs of the museum product with servicing visitor requirements within one location. However museum products attract audiences through audience participation and entertainment value.

As museums are part of the not-for-profit sector, and depend upon government funding for up to 70 per cent of their income, they also need to offer clear value to government by attracting increasing numbers of people.

Managing museums entails balancing the custodial role with the need to attract visitors. Museums often experience financial difficulty, indeed many cultural organizations cannot exist on earned income alone. Funders, both corporate and government, and foundations, now expect greater accountability for money granted. The context characteristics of museum services are illustrated in Table 4.1.

Museums as public services have unique characteristics and over the past decades their role has been changing and expanding. In tandem with this they have become more involved in developing marketing techniques to help them become more successful.

Within the recent history of museums there has been considerable change in how they perceive their role within society. This has led to many changes in how they are managed. The evolution of museum marketing has been conceptualized in three main stages, each with a different theme and discourse (Rentschler, 1998). The chronology involves the foundation period (1975–87), the professionalization period (1988–93) and the creativity period (1994 to present). Research of the foundation period (1975–87) found that studies in museum marketing were dominated by those on educating visitors, on raising the awareness of museum staff and on the economic impact of the arts on the community. The studies in the latter group had a data-collection focus rather than a strategic action-oriented focus. The modus operandi at this time began to be challenged from a number of sources and this heralded the beginning of a more professional period.

Cultural change has occurred in museums as they became more democratized. These changes forced the recognition of the applicability of marketing to non-profit museums (Andreasen, 1985). During the 1980s marketing departments were added to some museums. Restructuring of the public sector also had an impact where a shift in power and authority from producer to consumer occurred, funders demanded greater accountability, and contracting out of services occurred at the local level. All these things empowered 'a new managerial elite', less focused on 'cultural gatekeeping' and more engaged with the 'celebration of entrepreneurship' (Volkerling, 1996: 202–3). However changes indicated by the more 'professional' approach are not complete. Marketing in museums is in transition, heralding the beginning of a so-called creativity period where collaborative marketing activities and a new view of visitors as customers is in evidence.

In today's climate of change and requirement to become more profitable or efficient, the need to understand the nature of the museum service has never been greater. There is increasing pressure on museums to widen their appeal in order to attract larger and more diverse audiences.

Service dimensions for museums

As discussed in Chapter 1, services are characterized as being intangible, perishable, inseparable and heterogeneous. Like most services, the museum 'service product' is delivered in a physical environment or site that may encompass land or building space, shape and lighting, and requires some means of directing or orientating the visitor and methods of stimulating interest and involvement. Also a museum service is delivered in the context of a public sector environment. Within this complex service context, it is useful to consider multi-dimensional criteria in the overall conceptualization of the service.

The multi-dimensional nature of services is as evident in a public service such as a museum as in the profit-oriented services discussed in the last chapter. The scope of service dimensions ranges from the tangible aspects (those relatively easy to measure and evaluate, such as physical site and environment) to the intangible (those more difficult to measure and evaluate, such as the degree of visitor orientation, stimulation and involvement). A balanced focus on both tangible and intangible dimensions of marketing offerings is desirable in this service context also. This means that a range of marketing activity needs to be offered and evaluated in the overall service delivery process. Services marketing dimensions of how and what the customer experiences are very relevant to the overall perception of the museum service concept.

So what are the important service dimensions for museum marketing? The relevant elements of services delivery in a museum context are illustrated together in a model of 'dimensions of the museum service product delivery' (adapted from Figure 1.6 in Chapter 1). The scope of these dimensions ranges from the tangible aspects, such as physical facilities and range of collection, to the intangible aspects, such as communication and interpretation for visitors. Both tangible and intangible dimensions of services marketing offerings need to be addressed in order to achieve a balanced approach to the delivery of the services marketing mix. Each of these aspects is illustrated in Figure 4.1 and briefly described below.

The Collections

The scope and range of the museum collection are of course central to the entire museum service product. The extent of the core collection will have a direct impact upon the choice and quality of service to visitors. In addition the relevance, frequency and quality of special exhibitions are central to the drawing power of a museum, especially for repeat visits by local and regular users.

Accessibility/Availability

Accessibility and availability of the museum service include physical facilities, the proximity of core product for visitors, range of offerings of different markets and availability of museum services.

The physical facilities include the style and layout of a museum, the spaciousness in which visitors can browse around the collections and the quality of ancillary facilities offered, such as a shop, café and services for disabled users. These are important aspects of the service as they contribute to the overall comfort and freedom of movement of visitors. In some cases the museum may even include an art school, public education programmes and conference or lecture theatre facilities, valuable in attracting additional business and therefore contributing to the overall viability of the museum.

Accessibility of core product is closely linked to the quality of the physical facilities and is dependent upon the amount of space available and the efficient planning of visitor flow-through and ease of movement. Accessibility is very closely related to availability in that it impacts upon how easily visitors can assess the museum's offerings, it includes ease of viewing and how this is influenced by the numbers of other visitors. This will have repercussions for how closely visitors can view exhibits, as well as the ease of reading and following information. The pricing of both core and peripheral products will also influence how accessible the service and facilities are for potential visitors.

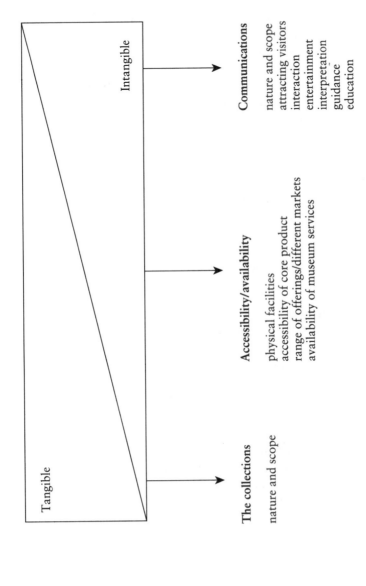

FIGURE 4.1 Tangible and intangible dimensions of museum service delivery

The range of offerings for different markets needs careful consideration as museums clearly need to offer a variety and range of offerings in terms of both collections and important aspects of service delivery to suit different groups of visitors – for example, different interest groups, school groups, repeat visitors, tourists and new visitors.

The availability of the museum collection is important in terms of being open at times to suit the market. This often means six- or seven-day opening during working hours and in some locations and seasons it will include opening in the evenings to suit as many visitors as possible.

Communication

Given the wide range and scope of collections in a museum, visitors need a variety of communication activities to help them decide which parts of the museum to visit. Often there is too much visual or textual information to absorb in any given collection or exhibition within a single viewing, resulting in visitors feeling overwhelmed. For this reason, many visitors seek interpretation of the collections to help them make sense of what is on offer and to help them plan their priorities for the visit.

Communication of the museum service includes the nature and scope of interactions, entertainment, interpretation and education. Interaction and guidance at different contact points between the museum's staff and its visitors are important contributors to the experience of the visitor. Also interpretation is important in adding value to the collection. It is needed to help visitors understand and appreciate the tangible aspects of the service.

Interaction and entertainment can add considerable value to the museum experience. Visitor experiences occur and need to be managed at the interaction points between the museum's staff and its visitors. Inherent in these interactions are visitor communication messages that occur in an intangible and impersonal way. These consist of all organizational communication offerings including information and guidance informing visitors about the relevance and meaning of the collections and other contributions to visitor relations. Related to this is the need of some visitors to be entertained or to participate in the exhibition in some way. Therefore, service activities need to be organized to maximize visitor interactions and experiences of the museum service and to allow different visitors to interact in different ways.

Interpretation and guidance are important in adding value to the collection, helping visitors understand and appreciate the tangible aspects of the service. Different types of communication are required to reach out to visitors, make the exhibition 'come alive' and to offer the visitor a memorable experience. This often entails visitors having historical knowledge or understanding of the context in which the collections are set. This calls for careful consideration of the level of interpretation provided to different types of visitors, according to their needs (for example, school groups, foreign visitors, local users). The effectiveness of communicating historical information related to the collection (the essential or core product) relies on the ability to construct images, convey information, and engage the visitor, through either staff–visitor interaction or more traditional textual or visual methods.

All of these dimensions are interlinked and therefore the effectiveness and quality of the museum service offering depends on the attention to detail of all aspects. These dimensions of the museum service delivery can be expanded and adapted to suit different museum service situations and contexts, depending on the nature and purpose of the museum. The design and management of the museum's total offering will depend on how it perceives its strengths and limitations in relation to the threats and opportunities in the market and environment in which it is to compete. In any case museum managers need to focus attention on all dimensions encompassed in the overall offering of the museum service product.

CONTEXT 2 – SERVICE MARKETING FOR CHARITIES

Charities exist in a very competitive environment. To be successful they need to constantly seek funding and public support in all that they do. In this section the discussion features the specific characteristics of marketing in the charitable sector and outlines the predominant market segments. The service dimensions for charities are then described in the context of each market segment to illustrate the scope of activities required in the management of charitable services.

To shed light on what is different about managing a charity and what is likely to impact on its marketing activities, the characteristics of charities are considered. Charities as non-profit organizations have some unique characteristics. They have a distinctive purpose in that they generally pursue social goals and they have a distinctive culture including an emphasis on value-based or ethical decision making. Charities have a broad variety of stakeholders; a reliance on voluntary or short-term labour to a greater or lesser extent; they fill gaps in statutory service provision and are used by that sector to provide service delivery. In addition they can be inward looking and behave in a traditional or bureaucratic manner. While these characteristics are significant they are superseded by the fact that in all cases demand for charitable services exceeds supply and the limiting factor is the availability of money and/or resources. The context characteristics of charitable services are illustrated in Table 4.2.

However from a service marketing perspective the foremost characteristic of a charitable organization is the fact that there are two constituencies: clients to whom goods or services are provided and donors from whom it receives resources. Consequently they serve at least two client groups, funders and end users, both of which require marketing activity.

Shapiro (1973) argues that the marketing task in non-profit organizations is more complex than in typical commercial organizations. In contrast

Table 4.2   *Context characteristics for charitable services*

Characteristics	Impacts upon	Leads to
Generally pursue social goals	Scope and range of activities	Many diverse activities
Broad range of stakeholders	How they respond and communicate to different groups	Many diverse activities, need to tailor messages for each group
Demand exceeds supply	Ability to reach all 'markets'	Need to focus on core activities

with the profit-motivated company whose marketing function could be described as facilitating a direct two-way exchange, which simultaneously includes both resource allocation and resource attraction, the charity must approach these two tasks separately. Although this duality of tasks increases the complexity, it can give the charity organization flexibility in its marketing since its approach to clients need not be the same as for donors.

Additionally most charities are services and this affects their marketing behaviour as services are predominantly intangible making them more difficult to evaluate and standardize. Charitable service providers therefore need to take this into account when designing their marketing activity.

Service marketing and management in the charitable sector, therefore, need to take account of the duality of publics with respect to resource allocation and resource attraction, and the specific characteristics of services marketing. Consequently, the purpose of marketing in a charitable services situation is to ensure that effective and efficient management activity leads to a consistent and effective delivery of suitable marketing activity to all of the company's target markets.

Service dimensions for charities

What are the most suitable service dimensions for the charitable sector? Obviously consideration needs to be given to the specific situation of each charity in order to refine the delivery of the service marketing dimensions. Initially an examination of the general situation will help focus on the key variables.

Earlier work has considered the value of market segmentation within the charity market (Schlegelmilch and Tynan, 1989). Often the traditional marketing mix using descriptions of the product, price, promotion and place has been used and modified for non-profit marketing by adding more Ps. These have incorporated additional factors essential to the specific service contexts of charities, such as people and process dimensions. More recently, some aspects of the relationship marketing approach have been considered appropriate for the charitable sector. For example, aiming to develop and maintain customer relationships by fulfilling the objectives of both donors and charities through various exchanges between the two sides and recognizing the importance of keeping existing donors and cross-selling to them rather than viewing them as a series of discrete transactions.

The different market sectors of any charitable organization will require specific service marketing dimensions and particular emphasis on the dimensions most appropriate for the specific situation in order to contribute to the building of long-term relationships.

There are many dimensions of services marketing that may be relevant for charitable services and concentration of service activity around those that will lead to more effective performance and interactive service delivery will be incorporated. The dimensions for charities need to be based on a set of interrelated elements and made specific for each market segment. The most relevant service dimensions will incorporate the more intangible and interactive aspects of a charitable service. Consequently, service marketing in this context will revolve around building relationships through the service suitability and service accessibility of the service product, communication and the perceived value of the charitable service. These four components are described below in a little more depth.

Service suitability

Fundamentally a charitable service is determined by the need or purpose it seeks to serve. It is usually a service that fulfils or makes a contribution to the supply of a vital and sometimes lifesaving need or requirement and/or it may be a service that fills a gap in the statutory service provision. The charitable service 'product' is therefore very much tailored to the needs and requirements of the end user(s). Service suitability has been chosen as a descriptive term because it explicitly reflects that charitable organizations offer a specifically designed service with the need or requirement of particular users in mind. The whole reason for the charitable organization's existence is built upon the desire to fill that need or change a specific circumstance. Therefore the service should be adaptable for a specific individual's or community's requirements, and should be reviewed regularly for relevance and appropriateness for each market segment.

Service accessibility

The location and timing of the service is often vital to a charitable organization's offering. It is not only important to have the service available in the right location for both of its market constituents, but it is important that the level of service is delivered in the right amounts. For example, the organization's staff should be willing to help, be at the right place at the right time, be responsive, and have relevant expertise or experience for the specific situation. Similarly donor segment markets must be appealed to when donors are most receptive and of course receiver segment markets must receive the charity's service when they need it most.

Communication

Primarily a charitable organization's communication and public relations activity needs to be stimulating in order to create interest in their purpose and activities and to encourage funding. Consequently, messages should be creative and interesting. Communicative information should take account of users' needs and requirements and exhibit empathy in their tone and content. All communicative activity should be proactive, friendly, and aim to develop short- or long-term relationships depending upon the nature of the charity and for whom the message is being designed.

Communication for the charitable sector has a variety of functions and involves many aspects. First, it provides an important role in gaining public support and to achieve funding. It is also essential for providing information about the benefits of the service to the individual user and, on a more holistic level, to the community in general. This information will involve explaining the benefits of the charitable activities and the importance of contributions and support to the charity's activities. Additionally it provides information to the referring agents or to the gatekeepers who are in a position to know who needs the service most, and therefore can provide useful feedback on how to prioritize activities and resources. Secondly, a charity's communication activities can be used to establish and monitor the expectations and most needed requirements of the end user and can facilitate the adaptation of the service to suit specific individuals or communities.

Perceived value

The important issues in relation to perceived value are value for money and efficient and effective use of funds. This term has been chosen because it explicitly reflects that a charity must always consider how the end user customers and donor customers perceive the handling of both the funds they attract and the money spent on end users. The charity needs to be seen to be carrying out a valuable service, doing a worthwhile job, fulfilling a need not already addressed by commercial organizations; and doing it in a responsible, non-wasteful manner. This will reflect upon the credibility of the organization and its ability to maintain and attract donors and sponsors. The service dimensions for charities are illustrated in Figure 4.2.

It could be argued that other service marketing dimensions are important. However for the purpose of effective and efficient management most of the service marketing activity in which a charity becomes involved could be absorbed within the headings above. Therefore the marketing activity of a charitable organization should concentrate on building relationships with its various customers through these key service dimensions – service suitability, service accessibility, communication (and PR) and perceived value. These variables require most emphasis and attention for service delivery in the charitable sector, although some may be more important than others depending on the needs of each market segment.

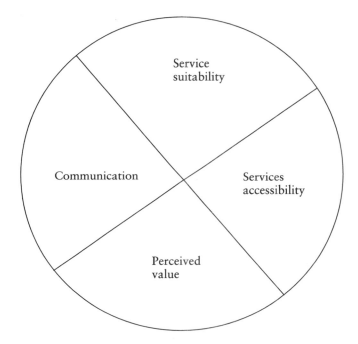

FIGURE 4.2   Service marketing dimensions for charities

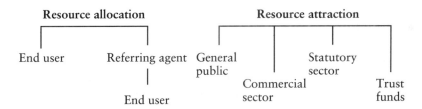

FIGURE 4.3   Charities' end user and donor customers

Market segments in the charitable sector

As mentioned earlier, there are essentially two categories of customers for charitable organizations: end user beneficiaries and donors. Within these two categories there are at least seven key marketing sectors, each requiring appropriate marketing mixes specific to its needs (Gilmore and Carson, 1994). These two 'customer' groups and the marketing sectors which relate to them are described below and illustrated in Figure 4.3.

The end user customer market includes:

- the end user who has a choice
- the end user who does not have a choice
- the referring agent.

The end user or client is the recipient of the charitable service. For the end user customers the emphasis of marketing activity is primarily on service accessibility, communication and service suitability. The aspect of perceived value is of less importance to these customers. The referring agent will most probably have a strong influencing role in the choice of service for the end user customer. There may be a different emphasis or focus on each of these marketing activities depending on which type of end user customer they may be. For example, the communication activity may require a different emphasis and use different messages for each of the user customers.

The donor customer market includes:

- the general public
- the commercial sector
- the statutory sector
- trust funds.

A charity may have a variety of 'donor' markets, the most common being the general public, the commercial sector, the statutory sector and trust funds. With regard to resource attraction the overriding key variable is communication in order to maintain a high profile and enhance the positioning of the charity and the funding agent. The emphasis and focus of the communication message delivered to these donor customers needs to be very specifically suitable. The aspects of perceived value and service accessibility are also important. Service suitability may be of less importance to the donor customer.

Although each of these donor markets may have a similar emphasis in relation to the service dimensions, each dimension may have a different focus or activity. The communication dimension for example may be important for each donor market but require a different method of communication and a different message and focus on different features and benefits of the service product. Therefore careful consideration needs to be given to how to approach each different donor market in order to build and maintain mutually satisfying relationships.

The two types of markets for the charitable organization, the donor customer and the end user customer will require completely different approaches and the different segments within these will also require different treatment. The different service dimensions for each of the charities' customer groups are represented in Figure 4.4.

Figure 4.3 illustrates the possible different customer segments of a charitable organization and Figure 4.4 shows the different emphasis of service dimensions for each customer segment. These are illustrated in the context of their two overall types of markets, the 'end user customer' market and the 'donor customer' market. The end user customer market (receiving resource allocation) includes the end user who has a choice, the end user who does not have a choice, and the referring agent. The donor customer (required for resource attraction) may include the general public, the commercial sector, the statutory sector and trust funds. These are discussed below.

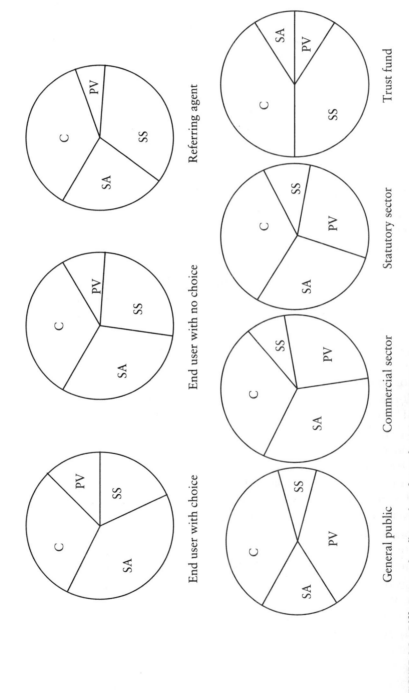

FIGURE 4.4 Different service dimensions for each customer group

C-Communication
PV-Perceived value
SA-Service accessibility
SS-Service suitabilty

End user customer with choice

The emphasis of the service dimensions for this type of charity user are primarily on service accessibility, communication and service suitability. First, the charitable service needs to be accessible in terms of location and timing. It needs to be easily obtained by the end user customer or their representative, and to be delivered efficiently and reliably when it is required.

The communication dimension should entail stimulating the end user customer's interest in order to encourage recruitment, and provide appropriate and specific information which would make the decision-making process easier for them. Initially, the charity needs to inform the end user about service availability, entitlement and suitability. Secondly, some consideration must be given to matching the customer's requirement to the service products available and communicating this to each end user in a positive manner in order to encourage their sense of identity and positive desire to belong or be a recipient of this service.

Obviously the end user customers need the charitable service to be very specifically tailored to requirements, therefore it needs to be the most suitable service available.

End user customer with no choice

Often the end user may not be in a position to make an informed judgement on the service delivered for a variety of reasons such as their state of health, their social circumstances, deprivation or lack of other choices. The emphasis here is on service suitability, service accessibility and communication.

Service dimensions should emphasise how the charitable service matches the customer's need in order to make it easily identifiable by the customer or someone acting on their behalf. The charitable service on offer also needs to be available at the specific time required for the end customer. Ease of use is important, therefore the service needs to be available within the locality for the user's convenience. Consequently, the emphasis on the communication message is important, together with the interactions with the end user and representatives. Communication messages should stimulate interest and aim to build a reliable and stable image of the charitable service for the user customers' representatives. The communication message should also focus on providing information and educating the end user's representative in order to encourage positive interaction and enhance participation and successful outcome. Therefore the emphasis must be on communicating with empathy in order to reinforce understanding and feelings of belonging – focusing on a sense of wellbeing, and client security and satisfaction.

Referring agents

The service dimensions here should focus on service suitability and communication. Service accessibility may have a secondary importance.

The referring agent is most likely to be a professional person such as a doctor, nurse or social worker. The service must be perceived to closely match the agent's end user-specific requirements, for example, childcare, or training for the disabled. The charitable service must fill a niche in the statutory provision. Therefore the charity needs to constantly revise its offering to maintain a close fit with end users' perceived needs.

The focus of the communication message is again important. In particular all communication should have the objective of building long-term relationships with referring agents. The charitable organization should provide a two-way mechanism for communication, encouraging frequent dialogue and involvement of the referring agent in some end user-related decisions. Communication needs to be informative, involving specific information about improvements in the service provision and any independent evaluations of the service, in addition to more general communication in order to raise overall awareness of the service. In developing and maintaining long-term relationships with referring agents the most important dimensions of service marketing activity include providing specific information about the services available and developing the reputation of being reliable and efficient.

The availability of the service within the immediate locality and the existence of facilities to deliver the service are relatively important in order to ensure accessibility to the end user customer. The service must also be a reliable one in order to ensure the referring agent's support.

The donor customer – the general public

The service dimension emphasis here is on perceived value and communication. Service accessibility is of secondary importance.

The service needs to be perceived to be worthy enough to attract a donation, therefore some intangible reward must be identifiable for the donor, such as a 'good feeling' or appealing to a sense of responsibility for the misfortunes of others. The charity needs to help the donor identify with the service and the organization and achieve some level of 'common ideals'. This will provide a necessary backdrop for nurturing a relationship in the long term. Clarity of purpose provides the best possible understanding of the aims of a charity and therefore communication is important in order to achieve a positive and focused profile of an organization. The method or location of charity collections may also send strong messages to the donor. For example, collecting boxes on the street corner will attract contributions of coins (small units) whereas using a mass medium such as TV calling for credit card donations will attract larger individual units of contribution. Therefore the place and method of resource collection is important.

All communication must achieve public awareness and liking for the charity, and provide information which will facilitate and encourage giving. Additionally communication needs to focus on all the charity's activities not only to create further awareness of its cause but also to nurture a sense of belonging and shared values amongst the donors.

Within the past few years charities have begun to use the worldwide web to promote and communicate with a mass market. Many charities have created sites that make it easy for the general public to make a contribution to support the fight against hunger, poverty and disease. For example, by visiting a site and clicking a button on the home page anyone can provide funding to feed a child or family for one day or week or year. Also new or temporary charities set up after a particular disaster or world event can be created on-line to help gather funding and support in the short or medium term. For example a charity portal was created as a collaboration between AOL Time Warner, Cisco Systems, Yahoo and *www.helping.org* in order to fundraise after the 11 September (2001) tragedy in New York. As in the previous example, some charities work together with corporate partners and so combine the charities' activities with links to business activity.

The charity's location is important so that the public can identify it geographically or indeed actually 'see' the service in operation and hence make the intangible more tangible. The use of communicational messages and mediums which show aspects of the service or the need for the charity are clearly very influential in attracting donations from the general public as evidenced by the effect of the extensive television reporting of starvation in Ethiopia in the early–mid 1980s. Also Internet access is equally important in today's e-environment. Secondly, the marketing emphasis will also be one of venue, such as Saturday afternoon collections in a shopping mall, or using a special evening event for resource attraction.

The donor customer – the commercial sector

The important service dimensions for this market are perceived value closely linked to service accessibility. Communication is also an important service dimension here.

Attraction of donors from this sector will depend on the perceived value of association with the charitable service to enhance the commercial company profile within the community and the company's markets. Consequently the location of the charity is important in terms of whether it is well known within the company's market coverage. Much will also depend upon the ability of the charity and the commercial organization to attract media coverage, advertising and PR opportunities together. Therefore charities must work in a close relationship with donors from this sector to ensure this is achieved.

The communication message to the commercial sector will need to emphasize the important role the service contributes to the wellbeing of the surrounding community. Additionally the amount of the donation will depend upon the company's profile, the charity's profile and the company culture. Therefore the communication message is vitally important in order to proactively promote the advantages of the charity to the company, to gain suitable media coverage in relation to the donation and PR for the company in question, and in order to build a long-term mutually satisfying relationship.

The donor customer – the statutory sector

The important dimensions of services activity in this sector are on service accessibility, perceived value and communication. In this case, the charity service must be seen to meet a shortfall or gap in the statutory provision, match funding criteria, be cost effective and be delivered by a professional and trustworthy organization. Geographically, it must be located within the funding bodies' geographic boundaries. Although funding may range between 75–100 per cent depending upon the perceived need of the charity and funds available, it may be sensitive to the contract culture and government cutbacks, therefore demonstrable value for money for the purpose of public accountability is very important.

Any promotional activity must be seen to be value for money, (not wasteful), honest and above suspicion, provide a good overall image of the charity, and be politically correct and acceptable. In addition communication through personal selling or lobbying with the 'gatekeepers' within this sector in order to emphasize the importance of the service the charity is providing is vitally important.

The donor customer – trust funds

The emphasis of service delivery for trust funds will be on service suitability and communication. Generally these funds have very specific criteria for what they will support, where they will support it and the size of the grant available. Thus the service is very much tailored to the stated criteria and can be repositioned to suit the funder. Promotional messages will involve highlighting competitive advantage over competitors, the charity's excellent track record, greater value for money and fitness for purpose. Most promotional activity will be carried out through personal contact.

Consideration of the key user and donor customer segments contributes to an understanding of how the different service dimensions are appropriate for each segment and how different aspects of each dimension are emphasized in different contexts. The previous discussion highlights the extent and versatility of service delivery that charities need to be able to maintain, balance and manage. Clearly this requirement for such diversity of service delivery will have implications for managers in these organizations.

This discussion has illustrated the relatively complex market sectors of charities and the subsequent complexity of tailoring service dimensions for each of these sectors. Of course, each sector, indeed specific charities, may want to reshape such service activities but such reshaping should emphasize the basic and fundamental concept, that charities with careful and considered thought can and do deliver a service that is tailormade to suit specific purposes and market requirements.

SUMMARY

This chapter has highlighted the complexity of delivering and managing appropriate service dimensions for two not-for-profit situations – museums and the charitable sector. Services marketing and management involves carrying out a careful 'balancing act' in these non-for-profit sectors, one that balances the tangible and intangible service dimensions. In particular these contexts illustrate the need to balance spending and attracting funds, focusing on each museum and charity's purpose and attracting long-term support via the public and repeat visitors in the museum context and donors and volunteers for the charitable sector, while operating in very competitive and very public environments. Building and maintaining a reputable image is crucial to the long-term success of any charitable and museum service.

DISCUSSION QUESTIONS

What are appropriate service dimensions for marketing to the charitable sector and how are they different to those for museum services? Why?

How can museums provide an excellent service to customers while maintaining unique and valuable collections?

Describe at least three different markets to which charities may need to offer and deliver appropriate service dimensions simultaneously.

REFERENCES

Andreasen, L. (1985) 'Marketing or selling the arts: an orientational dilemma', *Journal of Arts Management and Law*, 15(1): 9–20.

Gilmore, A. and Carson, D. (1994) 'Tailor made marketing in the charitable sector', Marketing Education Group Annual Conference proceedings, Coleraine.

Rentschler, R. (1998) 'Museum and performing arts marketing: a climate of change', *The Journal of Arts Management, Law and Society*, 28(1): 83–131.

Schlegelmilch, B.B. and Tynan, A. (1989) 'The scope for market segmentation within the charity market: an empirical analysis', *Managerial and Decision Economics*, 1: 127–34.

Shapiro, B.P. (1973) 'Marketing for nonprofit organisations', *Harvard Business Review*, Sept.–Oct.: 123–32.

Volkerling, M. (1996) 'Deconstructing the difference-engine: a theory of cultural policy', *European Journal of Cultural Policy*, 2(2): 189–212.

ADDITIONAL USEFUL REFERENCES

Alexander, V.D. (1999) 'A delicate balance: museums and the marketplace', *Museum International*, 51(2): 29–34.

Ames, P. (1988) 'A challenge to modern museum management', *Museum Studies Journal*, 3, Spring/Summer: 10–14.

Balabanis, G., Stables, R. and Phillips, H. (1997) 'Market orientation in the top 200 British charity organisations and its impact on their performance', *European Journal of Marketing*, 31(8): 583–603.

Berck, B. (1992) 'Museums: rethinking the boundaries', *Museum*, 174(2): 67–72.

Callen, J. (1994) 'Money donations, volunteering and organisational efficiency', *Journal of Productivity Analysis*, 5(3): 215–28.

Cermak, D., File, K. and Prince, R. (1994) 'A benefit segmentation of the major donor market', *Journal of Business Research*, 29(2): 121–30.

Dickman, S. (1995) *The Marketing Mix: Promoting Museums, Galleries and Exhibitons*. Melbourne: Museums Australia Inc.

DiMaggio, P.J. (1985) 'When the profit is quality: cultural institutions in the marketplace', *Museum News*, 63(5): 28–35.

Falk, J.H., Koran, J.J., Dierking, L.D. and Dreblow, L. (1985) 'Predicting visitor behaviour', *Curator*, 28: 249–57.

Fine, S.H. (1990) *Social Marketing: Promoting the Causes of Public and Non Profit Agencies*. Needham Heights, MA: Allyn & Bacon.

Giunipero, L., Crittenden, W. and Crittenden, V. (1990) 'Industrial marketing in non profit organisations', *Industrial Marketing Management*, 19(3): 279–85.

Goulding, C. (2000) 'The museum environment and the visitor experience', *European Journal of Marketing*, 34(3/4): 261–78.

Griffin, D.J.G. (1987) 'Managing in the museum organisation. Leadership and communication', *The International Journal of Museum Management and Curatorship*, 6(4): 387–98.

Janes, R.R. (1999) 'Seven years of change and no end in sight: reflections from the Glenbow Museum', *International Journal of Arts Management*, 1(2): 48–53.

Kotler, N. and Kotler, P. (1998) *Museum Strategy and Marketing: Designing Missions, Building Audiences, Generating Revenue and Resources*. San Francisco: Jossey-Bass.

Laczniak, G. and Murphy, P. (1977) 'Marketing the performing arts', *Atlanta Economic Review* (Nov/Dec): 4–9.

Lampel, J., Lant, T. and Shamsie, J. (2000) 'Balancing act: learning from organising practices in cultural industries', *Organisation Science*, 11(3): 263–9.

McLean, F. (1997) *Marketing the Museum*. London: Routledge.

McLean, F. (1998) 'Corporate identity in museums: an exploratory study', *International Journal of Arts Management*, 1(1): 40–9.

Moscardo, G. (1996) 'Mindful visitors: heritage and tourism', *Annals of Tourism Research*, 23(2): 376–97.

Navarro, P. (1980) 'Why do corporations give to charity?', *Journal of Business*, 61(1): 65–93.

Oliver, G. (1999) 'Corporate sponsorship: a sea change for French museums', *Museum International*, 51(2): 24–8.

Silverman, L. (1995) 'Visitor meaning-making in museums for a new age', *Curator*, 38(3): 161–70.

Stapp, C.B. (1990) 'The "public" museum: a review of the literature', *Journal of Museum Education*, 11: 4–10.

5

Organizational Influences on Services Management

The next four chapters consider important organizational and managerial issues that impact on how service marketing is carried out. In this chapter organizational influences on services management are discussed in some detail. Chapter 6 discusses the different managerial approaches and styles to managing and motivating service staff. These include production-line and empowerment approaches to managing service staff and managing with a custodial and/or a customer-focused emphasis. Chapter 7 considers the value of internal marketing concepts to service marketing organizations. Chapter 8 debates service management competencies for the many different aspects of service planning and operations.

This chapter focuses on managing change in service organizations, in the context of organizational structures and their effect on management decision making and activity. Then the chapter discusses the implementation of service marketing delivery and the operational issues that arise. In this context managing the tangible and intangible balance of service dimensions, managing people interactions and establishing proactive communication are considered. The requirement to manage such issues will be influenced by the management style and each manager's competencies for service management as discussed in more depth in later chapters.

The chapter concludes with a case example illustrating how changes in the organizational structure of a large service company impacted upon management decision making and the implementation of service delivery. The case highlights the need to manage change in service management – both in terms of organizational change and change in the priorities and focus of key service managers.

NEED TO MANAGE CHANGE IN SERVICE ORGANIZATIONS

Good management performance particularly in relation to management decision making and service marketing delivery is vital for any successful service organization. However all managerial activity occurs within the context of an existing organization, its culture and structure. Decision making will be strongly influenced by the nature and characteristics of existing managers and any situational circumstances of the service organization.

Few would dispute that managers today operate within a climate of change, both internal and external to their organization. Indeed given the changing environment in which many service industries operate, there will be a continual quest for the development of and improvement in management performance. This means that service managers need to be flexible and versatile, ready to adapt to changing needs and environments. Often studies of management development and organizational improvement are perceived as being either oversimplified or academically inaccessible, given the complexity of organizations in practice and the difficulty in studying such complexity (Buchanon and Boddy, 1992). During changing circumstances, organizations tend to focus solely on strategic management and the development of new strategic plans. However focusing on strategic issues alone diverts attention from the operational aspects of company activity and will result in weak implementation. In service organizations this will have a major impact on the nature and quality of service delivery.

Many studies of how organizations can successfully adapt and benefit from change emphasize the importance of 'change agents', or managers of change. Ottaway (1979) divides change agents into three categories: 'change generators' (unfreezers), 'change implementers' (changers) and 'change adopters' (refreezers). Change generators have the initial task of motivating change. They will often work outside the organizations and their role is to tell the organization that it must change if it wants to survive (sometimes carried out by a consultant, an accountant or a development agency). When the organization takes this message on board then the unfreezing phase is complete and a new type of change agent, a change implementer, is needed for the second phase. Change implementers may involve people both inside and outside the organization. When the final phase, the refreezing process, is reached, the success of lasting change will depend on the commitment and ability of the change adopters to adopt and maintain the changed behaviour. This approach to changing organizations is all-embracing in that the adopters or recipients of change are included as well as the motivators and the implementers. Without the motivation for change, the implementation of change will not happen. Today many service organizations employ consultants and advisers to help them change and evolve in the context of a volatile business environment.

Many other studies in this area have concluded that organization and people issues, not technical areas, are the real barriers to organizational success (Anderson, 1982; Bonoma, 1985; Buchanon and Boddy, 1992; Deshpande, 1982; Deshpande and Zaltman, 1984). Given the importance of people in the planning and delivery of the whole service process, the main factors influencing good service management are related to 'people issues' within the context of organizational and management structures. Thus the roles and activities of managers involved are implicit in any change situation. These will be discussed further in the context of organizational structure and its impact on managerial decision making and performance.

EFFECT OF ORGANIZATIONAL STRUCTURE ON MANAGERIAL DECISION MAKING

Organizational structures are often based on the division of labour, tasks, positions, interrelationships and interdependencies among positions. The degree and level of managerial decision making within an organization has an influence on the structure. Responsibilities will depend to a large extent on the organizational structure within which managers operate and the degrees and levels of managerial decision making inherent in the structure. Management structures can vary between the extremes of being either centralized and formalized or decentralized with a more informal structure. Traditionally centralized organizations have hierarchical structures with many lines of command and consequently have many middle managers controlling operations. An organization that is more decentralized, with responsibility for decision making pushed further down the structure to the managers closest to the functional activity, traditionally encourage and favour flatter organizational structures.

Organizations with long hierarchical structures emphasize control and are likely to have more distortion occurring as information flows upward from junior through senior managerial levels. This is often due to several factors. For example, from the selective perception of information by different individuals, new knowledge can take on different interpretations as it passes

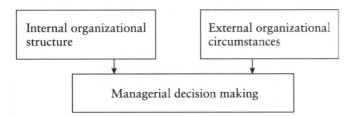

FIGURE 5.1   Influences on managerial decision making

from one person to another. Also, lower-level managers tend to show themselves in a favourable light to their superiors. So although senior managers may intend to exert more effective control by centralizing information, the knowledge with which they are provided may be very different from what was initially gathered (Wilensky, 1967). In this way, organizational structures have a powerful effect on decision-making activity (Deshpande, 1982; Heller et al., 1988; Simon, 1965).

Organizational structures can revolve around the major decision makers in the organization. When this happens 'quasi-organic' structures are formed within hierarchical organizations in order to manufacture a democratic atmosphere while at the same time strengthening central control. The effectiveness and efficiency of this type of 'looser' structure occurs where managers are trusted to do the job. Often quasi-organize structures have evolved around the key decision makers in an organization, in particular those managers who have proved to be competent in a specific functional area or role.

So changes in managerial structure often necessitate a change in the nature of decision making or conversely a change in the nature of decision making may necessitate a change in the organizational structure as an organization evolves through its life cycle or adapts to a dramatically changing environment (Weinshall, 1975).

Internal and external circumstances of organizational change

Organizations change as a result of circumstances that occur both internally and externally to the organization, as illustrated in Figure 5.1. Internal changes occur as the organization develops, management decision making evolves and managers change. External changes to the environment will also have an impact on organizational structures and practices.

Internal and external circumstances can have an effect on the quality of management decision making and marketing activity. In times of either internal or external change organizational structures can be described as being in a state of flux, with issues such as the nature of the decision-making roles of the manager and levels of responsibility constantly changing, thus having implications for the competence requirements of individual managers.

In times of change, organizations may function in a different way. When the external environment changes dramatically large companies put long-term plans on hold and regress to ad hoc decision making (Taylor, 1975). Mintzberg (1973) describes 'muddling through' where decisions are made incrementally on the best available information while managers try not to pre-empt any long-term strategies. A continued circumstance of change where such decision making occurs will eventually have an impact upon the organization structure.

Internally an organization is in a continual state of change however slowly this may appear to happen. There has been a variety of studies to suggest that organization structure is affected by such internal variables as size (Child, 1972) and innovation (Moch and Morse, 1977). Some studies have illustrated that organizations often overlook internal variables and fail to change in keeping with the developmental requirements or in a timely way (Greiner, 1972). When this happens a company can become frozen in its present stage of evolution regardless of potential marketing opportunities. Current relationships, interactions and interdependencies within an organization at any given time have an impact on the organizational decision-making processes and these in turn will depend upon the structure of that organization. Therefore changes in the organizational direction and purpose will have an impact on the management structure. In fact, structural change often follows strategic change (Chandler, 1962; Mintzberg, 1979; Rumelt, 1974).

Organizational structure may result from informal or emergent patterns of behaviour as well as from formally prescribed positions, for example, where employees may informally modify the prescribed work flow or engage in information exchanges that do not follow the usual or formal communications channels. These emerging interactions may become recurring patterns of behaviour and eventually further structure is added to the organization. Therefore an employee's structural position within the organization can be the result of the particular combination or interaction of the formal and emergent interdependencies. In this way an organization can be conceptualized as networks of interrelated structural positions, with individual employees occupying these relational positions, within the context of a more formalized structure (Brass, 1984). Often employees operate informal networks in order to get work done efficiently within an organization.

External influences such as environmental uncertainty and technological changes can also impact upon organizational structures and decision making activities. Organizational structure will have a powerful effect on decision-making activity, it will have an impact on how managers make decisions, the nature of the decisions they make and the overall level of management performance.

Effects of changes in organizational structure, management decision making and individual managers' responsibilities over a three-year period in a large company.

In the first year of a three-year period, a large transport company operated a centralized structure with four divisions in different geographical areas and a UK headquarters. The major managerial decisions relating to marketing and operations were made at headquarters. The divisional structure was built around control rather than responsibility and emphasized directives from managers in headquarters in relation to each specific operational activity. Managers at divisional level focused upon operational activities and were generally reactive to any changing circumstances. In year two of this period the organizational structure was decentralized. During years two and three decentralization gradually led to increased management responsibility and accountability, with some management groups becoming more proactive than others. Over time, the managerial decision makers developed a level of knowledge and experience in terms of specific role responsibilities, and gradually gained some expertise in decision making related to specific areas of marketing activity. In this way, over time, they became more competent managers in the context of the company's specific situation within a changing external environment.

The overall effect of the changing organizational structure was that marketing decisions specific for the local division were made at divisional level rather than headquarters level. There was a gradual move from headquarters control to divisional level managerial responsibility and accountability. Over time, the key decision-making managers at local level progressed and adapted to meet new challenges. This compared favourably with some of the original middle managers from headquarters who did not take full responsibility for planning or decision making and preferred to be directed by higher management.

APPROPRIATE ORGANIZATIONAL STRUCTURES FOR SERVICES MANAGEMENT

Researchers and practitioners have given some consideration to what the best type of organizational structure for services might be. There is general agreement that a traditional hierarchical structure involving different departments may not be entirely appropriate for a service organization. Separate departments responsible for different aspects of marketing may be too restrictive for the planning and implementation of complete service delivery. Such a structure may result in the inappropriate segregation of service tasks and responsibilities.

In addition, many service organizations are multinational and part of large chains such as hotels, fast-food restaurants and banks and so the

Table 5.1   *Organizing for services management*

Usually provided by people for people
Services will be influenced by 'contactors', 'modifiers', 'influencers' and 'isolateds'.
Services staff will include full-time and part-time marketers
Importance of support staff as well as front-line staff

company's service delivery sites may be located across a region, country, continent or the whole world. This means that organizing service companies and activities needs a more creative or holistic approach.

Given that services are usually performed for people by people they are more like people-processing organizations than product-creating organizations. The requirement for service deliverers to make contact with customers means that services need to be convenient, available and accessible to the marketplace. This has implications for how such an organization should be structured. In a service organization staff may be organized in relation to their role in providing a service to customers. In fact, Judd (1987) categorized service staff according to the degree of customer contact experienced in carrying out their role. 'Contactors' are those who are in direct, frequent or periodic customer contact such as the front-line service desk and reception staff on a hotel service. 'Modifiers' have less direct contact or have periodic contact with customers. In the hotel example, these may be the supervisors or office staff who organize billing and service systems. 'Influencers' traditionally have no direct contact but will make many of the decisions about the service ultimately received by customers. These may be the overall managers or the owner of a hotel. 'Isolateds' have no customer contact at all and may include the hotel accountants, flower arrangers and menu planners.

Recognition of these categories of staff encourages the development of appropriate roles and responsibilities within a service organization. The overall effect of this is that the service marketing function is closely interrelated with and dependent upon the procedures, personnel and facilities managed by the service operations function. Hence the service operations function is vital to the management of efficient service delivery.

Gronroos (1980, 1989) and Gummesson (1991) argue for an organizational structure that takes account of the different people involved in the whole service delivery and one that recognizes that service marketing activities are carried out by many in the organization, not just the marketing department. Thus isolating marketing planning activities to one department in a large operational company may be too restrictive given that a traditional marketing department can control only a minor part of the marketing function and it is usually removed from the buyer/seller interface.

Service organizations need to recognize explicitly the role of part-time marketers, those who do not work for the marketing department but are involved in marketing-related activities, either in a back office support role or in interactions with customers at some stage in their dealings with the company. These issues pertinent to organizing for services management are illustrated in Table 5.1.

SERVICES MANAGEMENT DECISION MAKING

At best, decision making can be an incremental and a sequential process. It rarely happens at only one point in time. In organizations where many people may contribute to any major decision, it will involve discussion and progression from one stage of planning to the next, where plans move along and develop in relation to the decision and implications of what is being considered.

The management literature recognizes that decision making occurs in stages or steps. Effective decision making occurs where managers actively select situations that require decisions and seek information regarding those decisions (Longbottom, 1972; Mintzberg, 1976). However, in a services context decision making will entail planning, that is reaching decisions about marketing activity, and implementation, acting on those decisions. Traditionally many management texts and research focused on the planning aspect of decision making. In more recent studies there has been some specific focus on the actions relating to implementing decisions and consideration of 'how to' put plans into practice.

Planning begins with an analysis of what is actually wrong or needs to be changed, developed and refined. That is, the initial 'problem' identification. Within an organization, the need for change must be recognized by service decision makers otherwise nothing new will be done. At this time, possible options for change need to be considered before a most relevant option can be chosen. This stage of decision making will be successful only where individual managers with responsibility for specific tasks actively accept the responsibility for the job function, fully understand and have strong empathy with the need to change and improve, and engage in positive activities. These managers need to take initiative for change, proactively seek ideas for improvement from their staff teams and look for different options or alternatives as possible solutions.

Management performance and the competencies of managers within the context of their responsibility for the delivery of specific marketing activity is important. Good management performance will therefore require managers to be both partly 'reactive' by responding to environmental and contextual threats and partly 'proactive' by exploiting contextual opportunities to promote change.

The willingness and ability of individual managers to adapt and change is a prerequisite for successful managerial development. In contrast, a built-in natural resistance of management to change can cause many problems (Kotler, 1990; Piercy and Morgan, 1990). Given that an organization's daily life can be designed around the implementation of past plans, any new plans will require different company patterns and habits and these are often difficult to develop.

In such a circumstance, any new initiative will depend on managers becoming proactively involved in making something happen. This may be very different from past activities and habits. If new plans entail very different activities from previous ones then managers and staff may require very specific guidance and encouragement while trying to implement them. This often creates a situation of managerial uncertainty, particularly in relation to individual managers' changing roles where the levels of responsibility for decision making may be relatively unfamiliar.

IMPLEMENTATION OF SERVICE DELIVERY

Service marketing plans, however good, often fail to be realized. After the planning stage, the process of implementation begins. This entails managing the actual detail of the decisions made and putting plans into practice. Some action and direction is required from managers in order to get a decision implemented. Implementation is the process that turns marketing strategies and plans into marketing actions in order to achieve objectives. It involves getting people into action, particularly in service situations. Often this is the most difficult task managers have as they need to believe in the plans they have contributed to and see the value of encouraging change in how services are delivered and this needs to be passed on to all the staff involved in the service delivery.

The implementation of service plans and the management of service staff requires active leadership from managers with the ability to direct and organize the sequence of service activities. It entails harmonizing activities, co-ordinating efforts, supervising work plans and human involvement in those plans, overseeing and co-ordinating activities, responding to change quickly and having alternative plans. An important aspect of good service management is for the manager to provide clear information to staff and give active direction. This will often entail continuous support and encouragement in addition to reinforcing active direction until the objective has been achieved. Also successful implementation will include some room for adaptability and flexibility so that a service organization's system can respond to customers' and competitors' activities in times of change.

An important aspect of successful service planning and implementation is persistence and perseverance on behalf of managers and service deliverers. Continuous improvement is a necessity for competitive services as a defensible market position is based on the company's strengths relative to its competitors. The only way this can be achieved is through ensuring standards and consistency are always maintained and frequently updated.

Operational issues and individual responsibility

Organizing and managing operational issues are a large and vital part of service management. Indeed managing the implementation of a service operation can be very time consuming and fussy. 'Attention to detail' should be the motto for service deliverers. There are some common barriers to successful implementation of otherwise well devised plans. Often managers who are good at planning strategies for business and marketing development tend to overlook the implementation issues. Such isolated planning may occur where planners are 'professional' planners or 'ivory tower' planners in a head office or away from the service front-line, where they have little direct contact with those who must implement the plan. These planners are often concerned with broad strategy and may prepare plans that are too general. The local and operational managers who face the tactical, day-to-day operations may not fully understand the plans or they may resent what they see as unrealistic plans made by 'ivory tower' planners and misinterpret them.

Another barrier to planning occurs where decisions are made in relation to a previous plan or the previous budget. In this case the planning task can degenerate into negotiating minor changes from the previous year, rather than the creation of new strategies based on current requirements. This type of incremental planning has a tendency to become repetitive and is often ineffective.

Effective decision making and implementation requires ownership and commitment from individual managers. Some studies have found that good plans are often produced but in the absence of 'champions' determined to make them work, nothing ever happens as a result of the planning effort. These champions will perform the role of the 'finisher' as described by Belbin (1981) in his study of managerial effectiveness, and are necessary to ensure that all agreed activities are carried out to completion. Managers who are involved with the implementation of plans need to prepare or contribute to the creation of a detailed implementation plan that explicitly states the specific activities needed to put the plan into action.

To ensure effective implementation of service delivery it is important to ensure that all initial planning and creation of new ideas for service improvements include and involve different levels of managers, operational supervisors and staff involved in the service delivery. Implementation plans need to recognize explicitly the need for participation, joint effort, involvement and ownership of all concerned in the new plans and their execution.

Managing and delivering the tangible and intangible balance of service dimensions

Managing service quality consistently also requires consideration to be given to both the tangible and intangible characteristics of the dimensions involved in marketing activity. Front-line operational managers and staff should be aware of dealing with both dimensions of service delivery and this should be explicitly recognized in all original plans at strategic management level. Indeed, all service marketing planning and implementation should be aware of the multi-dimensional nature of the service being offered and ensure that a balance of these dimensions is always delivered.

From a managerial point of view, the importance of maintaining and improving the quality of tangible aspects is well recognized, both in the literature and in practice. Capital expenditure and improvement in such tangible aspects as physical facilities, furnishings, high-quality brochures and communication material, are often used as major competitive activities. For example, companies in the retailing and banking sectors often improve the physical aspects of their service outlets in order to create a more 'high-quality' image than that of their nearest competitors. Similarly, tangible aspects of product improvement often include the use of better materials and better design, additional features, and an improved overall presentation of the product in order to compete on the 'quality' label.

However, the maintenance and improvement of the intangible aspects of marketing activities are vitally important also and often are given less specific emphasis at the planning stages and so are lost in the day-to-day operational business when service implementation occurs. In particular, the importance of delivering such intangible marketing aspects as added value in terms of time and quality of attention given to customers, manager-staff-customer interactions, and proactive communications cannot be over-emphasized. To deliver such intangible aspects consistently will require positive attitudes and proactivity on the part of management decision making as well as during front-line involvement. Indeed, attention to the intangible service dimensions will contribute to the overall perception of added value by giving customers more than the competitors.

Managing people interactions

Managing people interactions involves a range of constant customer-oriented behaviour. In a service organization this includes ensuring that staff attitudes exhibit a willingness to relate to customers. This can be encouraged through hiring the right people in the first place, but also through training, proactive managerial activity and rewarding appropriate behaviour (discussed in Chapter 6). Also the use of dedicated staff available to customers at all times of the service delivery process is important in managing the overall service experience. Action-oriented managers, supervisors, and front-line staff who are proactive in their dealings with customers throughout the service delivery are also conducive to excellent management of human interactions. Involvement at all stages through the service delivery process will aid the early anticipation of problems and allow staff to solve these before a major issue occurs.

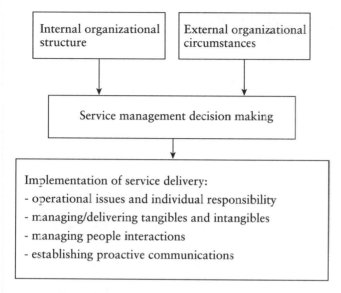

FIGURE 5.2   Service management and implementation

Establishing proactive communication

Effective service management requires proactive communication. Often good plans fail because the flow and clarity of communication within organizations may not be conducive to the effective implementation of plans. Many traditional or multinational organizations have tall hierarchical structures that emphasize rank; these organizations are likely to have some distortion occurring as information flows upward from junior through senior managerial levels. Often differential selective perception of information by different individuals occurs, where new knowledge takes on different shades of meaning as it passes from one person to another. This can be further accentuated by the tendency of lower-level managers to try to cover up any problems and only show a good side to their superiors. Conversely, effective, consistent and complete service delivery requires every aspect of the service package and everyone involved in the service delivery to work together in a fully integrated way. This is dependent on clarity of communication throughout the organization.

Communication needs to be proactive at all levels; that is, on the part of, managers, supervisors, front-line staff and customers; and at all stages through the service delivery process. Effective and timely communication will aid the early anticipation of problems and allow staff and managers to solve any problems that arise.

An overview of the focus of service management and implementation is illustrated in Figure 5.2 in the context of organizational and external circumstances.

CHANGES IN MANAGEMENT DECISION MAKING AND THE IMPACT ON SERVICE DELIVERY

The management decision making and service implementation issues discussed above are explored and illustrated in the context of a company which changed its organizational structure, in an attempt to improve the level of responsibility and authority of managerial decision making, twice over a three-year period. This occurred against the background of an increasingly competitive environment as illustrated in Table 5.2.

The company used as a case example for this study is a large, UK-based company offering a consumer travel service. At the beginning of this study this company was not structured around management responsibility; instead the traditionally centralized structure was built on a hierarchical system with directives being given from headquarters. All decision making either emanated from headquarters or had to be approved by managers there before any action could take place. The organization was built around different levels of hierarchical management which meant that operational managers working at divisional (regional) level had three or four middle managers to approach in order to have action taken or consideration given to any problem area. The company's UK operation was divided into four divisions each with responsibility for a particular geographical area. Each division had an overall manager, the Divisional Manager, who had control over the division's management, with considerable input from headquarters in relation to corporate policy and decision making. Most long-term corporate decisions were made at headquarters. Decisions in relation to the core product, the corporate advertising campaign, choice of products and services offered and the pricing of these products were made centrally and dictated to each Divisional Manager.

Top management at headquarters managed by issuing directives to their middle management in each division thus controlling the organization's activities. Their plans revolved around setting budgets for each year in relation to the operational activities that would be carried out. Each division had a cost centre that set limits to the amount of money which could be spent each year on each aspect of operational activity such as promotions, sponsorships and refurbishment of physical facilities. Some tactical decisions were made at divisional level. For example, decisions relating to which advertising agency to use for leaflet and brochure design, poster and newspaper campaigns; which PR agency to use for local work; promotion to the local travel trade and handling customer complaints.

In order to illustrate the impact of organizational factors on management decision making the following case description focuses upon one of the four UK divisions of this company over a two-and-a-half-year time period.

Table 5.2 *Case Study – overview of key changes in management decision making and service delivery over time*

	At beginning of study	Situation after 2 years
Internal context	Centralized organization	Decentralized organization
	Centralized decision making	Delegation to specialized units
	Top management directives	Key managers responsible for each unit team
External context	Inactive competition – share with 1 competitor	Aggressive competitive activity (2 competitors, one with hi-tech product)
	Static market demand	Growing market
Services management decision making	Reactive to internal circumstances, and external threats	Proactive identification of problems
	Minimal information search or evaluation of alternatives	Collect information, consider options
	Focus on tactical issues	Choose between several options
Implementation of service delivery	Follow top management directives	Delegation of responsibility
	Look to next in line for responsibility	Responsibility and advertising for activity
	Focus on tangible aspects of service	Focus on both tangible and intangible aspects of service
	Minimal or intermittent communication between functions	Liaison between functions
	Mostly media advertising	Advertising plus promotions and informational material
	Reactive approach to communication with customer and problem solving	Proactive approach to welcoming customers and problem solving

The organizational structure and its effect on management decision making at the beginning of the study

The nature of the organizational structure and influence on the key characteristics of the management decision making at this time are described here and summarized in the central column of Table 5.2.

Internal context/organizational structure

The organization had a hierarchical structure at the beginning of the study. Although the Divisional Manager had overall responsibility for the region, various managers from headquarters had joint authority with the Divisional Manager over specific aspects of the service. All line managers either directly or indirectly reported to and were accountable to headquarters.

The structure of management created a 'control' type of management rather than a decisive and action-oriented management. Overall the management structure tended to restrict the decision-making process and hold up activity until everything had been checked by each level of management. The structure also meant that there were at least two levels of managers between the Divisional Manager and the functional teams with responsibility for the various marketing tasks, creating two reporting levels before the Divisional Manager received information from the front-line. The position of the operational managers and supervisors meant that both headquarters and the Divisional Manager had authority for their management and this led to many conflicting decisions. Furthermore the structure resulted in a remoteness of decision making and inability to respond quickly to market changes. This dual level of both headquarters and divisional management created a system that encouraged and emphasized control rather than active decision making.

External context

At this time there was little external change to the marketing environment. The company shared the market with one competitor whose marketing activities rarely changed and the marketplace was relatively static.

Service management decision making

As a result of the organizational structure all decision making was influenced by headquarters. Decisions were reached in relation to suitability for all divisions and therefore the overall nature of decision making focused on very general policies and the setting of standards and rules that could be widely applied.

The decision-making process at divisional level focused on issues with which the managers felt more comfortable, such as dealing with familiar aspects of operational activity, and planning repetitive annual events. Most decision making was preceded by the collection of some convenient information (information within the office or easily found within the company), with no real in-depth search for information, consideration of the information or a convenient choice made which would not involve much change. Divisional decision making also involved following directives from headquarters and taking advice from their current advertising and PR agencies, with little new thought about the future requirements of the industry. Decision making also followed the bureaucratic traditions and priorities of the organization. Headquarters focus was on the overall control of divisions, standardization of activities across divisions, maintaining market share in each geographical location and stability of operations.

Strategic decision making was carried out by top management at headquarters. Directives were given to each region for their operational activity and these were given to Divisional Managers to carry out according to the rules and procedures accompanying them. For example, pricing structures and levels, the corporate message for advertising and promotional activity, and the choice and range of service products were standard for all divisions.

Decisions relating to specific tactical issues were carried out at divisional level. These included decisions about which PR and advertizing agency to use, any newspaper and poster campaigns to be used in tandem with corporate advertising, and how to deal with customer complaints

Implementation of service delivery

There was little responsibility taken by local managers for service delivery. Marketing activity at this time focused on the maintenance of traditional standards and offered the same level of activity as competitors, as directed by top management. In particular, marketing activity concentrated on the tactical/operational aspects of maintaining the tangible, physical features of the service delivery, with little consideration of the intangible dimensions of customers' experience. For example, many customer complaints were recorded regarding:

- staff unhelpfulness and rudeness in relation to giving information and helping customers with problems;
- the prices of services and products in relation to the quality, presentation and choice of items;
- difficulty in communication with the company in terms of telephone answering, replies to queries, and availability of services.

Overall front-line customer service staff were often inaccessible when required, reactive to customer requests, and frequently unhelpful.

Communication occurred through formal meetings and memos from headquarters; operational planning was fixed around the allocated budget for each traditional annual activity such as physical facility refurbishment, trade functions and advertising and promotional activities. Communication between functions was intermittent and occurred when a service problem arose.

Promotional communication with customers used mass advertising campaigns. Front-line staff were reactive to customers and only became involved in problem solving when requested.

The Divisional Manager wanted his managers to become more involved in the divisions' operations, have more direct contact with the local market, and develop more specific knowledge of the operational aspects of the business. Managers and staff were often torn between following head office procedures and ignoring them when they felt they were inappropriate. However these managers were not accustomed to making decisions for themselves and often were unsure when confronted with a different situation. At this time corporate management designed a more streamlined organization. Divisional Managers used this as an opportunity to change the structure at divisional level with the long-term aim of creating promotional opportunities for some younger, more enthusiastic managers. This led to organizational restructuring.

Changes to the organizational structure and its effect on management decision making

Decentralization was introduced as a result of corporate rationalization and because corporate management had recognized the diversity of the different divisions, requiring management from the people closest to the market and those who understood the local variations in demand for the service product. Headquarters was restructured and some headquarters functions were moved out to each division to increase divisional responsibility for managerial decision making and marketing activity; some longer-serving headquarters managers accepted voluntary redundancy packages. It was intended that this would ensure the organization could respond quickly to local conditions and improve the responsibility and accountability of the middle and senior managers in each division.

Consequently the overall influence of the UK head office was reduced. This gave the local divisions total autonomy; with the main decision-making responsibilities and tasks pushed down to each division so that each Divisional Manager had complete responsibility and authority for his own division. To benefit most from the corporate restructuring, the Divisional Managers devised a new divisional level structure. This was designed to improve local management responsibility and accountability for functional decision making and activity and to create some motivation and enthusiasm for role responsibilities. Functional management teams now had complete authority and responsibility for planning, managing and implementing new ideas in their own functional areas. In particular the Divisional Managers wanted to increase the level of accountability and responsibility from the management team, with managers taking direct control of their specific functional areas.

With this in mind, the Divisional Managers reduced the number of hierarchical levels at local level (in line with the corporate structural change) and made each functional manager responsible directly to himself with all other members of their teams directly responsible to them. This simplified the organization structure by reducing the number of reporting evels and numbers of managers responsible for each functional activity. Each management function was given direct responsibility for its specific area in terms of both planning marketing tasks and ensuring that marketing activities were performed.

Thus the structure was now decentralized with each functional area becoming a management unit, with specific responsibility for its own area. Functions which had been managed or jointly managed by managers in the head office structure were now completely and directly managed at divisional level. In this new structure the five management functional areas relevant to the organization's business were formed into five management 'teams': product management, pricing management, advertising and promotional management, customer/staff interface management and administration/internal communication management. Each management team was responsible for its particular management function's overall planning and the implementation of operational activities. This was expected to stimulate and motivate interest in functional responsibilities. However the effects of this organizational structure and the changes it required for the key managers took some time to work in practice.

The new functional managers were positioned within one or more teams in the new structure and worked together in the same location. Therefore there was more opportunity for the discussion of all management issues and management liaison. In addition, as a team they reported directly to the Divisional Manager, with no intermediate or middle managers to slow down or impede communication and decision-making efforts. Within the decentralized structure some managers were involved in more than one function. For example, the financial manager and the information analysis manager were both involved in pricing decisions and in the preparation of better management systems and information.

By the end of this stage it was clear that while some managers were accepting responsibility for their functional area, there was a tendency for other managers to fail to co-ordinate plans, money, technology and manpower with the rest of the functional teams.

After a period of 11 months of trying to improve the quality of decision making and marketing activity through the encouragement of staff and management to improve their performance, the Divisional Manager decided that some further organizational restructuring was necessary. The lack of consistent progress in marketing management decision making and implementing marketing activities concerned the Divisional Manager. He wanted to see more integration and co-ordination of company functional activity and tried to promote and encourage the importance of careful co-ordination and planning of marketing activity to all the functional managers. So he decided to restructure the division to incorporate a smaller and more informal management team of the key managers who had proved themselves able to make and carry out decisions; with each manager having more responsibility for overseeing a variety of areas and operations. These managers were also chosen to have a more directive role with some members of the functional teams who had not performed well on their own and who had explicitly stated that they were not comfortable with having responsibility for decision making.

So this time the Divisional Manager wanted to strengthen the organizational structure by making sure his best performing people became the overall managers of their specific functional area. Some managers who had not performed proactively in relation to planning and executing their tasks were now placed in subordinate positions to the individuals who had developed and improved over the past year. These key managers and staff who had had a more subordinate role but had shown initiative and drive and outperformed their 'superiors' were now promoted to take over the management of the functional teams. The organizational restructuring was arranged around the managers who had proved themselves to be proactive decision makers and those who had demonstrated the ability to implement those decisions and instigate action orientation. In particular the Divisional Manager wanted managers who could improve all the intangible dimensions of the service, involving proactive communication and interaction between customers and staff that would result in the delivery of a more balanced and consistent service marketing mix.

Thus the organizational structure was now more closely matched with the past experience, skills and competencies of managers. It was designed around the grouping of managers and staff by their level of knowledge and skill and suitability for specific functional management tasks. This contributed to a situation where each functional team had a balance of the relevant and different competencies for their functional activity.

The effect of this organizational structure and the key characteristics of management decision making at this stage are described here and summarized in the right column of Table 5.2.

Internal context/organizational structure

The organization was decentralized, with the emphasis on delegating management decision making to special functional units or teams. Each functional team had a manager responsible for ensuring decisions were taken and the members now worked together in managing all decision making and operational activity. The functional teams planned their activities at regular meetings, and communicated with each other on a daily basis. This 'participative' style of management decision making resulted in the improved marketing performance of the whole team.

External context

The marketplace was much more aggressive with two large competitive companies, one with a new hi-tech service product on offer, and the market was growing.

Services management decision making

The decision-making process now became more immediate and effective. The key functional managers proactively aimed to improve their own performance and subsequently that of the company. Initially they were extremely busy as they spent considerable time ensuring that their staff were well informed and taking part in the decision-making process as far as possible, but always leaving meetings with a clear and specific task to carry out before a given time period. Thus management and supervisor tasks were agreed at regular meetings and consensus and encouragement were elicited from the entire team.

The second level of managers, responsible to the functional managers with overall responsibility for each aspect of marketing management, were involved in most decisions, particularly in relation to their own activities and in plans relating to the delivery of their activity. They were well instructed and directed in order to ensure results.

Co-ordination and collaboration were the key goals of management at this time. The new structure had been created with the emphasis on solving problems quickly through team action. The key functional managers were chosen because of their proven ability to take responsibility for decision making. These managers were deemed to have the ability to become a management team that would combine across functions for task-group activity. To support this, meetings of the functional managers were held frequently in order to focus on major problem issues.

At this time the management style was participative and aimed at dealing with problems or issues as they arose whilst planning ahead for the longer term. In particular each Division was proactively seeking new ideas for innovative products and investing in new innovative technology developments.

Effective market information systems were developed for division-specific information and were being integrated into daily decision making.

Implementation of service delivery plans

Managers were responsible for the decision making and activities of specific functions and teams within the organization. Each one assumed ownership of particular tasks and involved team members in different activities. At this stage all marketing activity was planned to take account of both the tangible and intangible aspects of service delivery and customer care and could be described as comprehensive. The intangible dimensions of service delivery now included proactive interaction between customers and staff, and the use of promotional materials such as posters, signage, electronic displays and verbal information at various interaction points. In addition any customer complaints were dealt with immediately, whereby customers were given an apology combined with some compensation (such as a voucher) to encourage repeat purchase.

Informal communication between the functional managers was used on a daily or weekly basis to achieve better teamwork. Such communication allowed these managers to grow accustomed to each other's methods of decision making and styles of management without resulting in conflict or lack of action.

The development of improved information systems, improved internal communication systems and speedier decision making were considered to be the priority of all managers. By giving the key functional managers overall responsibility for specific areas of management the structure created a simplification of the previous formal/informal systems and combined them into a single multi-purpose system.

At the beginning of this study the division operated within a centralized structure with the major managerial decisions relating to marketing and operations being made at headquarters. The divisional structure was built around control rather than responsibility and allowed for directives from headquarters management in relation to each specific operational activity. During the time of change decentralization gradually led to increased management responsibility and accountability with some managers becoming more proactive than others. In addition the key managers who responded to the additional managerial responsibility in a positive way became more effective and efficient in their decision making over the time period.

The overall effect of structural changes on management decision making was:

1 all marketing decisions specific to the local region were made at divisional level rather than headquarters level,
2 there was a gradual move from headquarters control to divisional level managerial responsibility and accountability,
3 the key managers progressed and adapted to meet new challenges in comparison to the remaining managers who did not take full responsibility for planning or decision making and preferred to be directed by higher management.

Thus the 'fit' between the organizational structure, management decision making and the development of functional managers changed over time. This resulted in key managers being established, supported by 'secondary' managers who preferred not to take responsibility for decision making, but to be directed.

SUMMARY

The existing organizational and managerial issues discussed in this chapter will have an impact on any company's overall service delivery. The organizational structure will have a strong impact on the nature and scope of management decision making and effective management decision making should take account of both strategic plans for an organization and the direction and implementation of those plans. In a service context this will include clear and comprehensive action plans for operational activity, taking account of both the tangible and intangible aspects of service delivery, excellent people interactions and proactive communication as illustrated in the case study.

DISCUSSION QUESTIONS

How can organizational structures impact upon management decision making?

Discuss the internal and external changes that can impact upon an organization over time.

What impact does organizational change have on managers and their ability to plan and implement service marketing activities?

NOTE

Some of this chapter is based on material previously published in: Gilmore, A. (1996) 'The impact of organisational factors on management decision making', *Journal of Strategic Change*, 5(6): 343–58; Gilmore, A. (1997) 'Implementing "quality" in a services marketing context', *Marketing Intelligence and Planning*, 15(4/5): 185–9; and Gilmore, A. (1998) 'Quality in management decision making within a changing context', *The Journal of Management Development*, 17(2/3): 106–20.

REFERENCES

Anderson, P.F. (1982) 'Marketing, strategic planning and the theory of the firm', *Journal of Marketing*, 46, Spring: 15–26.

Belbin, R.M. (1981) *Management Teams*. London: Heinemann.

Bonoma, T.V. (1985) *The Marketing Edge*. London: Heinemann.

Brass, D.J. (1984) 'Being in the right place: a structural analysis of individual influence on an organisation', *Administrative Science Quarterly*, 29: 518–39.

Buchanon, D. and Boddy, D. (1992) *The Expertise of the Change Agent. Public Performance and Backstage Activity*. New York: Prentice Hall.

Chandler, A.D. (1962) *Strategy and Structure*. Cambridge, MA: MIT Press.

Child, J. (1972) 'Organisational structure and strategies of control: a replication of the Aston Studies', *Administrative Science Quarterly*, 17, June: 163–77.

Deshpande, R. (1982) 'The organisational context of market research use', *Journal of Marketing*, 46(3): 91–101.

Deshpande, R. and Zaltman, G. (1984) 'A comparison of factors affecting researcher and manager perceptions of market research use', *Journal of Marketing Research*, 21, Feb.: 32–8.

Greiner, L.E. (1972) 'Evolution and revolution as organisations grow', *Harvard Business Review*, 50(4) July–Aug.: 37–46.

Gronroos, C. (1980) 'Designing a long-range marketing strategy for services', *Long Range Planning*, 13, April: 36–42.

Gronroos, C. (1989) 'Defining marketing: a market-oriented approach', *European Journal of Marketing*, 23(1): 52–60.

Gummesson, E. (1991) 'Marketing-orientation revisited: the crucial role of the part-time marketer', *European Journal of Marketing*, 25(2): 60–75.

Heller, F., Drenth, P., Koopman, P. and Rus, V. (1988) *Decisions in Organisations: A Three-Country Comparative Study*. London: Sage Publications.

Judd, V.C. (1987) 'Differentiate with the 5th P: People', *Industrial Marketing Management*, 16(4): 241–7.

Kotler, P. (1990) *Principles of Marketing*. Englewood Cliffs, NJ: Prentice-Hall.

Longbottom, D.A. (1972) 'Decision making – a review', *Management Decision*, 10, Winter: 224–42.

Mintzberg, H. (1973) *The Nature of Managerial Work*. New York: Harper and Row.

Mintzberg, H. (1976) 'Planning on left and managing on the right', *Harvard Business Review*, 54(4), July/Aug.: 49–58.

Mintzberg, H. (1979) *The Structuring of Organisations*. Englewood Cliffs, NJ: Prentice-Hall.

Moch, M. and Morse, E. (1977) 'Size, centralisation and organisational adoption of innovations', *American Sociological Review*, 92, Oct.: 716–25.

Ottaway, R.N. (1979) *Change Agents at Work*, London: Associated Business Press.

Piercy, N. and Morgan, N. (1990) 'Organisational context and behavioural problems as determinants of the effectiveness of the strategic marketing planning process', *Journal of Marketing Management*, 6(2): 127–43.

Rumelt, R.P. (1974) *Strategy, Structure, and Economic Performance*. Boston: Division of Research, Graduate School of Business Administration, Harvard University. (Cited in Mintzberg, H. (1979) 'An emerging strategy of "direct" research', *Administrative Science Quarterly*, 24, Dec.: 582–9.

Simon, H.A. (1965) *The Shape of Automation*. New York: Harper and Row.

Taylor, B. (1975) 'Strategies for Planning', *Long Range Planning*, Aug.: 27–40.

Weinshall, T.D. (1975) 'Multinational corporations – their study and measurement', *Management International Review*, 15(4/5): 67–76.

Wilensky, H. (1967) *Organisational Intelligence: Knowledge and Policy in Government and Industry*. New York: Basic Books.

6

Management Styles and Emphasis
for Services Marketing

Building on the theme of management issues in services, this chapter discusses different management approaches and the value of adopting an appropriate style for managing people in a service organization. First, the chapter focuses on the suitability of different management approaches and styles for service contexts. In recognizing the scope of service management roles the discussion includes the 'empowerment' and 'production-line' approaches to managing people and summarizes where each may be appropriate. The discussion will also debate whether it is useful to try to achieve only one or the other and will discuss the relevance and practicality of combining participative and directive styles.

Secondly this chapter debates how service managers in some contexts may have different perspectives and priorities within their managerial responsibilities. The discussion focuses on situations where a custodial management emphasis is useful and where a market-focused management emphasis is required. These are illustrated in the context of the changing demands for museum management.

The chapter summary highlights the key themes in relation to management styles and management emphasis and the implications they have for the development of managers and their specific roles in service management.

Production-line management:	Empowerment management:
managers design systems	managers encourage
employees execute activities	employee participation
work standardization	more customization
consistent work patterns and	more flexible work patterns
outcomes	and outcomes

FIGURE 6.1 **Production-line and empowerment management style**

IMPORTANCE OF USING AN APPROPRIATE MANAGEMENT STYLE

Given the importance of people in service management, supervision and delivery any management approach needs to consider how to manage people very carefully indeed. Many managers and CEOs of service companies often say 'our people are our most important resource'. However in reality this is not always felt or perceived to be true at the front-line. Often service delivery staff are part-time workers, have had limited training, are paid on an hourly basis and find it difficult to keep motivated.

There are two extremes of approach to managing people. At one extreme, there is the traditional, control or production-line approach which encompasses top-down, hierarchical, mechanistic, bureaucratic or control-oriented management that is production-led. At the other extreme is the commitment approach that involves staff in the management process and its effectiveness or otherwise depends upon the empowerment and participation of staff. These two approaches are summarized in Figure 6.1 and discussed below.

Production-line management style

The control or production-line approach is used in companies where managers design the systems and employees are expected to execute them. Generally this approach was designed for an industrial environment. However as Sasser and Arbeit (1976) explain, this low risk/high return mode of product preparation provided a soothing image to the harried service executive. For this reason many service organizations adopted the production-line approach in an attempt to streamline and control service delivery. There are advantages and disadvantages of using this approach in a service context.

The main focus of the production-line approach is to try to ensure consistency through work standardization. In a service context, this approach may be relevant when services are routine, 'simple', high volume and predictable. However, a production-line approach is unlikely to be relevant to a situation where services are more complex, non-routine, sometimes unpredictable and need to be personalized. It is thought to be effective when the tasks to be performed are simple, there is clear division of labour, there is substitution of equipment and systems for employees and there is little decision-making discretion afforded to employees. Many franchise services use this system to ensure that a standard product is delivered consistently at all locations. For example, this style of management is essentially the one used by McDonald's. The advantages of such an approach are that it minimizes human individuality and therefore 'interference' or human error in an otherwise efficient service system.

Empowerment management style

On the other hand, the empowerment or involvement style approach encourages employee participation. It entails allowing employees to take initiatives and then reward them accordingly. Empowerment focuses on how a task can be performed at its best and depends upon front-line employees to improve the service and solve problems in an effective way. It works best where the skill, expertise and diagnostic capabilities of staff are vital to the service delivery.

The empowerment approach is built on the belief that if the organization wants to improve quality and performance, then service employees should be involved. This is where a service is viewed as a special kind of product. A problem with the empowerment approach is that in practice many organizations suffer from a lack of clarity as to what empowerment actually is as it can mean many different things in different contexts. Some authors view empowerment as 'turning the front-line loose' and dismantling the managerial structure (Clutterbuck and Kernoghan, 1994; Zemke and Schaaf, 1989). Others see empowerment as giving direction, vision and leadership, sharing information about the company's performance and giving employees the power to make decisions (Bell and Zemke, 1990; Bowen and Lawler, 1992; Brandt, 1998a, 1998b). Empowerment can be summed up in three words – accountability, responsibility and authority (Burdett, 1996).

Each of these management styles is appropriate in different contexts. In some situations a production-line approach may be most efficient and in other situations an empowerment approach will be better. However there are cases in some services where a combination of both approaches may be most effective. That is, some aspects of the service might best be managed through a production-line approach while other aspects of the service delivery may benefit from staff who are empowered and willing to take the initiative.

In high-contact services customers will interact with one or more front-line employees. If one or more of these individuals are in a bad mood or fail to provide an efficient or friendly service then the customer will not be happy. This contact emphasizes the difference between front-line (or front-stage) employees and back-stage employees. Back-stage employees need to support front-line people and will have a strong impact on the level of service delivered to the customer. Therefore a management style should recognize this and use techniques to involve all employees in the constant goal of customer satisfaction. Also in many services the role of the employee involves some 'emotional' contribution or the requirement to act out a role of being compassionate, sincere, or self-effacing. This kind of service role will require an empowerment style of management rather than a production-line approach.

CASE STUDY

WHICH IS BEST – A PRODUCTION OR EMPOWERMENT STYLE OF MANAGEMENT?

The dilemma of using a production-line or empowerment style of management is illustrated in an example of a call centre operation where a production-line approach was being used for the benefit of management control. However front-line staff or call centre agents questioned this approach because of the perceived lack of service support for the varied and complex nature of customer queries. Many call centres' management styles are production-led with a priority on answering a high number of calls above any other aspect of service delivery. A study of a large call service involving four call centres was commissioned to investigate the problems in service delivery and identify the barriers to improving the call centres' service. The research findings illustrate the effect of a production-line approach on a relatively complex service delivery requirement. The impact of this is highlighted in the delivery of the service dimensions most relevant to a call centre operation. These dimensions are: number of calls answered, speed of response, length of call, standard responses, relevant information given, dealing with customer's problem, empathy shown, access to relevant service and responsiveness to individual customer's problem.

Number of calls
During observations of the call centre operation and interviews with managers and agents it became evident that there was a 'production-line' approach to managing this call centre operation. The main emphasis was on answering a large number of calls within a given time period. It was an explicit part of written company policy. In each of the four call centre locations there was a display on the wall which monitored/measured quantitative details in relation to:

- number of calls answered within past 10 minutes
- calls waiting to be answered, that is 'in the queue'
- number of agents currently taking calls

- number of agents waiting to take calls (free agents)
- number of 'not ready' agents
- number of agents on outgoing calls or on a call to another agent.

Observation studies revealed that agents focused close attention upon the display and would only go for a break if this showed the call situation was under control. The agents worked in small groups and organized themselves to cover each other for 'breaks'. Agents were also required to categorize each call by pressing a button on the telephone. There were ten categories in all, each indicating a different type of service response. Observations and focus group discussions revealed that the agents frequently forgot to press the call category button and therefore failed to record a call type. Discussions with staff indicated that many incoming calls were outside the ten categories and therefore were not 'logged'. Call centre managers stated that they required agents to record the number of calls but were concerned about agent error in recording calls as the agents often 'forgot' to select the correct category button.

Speed of response

Again there was a 'production-line' approach in the management and delivery of this aspect of service. The call centre's overall manager's ambition for the call centre was 'easy to reach and best to do business with'. He recognized that the first part of the vision was easy to measure; the goal was to answer 90 per cent of calls within 10 seconds (the '90/10 rule'). He felt that the 'best to do business with' was more difficult and complex to measure as deciding what makes the company best to do business with is dependent on the customer. The problem was finding ways to measure this on a day-to-day basis.

Interviews with line managers (one for each of the four call centres) indicated a difference in opinions and a variety of responses in terms of everyday running of the call centres. One manager indicated that the agents in his centre could deal with all customers' needs and should not need to pass calls on to be completed by anyone else. The other line managers indicated that if an agent could not 'wrap up' the call in 3 minutes, they might need to pass the call on to other departments (back-up offices). However, agents indicated that they had experienced major problems in finding someone in other back-up departments to take the call. Focus group interviews with agents concluded that they thought the organization did not fully recognize the need for back-up support.

One of the four line managers emphasized that overall performance was measured by the 90/10 rule but he recognized that an 'acceptable number of calls would be abandoned'. This manager commented that 'quality aspects of the calls are not measured ... I am considering how to measure this'. Another line manager thought that the people characteristics of the service made measurement very difficult as: 'each customer expects something different from a call'. For example, 'an elderly person may want to chat for a few minutes whereas someone else may want a short sharp answer'. Managers said that they sought to improve the service by focusing on things when they went wrong, in order to identify where the service had failed. Some acknowledged this did not resolve immediate customer problems.

The major issue which impacted upon the 'speed of response' measurement was the variety of calls. Observations and discussions indicated a wide variety of calls. Focus group discussions with agents revealed that in their experience customers have many different queries. This is often exacerbated by customers not knowing 'the type of service they require when they call' and 'a lot of the services overlap'. In addition many customers often did not know basic 'screening' information that would be required from them. This resulted in the agent adapting their standard approach in order to get appropriate information from customers before dealing with the specific problem.

Length of call

The production-line approach was in evidence in relation to the emphasis and importance given to this aspect of service delivery in the call centres. Managers expected agents to spend no more than 3 minutes on each call; the company guidelines specified this time limit. Agents said the focus was on 'finishing the call' and 'getting the customer off the line' rather than helping them with their problem. Observations revealed the difficulty in keeping to this time for all queries. For example a large number of calls were from customers who did not know their customer account number; some customers could not even quote their postcode. On these occasions the agent had to find this information from a book in the office.

Different customer accents on the telephone made call handling extremely difficult as it resulted in customers being asked to spell words, such as road names. Observations also indicated that some customers wanted 'a chat' rather than a problem sorted out. For example, an elderly lady spent considerable time explaining to the agent how she had got a new mobile telephone and how much she liked using it. Although the agent controlled the call carefully by asking questions to identify the problem, it took the lady over 2 minutes to find the bill which was the reason for the call.

Standard responses

Call centre agents were required to use a standard opening sentence: 'good morning/good afternoon, (name of company), how can I help you?' This was the only consistent part of the call; after this each agent determined the best way to deal with the customer. The overall Business Manager explained that: 'we do not want agents to be like robots' and 'employees could answer the call in their own way'. He perceived scripts to be 'robotic' and 'off-putting' to customers. However, not all line managers agreed with this policy. Two line managers agreed that 'agents should be encouraged to deal with customers in their own way'; while two did not because of losing consistency in dealing with customers. For example, observations discovered two different responses to similar customer queries. Two customers had received demands for overdue payments; each explained in great detail why they could not pay their bill. Agents had the power to make a decision about what was an acceptable time-scale for the payment to be received. Agents dealt with these calls very differently, thus manifesting an inconsistent service response.

One line manager explained that he would like some aspects of the calls to be scripted because agents sometimes took the 'easy option' and allowed the customer to dictate the terms for resolving a problem with payment options/time-scales. This managerial apprehension has been identified in other studies that concluded that managers often fear empowerment as it may result in employees giving away too much to the customer (Merchants Group, 1997). Agents commented that often there was confusion about how best to advise customers with problems requiring specific expertise, and they were often left to their own devices without appropriate back-up support.

Relevant information given

Agents perceived that they did not receive sufficient direction, information or guidance from management in relation to dealing with the quality of service. Most communication and direction from management was through e-mails or memos. Agents' comments included the following: 'Managers e-mail us lots of instructions and information'; 'Some days we can get as many as 6–8 pieces of paper that we have to read …' 'We are left to interpret these instructions in whatever way we can. It is a lot to take in at once when there are calls coming in. If we put our "not ready button" on while we read the information it is "frowned upon".' Interviews with managers revealed that they preferred to use e-mails and memos for communicating with agents rather than talking to them while they were on duty as this would prevent them from answering calls.

In this call centre the emphasis on the tangible aspects of service delivery described above had an immediate impact on the more intangible aspects of service in relation to dealing with customers' problems, empathy shown and responsiveness to individual problems.

Dealing with the customer's problem

Agents and some, but not all, of the managers agreed that agents needed back-up support from other departments for very specific customer queries that required explicit expertise and action. Agents agreed that: 'the service could be improved dramatically if the systems were better. We have many complex customer service queries to deal with, there is a complete lack of understanding of what we do and we are only measured on inbound calls'; 'the service could be better if the back-up services from other departments were improved'; 'the system is designed to get calls in and out as quickly as possible, the focus is not on handling the call in the best way possible, just the shortest way'. This system puts agents 'under more pressure and stress'.

In each call centre computer systems storing customer information were so slow there was a continual repetition of agents' voices saying: 'just bear with me', 'sorry for keeping you', 'thank you for holding'.

Empathy shown

The call centre agents in this study did show empathy to customers and did constantly try to resolve their problems. However this was not always possible for them when they did not have relevant information for the specific query. In spite of calls being answered within 10 seconds, calls lasting less than 3 minutes and agents showing empathy to customers there was poor customer service in many instances because of being unable to find the appropriate information or expert to advise customers.

Access to relevant service

Agents often lacked appropriate expertise for some complex problems; they also had little back-up support from different specialist departments with specific expertise and they had on-site management guidance and direction (as illustrated earlier). This led to customers being frustrated and having to 'call back' in order to get problems resolved. Agents felt that they needed better back-up systems and support from management in order to fulfil all dimensions of service delivery.

Responsiveness to an individual customer's problem

Although observations in this study indicated that customers were dealt with in an individual manner, focus group discussions with agents indicated that they felt the '3 minute' guideline given by the organization emphasized that the agent was being asked to focus on the company, rather than the customer. Agents felt 'under pressure' and 'torn in two' as they were constantly trying to please the customer and their employer. This finding supports Denny's (1998) study where he concludes that many call centres put pressure on agents to answer a great number of calls regardless of the quality. This led to work stress in relation to how they dealt with 'surprises' in the form of unexpected calls and requests.

In this case study agent frustration led to the widely held perception that the company was only concerned with the tangible measurements and was not concerned with the quality of the call centre's service. Agents felt that managers did not want to receive staff feedback or communications in relation to the drawbacks of the service encounter. For example, agents said that: 'We have not been asked how we think the service could be improved even though we are the front-line staff and we know the customers better than anyone; 'Management are only interested in the statistics not the quality issues.'

Line managers commented on how difficult it was to measure the quality of service delivery and that they were still considering how it might be done. Observation studies and focus group discussions revealed the inconsistencies in service delivery, particularly in relation to dealing with complex customer complaints where agents were often unsure how to cope.

The findings from this study of call centre services indicate a managerial or organizational problem, rather than one of agent motivation. The challenge for call centre managers is to decide what approach best meets the needs of the organization, the agent and external customer. In this example, there is a need to recognize the multi-dimensional nature of the call centre service, the existence of simple and complex queries and therefore a need for the delivery of both tangible and intangible service dimensions, using a combination of both a production and empowerment management approach.

Combining the Production-Line and Empowerment Approach

For efficient and effective management of services such as call centres, the use of a combination of production-line and empowerment approaches may be beneficial. However this needs some careful consideration in relation to how each aspect should be managed. The production-line approach would appear to work well with the delivery of tangible aspects of service delivery. All staff need to agree how each of these tangible measures is set (in accordance with customers' expectations) in terms of number of calls answered in a given time period, speed of response and length of call. The more intangible aspects of service delivery such as individual customer service, access to relevant help and seeing problems through to completion need to be dealt with, particularly where there are more complex service queries and problems to be addressed. A wide range of calls in terms of variability, and levels of customer service is a complexity inherent characteristic of this kind of services as is a wide variety of customer needs, requirements, perceptions, experience and ability to comprehend instructions and directions.

Therefore recognizing, measuring and managing the intangible aspects of services such as a call centre service is vital. Of course, an efficient customer information database and computer system are necessary prerequisites. For example, a mechanism for screening calls in terms of their complexity is one of the first steps in the effective management of a call centre given that some calls can be 'simple' and resolved within seconds and others are complex and need a high degree of expertise for their resolution. The more complex calls need to be directed to agents who are experts in the relevant areas; this suggests that some agents should be trained to become specialists in specific service areas, while others deal with the shorter, simple queries. The implication for call centre managers is that they become more 'hands on' managers who identify specific training needs for individual agents and help develop the call centre staff. This role would be similar to one of an empowering 'coach' rather than a production-led 'boss'.

There are a number of significant benefits of using a proactive and supportive managerial approach that incorporates an empowerment approach into the efficient production-line systems needed to deal with a large number of customer contacts or interactions in a consistent manner. By recognizing the multi-dimensional nature of service delivery in many service situations managers can ensure that the benefits of both production-line and empowerment management styles are used to achieve cohesion in a service operation. It is important to recognize all the key aspects of service quality requiring attention and how those aspects interact with each other.

IMPORTANCE OF USING AN APPROPRIATE MANAGEMENT EMPHASIS: CUSTODIAL MANAGEMENT VERSUS SERVICE MANAGEMENT

In other contexts of services management there are different choices regarding the style of management for specific purposes. Often managing the actual service site in itself is regarded as the most important aspect of a manager's role, particularly if the site or physical attributes of the site are unique or irreplaceable. This is particularly relevant in the context of managing museums, natural heritage sites and tourism sites.

Managerial conflict can occur where there is a need to run a successful enterprise and make some profit from allowing large numbers of visitors to have a positive experience of using such sites. In such circumstances there are two managerial roles: one to maintain a site, a valuable and unique collection of artistic works, or a natural and beautiful scenic area, and the other to deliver a service experience to considerable numbers of visitors or users of the service site. The following box illustrates this conflict in the context of a unique natural heritage site.

The effect of an increasing flow of visitors on a natural and unique site, the Great Barrier Reef.

Increasing numbers of visitors come to visit the site each year. They have been attracted by excellent opportunities for snorkelling, seeing the magnificent coral reef and its surrounding ecosystem, enjoying a natural environment and experiencing one of the world's unique attractions. This in turn has increased pressure on the coral reef and on-site physical facilities. The growth of visitor numbers will continually impact on the site and therefore needs to be managed carefully if sustainable tourism is to be achieved. Many visitors are not aware of the fragility of the site and do not behave appropriately. For example, some visitors stand on the coral even though there are signs to ask tourists not to do this because of the corrosive effect on the coral. The entire area surrounding the Great Barrier Reef in the north-east of Australia and similar areas in different regions around the world are extremely important to local and national economies and need to be sustained. Thus there is an increasing challenge for local management groups and both the private and public companies involved in the operation and maintenance of the site to manage the numbers visiting the site at any given time and to manage their behaviour. They need to ensure that the site is available, accessible and visitor-friendly while caring for and maintaining the sustainability of the site.

The managerial dilemma of managing a unique service and simultaneously encouraging visitors has been the focus of some public museums in recent years. However this has led to many differences in managerial opinion concerning the priorities of running a museum and how they should be managed. The implications for managers are discussed in the context of museum management to illustrate these two requirements of service management.

Custodial museum management in transition

Many museums are long established organizations where management performance has built upon tradition and past practices. This is evident where museums are in the process of change and are in transition from having a custodial focus to becoming more market-focused.

The custodial management style has been criticized for being too restrictive and not market-focused. This is because traditionally decisions were made centrally, following long-standing 'industry' practice, so managers at museum level often did not feel the need to plan or implement anything new especially in relation to attracting visitors. Also systems designed for gathering information were often based upon 'older' or traditional values and not always focused on gathering relevant data. Consequently museums have not always had appropriate and up-to-date information for their specific visitors and local market. Planning focused on familiar aspects of operational activity such as organizing annual events, with little thought of doing anything new or more relevant for different and changing markets.

This type of management has resulted in activities that focus on maintaining the collections for posterity, emphasizing the tangible aspects of the service delivery that are more easily measured, evaluated and operationalized by managers. So managing the collections and focusing on their maintenance and safety has been a priority. The intangible aspects of service delivery such as providing guidance and interpretation were not seen as a priority they this could interfere with the safety of the collections and were more difficult to manage. They were often overlooked in the day-to-day running of a museum and maintenance of a collection. For example, exhibitions may have focused on the art displays only and offered little attempt to provide suitable information and interpretation for different visitors' needs.

During a time of transition when the focus of management is changing to becoming more visitor-focused and service-oriented, the priorities of service delivery will create some difficult challenges for custodial-type managers. Changing from well-practised and ingrained patterns to one of focus on new aspects and service delivery priorities takes some time, patience and practice before a new pattern can emerge and become 'set'. A more participative style of management, encouraging staff at all levels to contribute to the development of service delivery, will be more useful at such a time. Different staff members can be involved in developing the new service and can adapt and learn within the changing context, with an aim to achieve integrated planning and co-ordination of specific aspects of marketing activity. Much of such activity can be encouraged through regular meetings and trying out and evaluation of ideas. In this way the management style can become more collaborative. During a period of change service delivery can be inconsistent given that some staff members and managers may carry out all activities while others may not. Some service areas may be more proactive, communicative and, interpretative than others, depending on how they have grasped the new service-oriented focus and direction of the museum.

Custodial-type managers and marketing managers often have different approaches to the service delivery dimensions as illustrated in Table 6.1. For example, for custodial managers the value and safety of the collection are more important than illustrating the relevance of the collection to visitors and creating a visitor-friendly environment.

However in a transition period elements of both styles of management will occur. During a change in the focus of management, the challenge for museum directors and managers is to decide what approach best suits the needs of the organization, staff expertise and the nature of visitor. The management approach needs to recognize the nature of the museum 'service/product' and the entire experience of the visitor. The curator-style emphasis would appear to work well with the delivery of the collections (tangible aspects of service delivery) while the marketing management style may be more focused on interacting with the market. However this needs some careful consideration in relation to how each aspect should be managed.

Table 6.1 *Custodial and service marketing approaches to the management of museums*

Product/service dimensions	Emphasis of custodial management	Emphasis of service marketing management
The collections	Value and importance in artistic terms	Relevance to visitors
	Maintained, designed for safety of collections	Create impact, differentiation, visitor-friendly
Availability and accessibility	Standard opening hours, limited proximity of customers to some valuable collections	Proactive staff-visitor interactions and proximity encouraged
Communication	Predominantly passive observation encouraged	Visitors encouraged to participate in experience
	Standardized messages/attention, non-personal approach, little attempt to involve visitor	More individualized messages/attention
		Personal approach and emotional involvement of visitor

Moving from a custodial emphasis to a service emphasis

In a recent study of museums the two different styles of management were evident within each of them. Although there was considerable emphasis on the safety and security of the collections, there was a drive to change the role of warding staff from one of security to one of interpretation. These front-line staff were trying to become more communicative in their interactions with visitors. However while some staff saw themselves as custodial and not involved at the visitor interface, others were more receptive to the idea of interacting with visitors. Any changes in the managerial direction had an impact upon the staff skills and competencies required and many staff actively sought some customer service training.

By recognizing the need to both manage the visitors experience and the welfare at the collections museum managers can ensure that the benefits of both curator and marketing management styles are used to achieve cohesion. All the key aspects of the museum offering and service quality require attention and how those aspects interact with each other requires the involvement of all staff in the change process. Participation and involvement will contribute to the commitment and co-operation of staff in the evolving service environment.

Although managers will be busy during a time of change, they will need to spend time ensuring that staff are well informed, can take part in decision making and always have a clear and specific understanding of the tasks to be carried out within a given time period. Tasks should be agreed at regular meetings and consensus achieved by the overall management team. Staff should be encouraged to learn from mistakes and actively seek to improve their performance for visitors.

SUMMARY

This chapter has discussed different management styles and different emphases of service managers. The value of adopting a production-line or an empowerment management style depends on the organizational context and the complexity of service delivery. The use of one or the other may be appropriate in either simple or complex service operations. However, often services have both simple and complex aspects and it may be useful to consider using both – each for different aspects of the service delivery. This is particularly true in situations of organizational flux where individuals may have different and changing responsibilities and work tasks to carry out.

Similarly the differing emphases of managers involved in managing important or valuable service sites needs careful consideration. Managing service sites such as museums or heritage sites requires both a custodial focus on maintaining the site in the long term and encouraging visitors to participate in a complete service experience. With the current competitive climate and funding shortages the need to understand the nature of services such as the museum experience has never been greater. Although significant changes have taken place over the past decade in museums everywhere, there in many cases appears to have been less emphasis on the marketing aspects of the museum service and how these could have been developed and managed.

Consideration of the scope of service delivery in any context should help managers adopt the appropriate management style and to ensure the appropriate emphasis for service management.

DISCUSSION QUESTIONS

What is meant by a production-line and an empowerment style to managing employees?

Outline a situation where a custodial management emphasis may be useful in a service context and discuss how this might conflict with service marketing objectives.

What are the disadvantages and advantages of each of these managerial approaches?

NOTE

Parts of this chapter have been previously published in Gilmore, A. and Moreland, L. (2000) 'Call centres: how can service quality be managed', *Irish Marketing Review*, 13(1): 3–11. I gratefully acknowledge Dr. Ruth Rentschler, Deakin University, Australia for assistance with the 'Custodial museum management in transition' section of the chapter.

REFERENCES

Bell, C.R. and Zemke, R. (1990) 'The performing art of service management', *Management Review*, 79, July: 42–5.

Bowen, D.E. and Lawler, E.E. III (1992) 'The empowerment of service workers: what, why, how, and when', *Sloan Management Review*, Spring, 33(3): 31–9.

Brandt, J. (1998a) 'IT and empowerment: a powerful duo', *Industry Week*, 20 April, 247, 8: 4.

Brandt, J. (1998b) 'Too much of a good thing?', *Industry Week*, March 16, 247, 6: 6.

Burdett, D. (1996) 'Empowerment defined', *The Occupational Psychologist*, 28: 33–4.

Clutterbuck, D. and Kernoghan, S. (1994) *The Power of Empowerment*. London: Kogan Page.

Denny, C. (1998) 'Remote control of the High Street', *The Guardian*, 2 June.

Merchants Group (1997) '*The 1997 Call Centre Benchmarking Participants Report*', March. Merchants Group, London.

Sasser, W.E. and Arbeit, S.P. (1976) 'Selling jobs in the service sector', *Business Horizons*, 19(3): 6–11.

Zemke, R. and Schaaf, D. (1989) '*The service edge: 101 companies that profit from customer care*', New American Library, New York.

7

Internal Marketing in Service Organizations

Although widely used, the term 'internal marketing' is often used loosely to describe many different managerial initiatives aimed at improving the effectiveness and efficiency of organizational resources, both people and materials. The use of the term 'marketing' in this context does not simply mean the application or performance of marketing activity. More specifically, it means a focus on marketing concepts and theories that can be adopted for application to the internal customer (employee); so that they can understand and value the philosophy of providing satisfaction for the external customer.

Internal marketing is based on the idea that employees represent an internal market within the organization and that they need to be educated and informed about the organization's mission, the benefits of its products and services and the expectations of its customers. Successful 'marketing' to this group is believed to contribute towards achieving ultimate success in the delivery of all marketing activity to external customers. Thus the overwhelming purpose of internal marketing is to 'involve' employees in the organization's mission and strategic direction and help them understand and value the corporate objectives. In so doing, it will achieve a 'balance' between operational efficiency and management objectives.

Internal marketing can be practised at different levels within an organization and with its suppliers and networks (Gummesson, 1991). For example, it can occur within the customer–supplier relationship, in the application of marketing know-how to personnel, in the activities which focus on encouraging a company to be marketing oriented, and the marketing that takes place between profit-centres inside a decentralized company.

In the context of a service organization, internal marketing needs to be based on negotiation and so depends upon joint or consensus planning and agreement, a focus on continuous value creation for all parties, and reciprocal rather than sequential interdependence (Joshi, 1995; Varey, 1995). It also needs to be based on the involvement of a number of individuals across functions and levels in the firm, including both general and functional managers, and encompassing all marketing and marketing-related activities. Such involvement needs to have a long-term perspective in that the duration of interactions should be continuous, ongoing, active and adaptive; formal and informal. To be successful internal marketing needs to build on relationships staff may have with each other or with others outside the organization, and involve management from across different functions and levels in the firm. For such interactions to exist or develop, empowerment should be inherent in the organization; that is, there should be some degree of 'experienced responsibility for work outcomes' (Hackman and Oldham, 1980) which encourages employees to be accountable and responsible for their results.

ORGANIZATIONAL CONTEXT OF INTERNAL MARKETING

The nature of the organizational structure will impact upon the degree of management responsibility (see Chapter 5). Organizational structures gradually change as a result of both internally and externally occurring circumstances. As an organization develops, grows and reorganizes, management decision making evolves, managers move and the structures change. Similarly, as the organization adapts to a changing external environment such adaptation will have an impact on organizational structure.

Typically, as organizations grow they develop more structure. Traditionally structure is built around the functional activities of an organization. This can create different departments, each being developed with individual emphasis and priorities. Often, as organizations become larger, they can become unwieldy and the overall goal or purpose of an organization can be overlooked or become vague. Different types of decisions will be required at different levels within a functional structure in an organization. For example, some levels of management will be involved in planning, different levels of managers will be responsible for making operational decisions and front-line staff will be involved in carrying out the operational activities.

Table 7.1 *Barriers to internal marketing*

Resistance to change
Inter-functional conflict
Intra-functional conflict
Lack of individual responsibility

Traditionally the purpose of an organizational structure is to create and support a system of management hierarchy, authority, power and control. Where there are many levels in the hierarchy from top management to front-line staff there are likely to be more standardized and formalized role definitions and demarcations. In this situation, decision making occurs at many levels away from the front-line. Often managers and staff in different levels tend to deal with their immediate areas of responsibility only, with little perception of the activities of the organization as a whole. In addition decision making in many organizations occurs against the background of 'political' power struggles and therefore is influenced by managerial manipulation, keeping control, and attempting to repress social interactions and informal negotiation. Such manipulative behaviour is often furthered by 'behind closed doors' communications. Many weaknesses are inherent in traditional hierarchical structures where managerial power and control is paramount. In this way hierarchical, formal structures restrict both individual and functional creativity and flexibility and limit any quick responses to environmental changes. Because such structures have been criticized for stifling individual role responsibility and managerial accountability, many organizations have attempted to reduce the number of managerial levels, devolve managerial responsibility and accountability and move decision makers closer to the (external) customer interface level.

Given that internal marketing occurs within an organizational environment the nature of organizational interrelationships and interactions need to be recognized. Organizations are internal networks of interacting groups where power dependencies and relationships occur between internal departments (Mastenbroek, 1993). Some of the more common barriers to developing and sustaining effective internal marketing in an organization are shown in Table 7.1 and discussed below.

Resistance to change
Many organizations suffer from an organizational 'resistance to change' at various stages in their lives. A 'built-in' natural resistance of management to change can cause many problems (Kotler, 1990; Piercy and Morgan, 1990). In many cases this results from a reluctance of management and employees to consider new ideas, at times when key managers (and gatekeepers) may feel their power could be eroded, an overall fear of the unknown, and concern about job security or future promotion. In association with this many managers' resistance to change is based on the protection of vested interests when they

have built departments and teams around them and want to keep this power. Thus in a large organization there may be a number of managers who feel this way and will do everything they can to maintain the established and traditional organizational infrastructure.

Furthermore resistance to change is often exacerbated if front-line and supervisory staff in an organization perceive that the organization is led by 'ivory tower' planners. This is when management are too far removed from the actual functional activity and operational delivery to understand the 'real' issues requiring improvement (illustrated at the beginning of the case example described in Chapter 5). Another barrier to change can exist when one level of management tries to control the degree of power and responsibility taken by another level of management. For example, in service organizations there may be an implicit need for managers to make timely decisions related to external issues such as new competition or increased labour costs. When this occurs there may be pressure from within the organization to limit individual proactive behaviour because of high-level decisions and exigencies of hierarchy.

Inter-functional conflict

Senior managers often have misguided assumptions about their organization's culture (Hofstede, 1991) in that they may be unaware of the problems and issues which impede co-operation and integration. Inter-functional conflicts may be one such area. In many organizations functional conflicts exist when one function fails to recognize that other functions may have different priorities. For example marketing's view of personnel, production and finance departments within an organization will be different from each department's perceived view of themselves.

Equally these different departments will have varying views of the marketing function (Ruekert and Walker, 1987; Weinrauch and Anderson, 1982). For example, marketing managers' emphasis may be on: increasing sales, offering many products, frequently changing product ranges, using pricing incentives, offering good value for money and requiring staff to work according to flexible work patterns. However production, finance and HR managers may consider managers implementing these practices to be either under or over selling, not cost conscious, flexible to a fault, ultra optimistic and uncontrollable. So functionally organized companies may in fact be working against themselves, the consequence of which will be inefficient performance.

Intra-functional conflict

Intra-functional conflict occurs when organizational and departmental goals are very different to individual and personal goals. It occurs because individuals may have different goals, desires and ambitions, and will be submerged in different social interactions that will impact upon their overall attitude and behaviour.

Such conflict often occurs when there are is a small number of internal promotions available for a large number of people, and colleagues become very competitive in their work-related activities. This often leads to secretive practices, for example not sharing ideas, work plans or initiatives with colleagues, and restricting flows of information. Work-related possessiveness entails poor communication in not letting others know the whole perspective in any work context such as a new development or initiative. In the worst scenario one-upmanship, where individuals try to be seen as the initiator of good ideas, in the context of playing down others' contributions occurs. Indeed this often leads to a 'blame' culture where individuals are 'accused' or linked to inefficiencies and mistakes; and 'personality clashes' interfere with best working practices.

Lack of individual responsibility

Lack of individual responsibility in an organization manifests itself when action is required but managers are unable or unwilling to take decisive action or make new decisions. In this vein, Piercy and Morgan (1990) describe the 'problem of incrementalization' where managers fail to take new decisions but instead just adapt the previous year's plans.

The problem of finding individuals to actively implement plans is well recognized in the management literature. Individuals need to have a clear understanding about where to fit in and to know about their duties and responsibilities. Indeed, managers who will be involved with the implementation of new activities need to be contributors to the design of action plans which explicitly state the specific activities needed at each stage of implementation.

Clearly there are a number of organizational barriers to internal marketing. Often these are created and manifested through the structure itself, particularly through a managerial resistance to change. Any change in the nature of management decision making necessitates a change in managerial structure and in the individual requirements and roles of managers (Weinshall, 1975). This will occur as an organization evolves through its life cycle and/or adapts to a dramatically changing environment. Thus the 'fit' between the organizational structure, management decision making and the development of managers is of vital importance. The effectiveness and suitability of this 'fit' varies throughout the life cycle of an organization, particularly in a situation of rapid organizational change in relation to internal or external circumstances (illustrated in the case example of Chapter 5).

Inter- and intra-functional conflict will impede any attempts to introduce or develop the benefits of internal marketing. Receptiveness to change is an important attribute for an organization aiming to successfully apply internal marketing, especially if it is to be an adaptive or learning organization (Garratt, 1987). Therefore the implementation of internal marketing cannot rely on organizational structure alone. Current relationships, interactions and interdependencies within an organization have an impact on the organizational decision-making process and this will depend on the structure and nature of interrelationships within the organization at any given time.

FIGURE 7.1   Requirements for internal marketing

Naturally any changes in organizational direction and purpose will have an impact on the nature of decision making. The use and recognition of informal networks within the organization are important if internal marketing is to be effective.

REQUIREMENTS FOR EFFECTIVE INTERNAL MARKETING MANAGEMENT

Internal marketing management involves proactively establishing, developing and facilitating co-operative relationships for mutual benefit. As illustrated in Figure 7.1, this entails internal relationship building and internal networking between relevant parties.

Within the services marketing literature (Berry, 1983; Gronroos and Gummesson, 1985), and the Industrial Marketing and Purchasing group's literature (Ford, 1990; Hakansson, 1982), and more recently in the relationship literature (Gummesson, 1995), 'interaction' in a marketing context implies face-to-face interaction between managers and managerial networks. Thus this type of interaction occurs at an individual level where 'personal contacts are made, bargaining and information exchange carried out, and individual relationships established' (Cunningham and Turnbull, 1982). Much of the relationship literature advocates that 'the focus shifts from products and firms as units, to people, organizations, and the social processes that bind actors together in ongoing relationships' (Webster, 1992). Internal marketing management involves handling these complex, personal interactions. Interactions are based on social exchange, involving mutual orientation, dependence, satisfaction, commitment and adaptation. Success or otherwise of internal marketing depends on getting people involved in two-way, interactive relationships, and developing interactions between people and various technologies and systems. All of these should occur in the context of, and within the priorities and purpose of the organization. Thus internal marketing management should be guided by having similar goals, and be developed through exchange processes and social exchange.

Internal marketing used to improve hotel employees' service delivery

As in any competitive marketing situation, hotels acknowledge the importance of high quality service delivery, and many differentiate their offerings by delivering different levels of service in different situations. However, emphasizing high quality service is one thing but delivering it is another. As the majority of service operations are provided and delivered by people, the service employees need to be included in all plans relating to service delivery and they need to be competent and motivated enough to work efficiently and effectively. To deliver the whole hotel service package, firstly it is important to market the product to the employee. Only then can they be sufficiently confident to proactively sell the hotel's products and services to guests. In order to support the hotel staff's role in selling to guests, the use of merchandising materials to sell across the different 'departments' or service areas are useful if developed and displayed effectively.

Employees' performance and attitudes play an essential role in selling the service. It is difficult for an employee to sell a product or service he or she does not value so one of the first tasks of internal marketing is to market the hospitality operation and the role the employees play in it to the employee.

Personal selling by staff can be encouraged through good internal communication from managers and supervisors and using practical internal marketing messages. These can include providing guidelines on when, where and how employees can be friendly and hospitable and how staff can make guests feel welcome. Guest contact by employees has an enormous impact on the profitability of an establishment. Direct interpersonal selling provides an opportunity to:

1   provide a personal impression of the product or service;
2   make direct contact with the guest;
3   show the product directly to the buyer;
4   correct misleading or false impressions and overcome any queries or confusions the guest may have;
5   answer questions directly;
6   ensure a commitment, a provisional booking, a sale.

Interdepartmental selling entails each department selling the other department effectively and it can be very useful for the whole range of hotel services. It is effective when employees do not only sell what is offered in their own area but also encourage guests to use the products and services provided in other departments of the hotel. This requires employees to know about and have some experience of each department's offerings and service levels. Merchandising activities using internal sales tools such as brochures, leaflets, signs and flyers are also useful means of promoting different service areas and offers. Many of these sales aids will help employees promote and illustrate the offering for the guest and will make the guest aware of other services within the hotel. Some of these merchandising tools may include:

1   in-house video promotions;
2   literature in guest's room;
3   clear and attractive signage;
4   table leaflets in different locations selling other locations;
5   guest comment cards and questionnaires;
6   menu clip-ons.

(Continued)

(Continued)

However the success of these will depend upon the commitment of both staff and management as this material and activity needs to be kept up-to-date and relevant and used as part of the overall strategy to serve guests while offering as much choice as possible.

REQUIREMENTS FOR INTERNAL RELATIONSHIP BUILDING

Managing business relationships involves combining the use of relationships, networks and interactions. Relationships require at least two parties who are in contact or interact with each other (for example, a provider and a customer). Although Gummesson (1995) believes that networks emerge when relationships increase in number and therefore become more complex, in many business circumstances, networking occurs first out of a particular business need and relationships develop over time. Business networks exist in the context of current and potential internal relationships involved in management and marketing within a company, its profit centres, owners and investors. Organizations are comprised of networks; the interactions within and between these networks involve the establishment and development of relationships on an on-going basis. Indeed, organizations can be comprised of 'imposed' relationships at varying levels. Therefore to manage the interactions of internal marketing effectively, a manager's aim should be to improve relationships by exploiting networks. Relationship networks can be improved and sustained through the explicit development and refinement of managerial interactions within an internal management network. This is discussed and described in the remainder of this chapter.

DEVELOPMENT OF INTERNAL MARKETING IN A SERVICE ORGANIZATION

Organizations encompass networks of interrelated structural positions, with individual employees occupying these relational positions, within the context of a more formalized structure (Brass, 1984). In an internal marketing management context individuals (managers, supervisors and front-line staff) can develop the skills and habits required to become more efficient at networking and relationship building. Networking in an organizational context can be defined as the interactive activities of a collection of individuals who may or may not be known to each other. These individuals may contribute in some way to the organization, passively, reactively or proactively, whether their contribution is specifically elicited or not (adapted from Gilmore and Carson, 1999). Bringing together the requirements for internal marketing and the advantages of formally encouraging networking will contribute to the management of service interactions and delivery through networking. Managing by networking is a naturally inherent aspect of managerial activity, whereby managers exchange and seek ideas, knowledge and market-related information through all their business activities and contacts. Internal managing by networking is based around people-orientated activities. It is informal, often discreet, interactive, integrated, habitual, reactive, individualistic and highly focused around the individual manager. The way in which managing by networking is carried out will be predetermined by organizational and industry behaviours and norms, through regular or irregular meeting occasions and industry activities or in just doing routine business. The frequency and focus of networking activity may vary depending on the nature of the organization, the industry and the nature of the markets in which the company operates. For example in service organizations, some networks may be more focused than others because of the reliance on specific people and their contribution to the overall service delivery and the need to manage the whole service process.

Internal networking should be encouraged by service managers to develop, progress and support all aspects of service activity and responsibility in relation to internal service providers, customers and potential customers, and industry and business networks. A natural extension of this is to use internal marketing activities in tandem with word-of-mouth communication, idea promotion and information-gathering activities involving staff. This clearly contributes to the holistic way in which managers can integrate their activities with the rest of the organization. The creation and existence of a network and networking will intuitively be concerned with maximizing management opportunities and directing all internal activities towards survival and development. Networking represents the intangible 'glue' holding people, functions and management activities together, matching different management functions, goals and operational activities with the more intangible interactive, communicative and personal characteristics inherent in the internal environment.

An internal manager can move in any way, between and amongst the various network groups represented in the organization depending on his/her requirements at any time. An outside observer might see only a fairly chaotic scene, including apparently haphazard or spontaneous activities, when in fact an 'invisible' framework of useful interaction exists.

Managing by internal networking will be enhanced and improved with the development of experiential knowledge. This is often manifested where managers use their networking abilities and what they know to be their strengths to overcome their inherent weaknesses. For example, managers may learn from mistakes by assessing what went wrong in a given situation and how to avoid such mistakes (both internal and external) in the future. Such experiential learning has very strong links with the learning of the organization as a whole, given that such learning is derived from the capability of an organization to draw valid and useful inferences from experience and observation and to convert such inferences to effective action (Argyris and Schon, 1978). Thus the internal manager has the power to create and sustain a 'learning organization'.

Doing internal marketing

Internal marketing can be developed and improved by a consciously proactive approach. Such an approach simply requires a manager to address an issue or problem of managing interactions around a two-part construct. First, by loosely defining the managerial issue or problem, then making a list of people who might offer an opinion on the issue. These people are likely to be regular contacts of the manager, although with a little concentration some lesser contacts, possibly from other organizational functions, may emerge. The manager is now in a position to trawl his/her newly defined network. Nothing much is different from normal activity except that the trawling process may be accelerated because it has been consciously defined and the trawl is now proactive, and not simply naturally occurring. The manager will intuitively know what information is relevant and make a judgemental assessment of the issue and a decision on how to address it. In addition the manager needs to communicate to all individuals involved at various stages of this process to keep them informed and open to the potential suggestions for change (adapted from Gilmore and Carson, 1999).

The impact of internal managerial performance on external marketing performance in a museum context

In a museum context the quality of managerial activities depends upon internal and interdepartmental communication and co-operation, the knowledge and ability of staff to communicate and deliver service to users, and feedback between managers and staff, and staff and visitors. Such internal performance strongly impacts upon the external performance, that is, the service experienced by visitors. This affects all aspects of the museum service delivery, such as the scope and range of collections and exhibitions, availability, accessibility, information and guidance provided, the interpretation of collections and artefacts and education of customers (as described above). This is illustrated in Figure 7.2 and discussed below.

FIGURE 7.2   **Effects of internal marketing on the museum service**

All of the organization's staff (managers, supervisors and front-line people) are responsible for delivering and implementing external marketing activity. That is marketing activities are delivered to the external market (visitors) by individual members of staff. Given that marketing is carried out by staff at all levels in the service organization (Gummesson, 1991), an organization needs effective internal communication and interdepartmental co-operation. To achieve this the museum needs staff who are able and willing to do the job and two-way communication with visitors; these are prerequisites of success for the museum.

Internal communication and interdepartmental co-operation

Internal communication and interdepartmental cooperation in a museum context implies face-to-face interaction between managers and with any other managerial networks. Interactions are based on staff and management exchange, involving mutual orientation, dependence, satisfaction, commitment and adaptation. Thus, this type of interaction occurs at an individual level where personal contacts are made, bargaining and information exchange are carried out, and individual relationships are established. Managing interactions involves handling complex, personal interactions; the use of internal performance techniques can be used as a vehicle or mechanism for this. Success or otherwise of managing interactions through internal marketing depends on getting all museum staff involved in two-way, interactive relationships, and developing interactions between people and various technologies and systems. All of these should occur in the context of and within the priorities and purpose of the museum. Thus, the management of interactions should be developed through dialogue and social exchange processes.

Interdepartmental co-operation is a prerequisite of a museum being able to deliver an excellent service in terms of collections, availability, accessibility and communications. Effective management will require formal procedures and both informal and formal communication to ensure co-operation occurs at all levels. For example, the views of all staff need to be encouraged and made accessible to senior management, and senior management should be seen to take these views into account and respond to them. In this way inter-departmental communication and co-operation will be more likely to occur. For this to happen, the museum director needs to share his/her vision for the museum with all staff. Regular meetings should involve all levels of staff to encourage participation and two-way communication.

Both internal communication and co-operation are vital to the evolution of a cultural change in any organization and essential for the achievement of effective external marketing. They encompass 'selling the staff' their role in providing service delivery and allow them to see how their role influences the overall museum experience. This impacts upon staff knowledge and ability to deliver service.

Staff knowledge and ability to deliver service

The development of key skills and competencies for all staff roles is crucial to the cross-functional dimensions of internal management performance and service delivery. In a museum context the competencies of communication and knowledge will be particularly important, for example, knowledge of the collections and historical context and communication with visitors and other members of the museum staff.

Front-line staff are involved in all aspects of service delivery, from knowledge of the collections to interacting with visitors, encouraging participation, and providing interpretation and information, they need to be able to contribute to all aspects of service delivery. That is, have the relevant knowledge and ability to interpret and proactively communicate information about collections and ensure availability and accessibility.

Feedback and communication between museum and visitors

Given the importance of repeat visits in any local marketplace there is a need to establish a long-term commitment (and build relationships) with visitors. Therefore it is important for a museum to undertake activities that encourage a longer-term relationship with visitors. To achieve this, useful market information is required. Regular visitor feedback is a valuable means of evaluating the success of collections and effectiveness of the overall service delivery. Supervisors and managers need to be closely involved and encourage feedback from the front-line staff and visitors. Information gathered in this way can contribute to the development and expansion of visitor interactions. Front-line staff are also useful sources of feedback from the visitor. Effective procedures for gathering such information need to be established so that comments can be passed on to senior management. For example, reception staff and clear signage should encourage visitors to complete comment cards or write in the 'visitor's book', and a clearly defined complaints procedure needs to be in place. Thus all museum employees can be visitor-orientated and have the potential to develop and strengthen customer–company interactions, communications and co-operation.

In summary, effective and successful management in a competitive environment should aim to develop and sustain long-term relationships with users of the museum. To achieve this aim museum managers need to co-ordinate the organization's resources to implement relevant strategies, develop successful communication methods both externally (between the organization and the customer) and internally (between management and employees) and at all stages of the service encounter.

CASE STUDY

INTERNAL MARKETING IN PRACTICE

A case example of a museum studied in relation to the framework shown in Figure 7.2 is given here in order to illustrate the service delivery of the museum service and how the internal performance of its staff and managers impacts upon the scope and range of its service delivery.

The museum in this discussion is a general museum. It has galleries covering five areas of interest: local history, antiquity and indigenous art, botany, zoology and geology. The museum is located close to a city centre. It employs 170 staff and attracts around 250,000 visitors per year, apart from those coming to see the special exhibitions. Many visitors are repeat visitors. The museum makes a conscious effort to continually provide new attractions to retain the interest and loyalty of this group of customers. Attention is focused on staging and promoting temporary exhibitions, rather than the sole use of permanent collections to attract visitors.

As part of the museum's development, it has introduced a programme of radical change which has resulted in leadership change, a refocusing of the image of the museum and cultural and administrative change resulting in significant organizational restructuring. Recent leadership change has emphasized the recognition that museum managers need to have expertise in improving the quality and professionalism of services provided within the museum as well as in museum scholarship. Such a focus has been implemented through the development of a wide range of exhibition programmes and special projects.

Currently management focus is on communicating the content of the collection to visitors and using promotional material to promote exhibitions. The museum recently employed two education officers and two part-time assistants with responsibility to improve communication, prepare an annual programme of events and make the collections better known to the public.

Internal communications and inter-departmental co-operation

The museum has four marketing staff, a marketing officer and three assistants. Marketing staff are a relatively new addition to the museum. However the marketing officer was appointed from inside the museum. This was thought to reduce any resentment among professional staff who may have traditionally regarded the care of the collections as taking preference over visitor needs and may have made it difficult for an outsider to come in to change the emphasis of some staff roles.

The marketing officer's responsibilities include all income-generating activities, such as the shop, the café and the sale of art reproductions for commercial use, as well as promotion. However the role of customer care is the responsibility of the head of museum services.

There is evidence of close co-operation between the various departments. For example, an exhibition is planned from its initial stages to its execution through interdepartmental communication and co-operation. The curator presents the idea for an exhibition to the senior management group. If it is acceptable to management it goes to an exhibition planning group. A project officer is appointed and he/she draws in people from relevant departments. The marketing officer is also involved at an early stage to give an opinion on what is a good idea, and what is not.

Staff knowledge and ability

The director and marketing officer are both aware that the museum is in direct competition with other museums and leisure and entertainment attractions for visitors' leisure time and therefore aim to be competitive by offering an excellent service delivery to all visitors. For example, the marketing officer makes a conscious effort to see the museum through the eyes of a visitor by regularly walking round the exhibits, noting any shortcomings, such as visitor guidance and access details and passes the information on to the appropriate curator.

Regular training is provided for front-line staff, particularly focusing on how they should approach and interact with visitors. The marketing officer emphasizes and believes that the front-of-house staff are the main communication link between the museum and the visitor, and that ideally all elements of visitor care and management should fall within the remit of the marketing department. However, this is still under the auspices of the head of museum services, although there is some consideration being given for change to happen. The marketing officer considers the planned change of role for front-line staff from one of 'warding' with an emphasis on security, to one of 'interpretation' of exhibits for visitors, would help develop a friendly atmosphere in the museum and strengthen the lines of communication with visitors.

The overall strength of the museum's staff knowledge is that recognition is given to the importance of providing a high standard of customer care by the director and staff. At present, the weakness of the museum's staff knowledge and ability is that the front-of-house staff do not have an 'interpretative' role and therefore are limited in their ability to interact at different stages of the visitors' experience.

Feedback/communication between museum and visitors

The museum makes a conscious effort to continually provide new attractions and so retain the interest and loyalty of repeat visitors. This is demonstrated by the focus on staging and promoting temporary exhibitions, rather than the sole use of permanent collections. Temporary exhibitions are regarded as being a major method of attracting both new and repeat visitors.

Although staff are aware of the value of feedback there are no regular procedures employed for obtaining feedback at present. Managers say they have plans to introduce a system as soon as resources permit. Currently consideration is being given to carrying out a survey of visitor opinions on the museum service. Guidance signage is being constantly modified and improved but still visitors become lost (according to the marketing officer).

The marketing officer uses much of the marketing budget for the development of public relations for the promotion of events as the museum does not have the budget for commercial advertising campaigns. Instead good links have been established with the media, and the marketing officer proactively sustains these relationships. Each year the events programme is presented with a press launch.

Special exhibitions are often used to initiate additional events. For example, a series of lectures for different groups of visitors or face painting for children may be linked to the theme and timing of a special exhibition. The purpose of these events is to attract people into the museum who will come back again and in this way build up a broader base of repeat visitors.

The director of the museum recognizes marketing's role in the promotion of the museum by communicating with visitors. He readily accepts the use of innovative methods to attract the visitor and feels there is a need to be very opportunistic in the marketing of museums and constantly look for new ideas. The focus of the museum service is to present information in an entertaining way so that visitors will learn something while they are there and will leave feeling that they have had a good experience. If this is achieved, visitors are more likely to come back.

In addition, the museum becomes involved with relevant activities and events organized by the Tourist Board or the city council and so benefits from shared and free promotion. The museum uses a varied range of promotional material aimed at reaching different visitor groups. First, it produces a programme of events, designed in the form of a two-sided poster. Secondly a brochure aimed at and promoted to schools provides information about the services provided by the education department. A souvenir guidebook is produced on a regular basis and is for sale in the museum shop.

The annual programme of events is designed each year and is the core method of promoting the museum to visitors. Its production and distribution consume the largest single part of the promotional budget. The events programme is distributed to a wide network of outlets, the list of which is constantly updated. Outlets include hotels, tourist attractions, and local educational and library offices. The programme is also distributed through a monthly mail-shot from the Arts Council, to selected households.

Single sheet flyers are produced for special exhibitions. The marketing officer liases with the curator involved, and negotiates a sum from the total budget to be used to promote special exhibitions. Together they identify specific interest groups with the purpose of bringing in new visitors with the potential to become repeat visitors.

An 'education pack' is used to promote the museum to schools. It contains a collection of current promotional materials relating to existing and special exhibitions. For example included are: detailed information about the services on offer and the exhibitions planned for the school year, the events programme, the souvenir guide, any 'flyers' for special exhibitions, art study sheets (based on current exhibition material) and leaflets promoting teaching packs available for sale. Information regarding opening times, ancillary services and facilities for disabled visitors is provided on all the material.

Overall effect of internal performance on external activity and service

A museum's performance depends upon the quality of managerial activities. (The quality of managerial activities depends upon the knowledge and ability of staff to communicate and deliver service to users, and communication, co-operation and feedback between managers and between staff, and staff and visitors. Such internal performance strongly impacts upon the external performance, that is the service experienced by visitors. This affects all aspects of the museum service delivery, such as the scope and range of collections and exhibitions, availability, accessibility, information and guidance provided, in the interpretation of collections and artefacts and education of customers.)

In relation to collections the museum in this study has tried to balance the need for maintenance and safety of collections and trying to create impact and differentiation. However the current focus is on maintaining safety and value of the permanent collection. Recent special exhibitions have focused on creating differentiation and impact with the chosen themes and quality of exhibition material. The director and marketing officer are actively aiming to create more impact and differentiation in the museum's service delivery. They are aware that the museum is in a period of transition. In particular they aim to focus on becoming more visitor-friendly through a change of front-line staff role emphasis and training. At present aspects of front-line staff interface with visitors need more development and participation. The value and importance of the tangible collections have traditionally been considered more important than the relevance of collections to visitors.

In relation to availability and accessibility this museum operates standard opening hours (9am.–5pm. weekdays, 1pm.–5pm. Sundays). In the case of particularly valuable collections visitors are limited in how close they may come. Observations illustrated that in some instances staff are more aware of their 'warden' role than behaving proactively with visitors and so positive interaction between staff and visitors and proximity to collections are not encouraged.

In relation to communication visitors are encouraged to engage in passive observation rather than participating in the experience. Overall the museum uses standardized messages and there is a non-personal approach with little attempt to involve visitors in any aspect of the museum experience. Given the overall lack of individualized messages, attention or personal approach the emotional involvement of the visitor is very limited.

However, some newly appointed marketing staff proactively liase with all the front-line staff and managers in order to improve internal communication and co-operation. With reference to staff knowledge and ability, clearly all new staff need to know the value, history and context of the collections as they form the core part of the service delivery. The more intangible aspects of service delivery such as interaction, interpretation, communications, accessibility and availability need to be addressed, particularly where there are more complex and interactive/social exchange service queries and issues to be addressed. Individual customer service requirements can be diverse, therefore a degree of variability in service delivery should be accommodated. A museum service that acknowledges and addresses the varying degrees of customer needs, perceptions, experience and ability to comprehend instructions and directions should be the ultimate goal.

Feedback and communication with visitors is important given the many intangible aspects of the museum service. Some aspects of the service can be 'simple' and dealt with easily and others are more complex and need a high degree of expertise in order to be resolved. The implication for museum managers is that they become more 'hands on' and market focused as well as managing the collection efficiently.

SUMMARY

Although there are many interpretations of internal marketing, it can be used in various ways to improve communication and internal working relationships within an organization and so impact upon how services are delivered to end customers. It is particularly useful in service-oriented organizations that rely on the specific abilities and attitudes of front-line service teams to maintain appropriate and competitive levels of service for their organization and long-term reputation.

Internally, it is important to recognize the significance of using and listening to both formal and informal networks. Managing internal customers should build upon the core building blocks of managerial knowledge and experience already in existence by focusing on 'how to' build networks between internal customers within the company. Over time, such development will lead to effective networking and positive relationships, and to internal marketing managerial interactions. This will create and sustain a suitable environment for staff responsibility and empowerment.

DISCUSSION QUESTIONS

Outline the scope of 'internal marketing' and discuss the value of this to service organizations.

What problems might a service manager have in attempting to introduce internal marketing in an organization?

Describe how internal marketing could be applied to a business of your choice.

NOTE

Parts of this chapter have been previously published in: Gilmore, A. (2000) 'Managing internal marketing interfaces', in R. Varey and B. Lewis (eds), *Internal Marketing. Directions for Management.* London: Routledge, pp. 75–92.

REFERENCES

Argyris, C. and Schon, D. (1978) *Organizational Learning: A Theory of Action Perspective.* Reading, MA: Addison-Wesley.

Berry, L.L. (1983) 'Relationship marketing', in L.L. Berry, G.L. Shostack and G.D. Upah (eds), *Emerging Perspectives on Services Marketing.* Chicago: American Marketing Association, pp. 25–8.

Brass, D.J. (1984) 'Being in the right place: a structural analysis of individual influence on an organization', *Administrative Science Quarterly*, 29: 518–39.

Cunningham, M.T. and Turnbull, P.W. (1982) 'Inter-organizational personal contact patterns', in H. Hakansson (ed.), *International Marketing and Purchasing of Industrial Goods: An Interaction Approach*. Chicester: John Wiley.

Ford, D. (1990) *Understanding Business Markets: Interaction, Relationships and Networks*. London: Academic Press.

Garratt, R. (1987) *The Learning Organization*. London: Fontana.

Gilmore, A. and Carson, D. (1999) 'Entrepreneurial marketing by networking', *New England Journal of Entrepreneurship*, 2(2): 31–8.

Gronroos, C. and Gummesson, E. (1985) *Service Marketing – Nordic School Perspectives*. Stockholm University, Sweden.

Gummesson, E. (1991) 'Marketing-orientation revisited: the crucial role of the part-time marketer', *European Journal of Marketing*, 25(2): 60–75.

Gummesson, E. (1995) 'Relationship marketing: its role in the service economy', in W. Glynn and J. Barnes (eds), *Understanding Services Management. Integrating Organizational Behaviour, Operations and Human Resource Management*. Dublin: Oak Tree Press.

Hackman, J.R. and Oldham, G. (1980) *Work Redesign*. Reading, MA: Addison-Wesley.

Hakansson, H. (1982) *International Marketing and Purchasing of Industrial Goods*. Chichester: Wiley.

Hofstede, G. (1991) *Cultures and Organizations: Software of the Mind*. New York: McGraw-Hill.

Joshi, A.W. (1995) 'Long-term relationships, partnerships and strategic alliances: a contingency theory of relationship marketing', *Journal of Marketing Channels*, 4(3): 75–94.

Kotler, P. (1990) *Principles of Marketing*. Englewood Cliffs, NJ: Prentice-Hall.

Mastenbroek, W.S. (1993) *Conflict Management and Organizational Development*. New York: John Wiley.

Piercy, N. and Morgan, N. (1990) 'Organizational context and behavioural problems as determinants of the effectiveness of the strategic marketing planning process', *Journal of Marketing Management*, 6(2): 127–43.

Ruekert, R.W. and Walker, O.C. (1987) 'Marketing's interaction with other functional units: a conceptual framework and empirical evidence', *Journal of Marketing*, 51(1): 1–19.

Varey, R. (1995) 'Internal marketing: a review and some interdisciplinary research challenges', *International Journal of Service Industry Management*, 6(1): 40–63.

Webster, F.E. (1992) 'The changing role of marketing in the corporation', *Journal of Marketing*, 56, October: 1–17.

Weinrauch, J.D. and Anderson, R. (1982) 'Conflicts between engineering and marketing units', *Industrial Marketing Management*, 11: 291–301.

Weinshall, T.D. (1975) 'Multinational corporations – their study and measurement', *Management International Review*, 15(4/5): 67–76.

8

Management Competencies
for Services Marketing

Following the previous chapters' discussion on issues for services management and different managerial approaches, this chapter focuses on the specific competencies service managers will require for the types of managerial and operational roles involved in service management. The increasing sophistication of services within an increasingly competitive environment means that managers need to constantly evolve skills and competencies to suit their managerial roles.

Initially the requirements for training and developing services marketing staff are explored in terms of different service delivery roles. This leads to a brief look at the use and value of creating formal standards for ensuring good service marketing performance.

The discussion on managerial competencies begins with a consideration of what are core and specific competencies. Then the debate focuses on how core competencies can be developed and refined to become more specific or distinctive in the context of different service roles. The remainder of the chapter discusses the specific competencies required for service managers with responsibility for product, pricing, promotion, administrative, customer–staff interactive management and service delivery.

TRAINING AND DEVELOPMENT FOR SERVICE MARKETING

Attracting, training and developing staff is vital for service organizations, given their reliance on people and their expertise in service management and delivery. Having the right staff starts with the recruitment process. Managers involved in recruitment should aim to recruit personnel who will help shape the organization's climate and culture. Once recruited, these employees need to be motivated to carry out all aspects of the service role with responsibility and enthusiasm. Positive and effective behaviour can be encouraged through rewards and incentives. Service companies use different varieties of rewards for good performance. For example, offering slightly higher wages than immediate competitors, cash rewards for specific behaviour/activities, bonuses, certificates of recognition thus encouraging employees to participate in aspects of service development and improvement. Of course, companies need to offer appropriate training programmes to explicitly develop employees' skills and knowledge for job performance. The importance of educating people who supply specific and distinctive services is evident in many service companies who establish their own service training schools. For example, hotel chains often have their own training schools and the Disney Corporation established the Disney 'university'.

Often staff empowerment is encouraged in service organizations to ensure that employees are service focused and motivated in their roles (see Chapter 5). One way to create an empowerment culture is by decentralizing organizational structures. Decentralized structures encourage staff at customer interface level to make decisions on their own initiative and take responsibility for their role (as illustrated in Chapter 4). Another way to encourage staff development and motivation is to create incentives for career advancement, where people can bring their best skills to even the simplest of jobs (Normann, 1991) and get recognition for that. This encourages staff competency development and allows individuals to grow and develop within the company.

USE OF FORMAL STANDARDS TO ENSURE SERVICE MARKETING PERFORMANCE

In the past, many service companies have relied heavily on formal service standards in order to ensure a certain level of service quality. Levitt (1976) described how service operations can be made more efficient by applying the logic and tactics of manufacturing. This is similar to the production-line management style approach described in Chapter 6. His recommendations included the simplification of tasks, clear division of labour, substitution of equipment and systems for employees, and little decision-making discretion for employees. For example, airlines and hotel chains use specific standards and procedures to ensure check-in waiting time, baggage labelling, cleaning of facilities and telephone answering all happen within a certain time period and to a pre-arranged standard. All these duties may have previously relied on intuitive behaviour of individual staff but by stipulating rigid procedures and minimum performance standards, these companies have considerably improved their service offerings. This production-line approach not only gives organizational control, but also creates uniformity of the customer-service interaction.

In addition to the focus on formal standards, service research and literature has focused heavily on service quality performance and measurement (as discussed in Chapter 3). Thus the bulk of the service quality literature features the performance outcomes and measurement of service quality. Less emphasis has been given to improving the quality of management decision making in different service situations. So in some ways actual management performance has been hidden behind the use of different and increasingly sophisticated measurement techniques and service standards.

This may be because it is difficult to measure management skills and competencies. It is difficult because managers behave differently and many managerial activities are different and will be different from one situation to another. However the quality of management decision making and marketing activity will depend on the competencies (skills and abilities) of managers within the context of their specific responsibilities and tasks. In order to identify what these management competencies might be the nature and characteristics of service management decision making should be examined so that the specific management tasks required for an individual service manager's role within an organization are recognized.

Developing competence for hotel front-line service staff in a small country hotel

In the context of a small hotel business competence is defined as ability of a member of staff to do their particular job efficiently and to the best of their ability, and to help out other staff when necessary. Examples in practice include dealing with customers professionally and helpfully, demonstrating the ability to sell to customers, having sufficient product knowledge in relation to hotel products and services (such as room capacity, service available at different times, etc), computer literacy and word-processing, general administration skills and ability to handle money.

In this small country hotel the main problem relating to 'competence' was manifested in the different levels of ability of staff. For example some staff were good at selling face to face and others were better dealing with customers on the telephone. Some staff were better at administration than others. The hotel was dependent on some contracted-in services such as security expertise

(Continued)

(Continued)

and catering for large functions. These companies offered poor wages or had poor induction procedures and a higher turnover of staff. This resulted in poorer service quality.

Recommendations to improve competence included providing continuous staff training in relation to using the computer for administrative tasks, sale techniques and customer care. In addition, occasional seminars on pertinent topics in relation to improving the hotel service package were offered. It was acknowledged that precise work guidelines needed to be agreed upon between the hotel and the contractors for security staff. Also managers acknowledged that the self confidence of the less well-trained members of staff could be improved through managerial encouragement and more individual attention in terms of constructive on-the-spot training.

In addition, given that change is a continual element in a manager's career, managers need to see their jobs as an ongoing process of learning in which they acquire new knowledge and skills. The further up the organization a manager progresses the greater his or her need to develop accordingly. A competent decision maker needs to have the appropriate mix of skills relevant to his/her position. If a manager promoted to a higher or different level does not acquire the necessary knowledge and skill, then he/she will be inefficient. The mix of skills required by a manager is dependent on a number of factors, including the size of organization, position and degree of responsibility and the specific responsibilities and tasks of the manager.

SERVICES MARKETING COMPETENCIES

Often competencies are described in terms of being technical and operational or managerial and related to decision making. Technical competencies relate to the functional aspects of service operations. Managerial competencies are more specific to the roles and issues important to service marketing decision making and management. A manager needs to possess both types of competencies. Often managers may be competent in the technical aspects of the delivery of marketing activity. This may be a result of having spent the early part of their career involved in service delivery. They may not be so competent in the managerial aspects of marketing decision making and management of people because of lack of involvement and experience in such a role.

Managers' competencies need to be specific to the responsibilities and roles they perform as competence is dependent on the context in which it is demonstrated (Smith et al., 1989). Therefore competencies should be defined according to the work situation and requirements. Also each functional manager's task will require a complex mix of competencies rather than a list of separate or discrete competencies. Thus distinct competence or expertise in each situation will call for a different mix of competencies.

Some competencies such as knowledge and experience in technical aspects of marketing activity can be described as fundamental or basic competencies upon which expertise and judgement are developed over time and these become the basis for other marketing-specific competencies. Basic competencies will include the fundamental competencies of knowledge and experience that most managers possess to some extent. Knowledge and experience of a particular industry and company circumstance provide a useful and important platform from which to build and develop competencies for a specific role. Competency in these two attributes will provide a starting point for a manager in a specific marketing decision-making situation to develop effectiveness in managerial performance. It should also be recognized that any manager will possess some basic competencies in relation to the knowledge and experience accumulated in carrying out management responsibilities to date.

Therefore competency development begins with the existing knowledge and experience or 'common sense' knowing of managers. Jackson (1991) argues that the starting point of any management development is to consider the common sense of the management team at a given time. A manager's common sense in relation to his work environment at any given time can be described in terms of his level of knowledge and experience of the current organizational situation. The knowledge and experience of managers are often based on some years working in the same environment, building up a general familiarity with the industry and executing repetitive planning, or operational and tactical activities.

Common sense knowledge will entail a clear understanding of the specific details and requirements of the job, the company's markets, competitors and different customers. In particular managers may have a knowledgeable understanding of the processes and activities required for the successful integration of their managerial responsibilities, of how each process impacts upon the others, of specific details of planning requirements and action-oriented implementation of the related issues. For example, in the case of developing new service products of a product management team will need to recognize when to extend their service product range and delete or modify old service products without losing or disappointing their core market.

Knowledge of the interdependencies between staff and departments will also be important as they will have an impact upon how 'things get done' within the organization.

Managerial experience is more difficult to describe and measure. Although managers' experience can be counted in years, in effect their experience could best be described as 'one year repeated several times' (Kolb, 1984). However, experience can be described in terms of both 'width' and 'depth'. The depth of experience relates to the circumstance of working in the

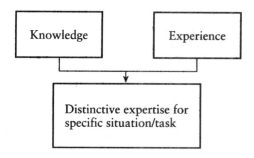

FIGURE 8.1   Development of marketing management competencies

same area over a period of time and entails concentrated involvement and understanding of specific tasks. This will contribute to a manager's experience. The width of experience is also important in relation to allowing managers to transfer their experience to other situations, contributing to the building and development of their overall performance. Managers can develop experience by having the opportunity to experiment, try out new ideas, learn from experience and have the ability to develop and expand their experience to build for the future. Clearly the variety of experience is also important in order to develop vision to see and understand all other possibilities in the specific managerial situation for which they have responsibility. These competencies of knowledge and experience can be used as a basis for building on the next level of competencies which will include the specific judgemental aspects of expertise in relation to each functional managerial team's or individual's specific tasks, that is, a 'distinctive expertise'. This is illustrated in Figure 8.1.

Therefore managers' common sense knowledge can be developed through the transformation of experience (Kolb, 1984). Dewey (1938) contends that what an individual has learned in one situation becomes an instrument of understanding and dealing effectively with the situations which follow. This is the core concept of experiential learning (Dewey, 1938; Kolb, 1984; Lewen, 1951, Piaget, 1970).

The development and evolution of competencies in any specific managerial situation will aspire to reach or achieve 'expertise' in that context. Although each managerial situation may require the same general competencies, such as knowledge, experience and expertise, these may be manifested quite differently in the performance depending on the specific responsibilities of the manager and situation in which he operates. Expertise will therefore involve a different mixture of competencies in each situation; this will involve the judgemental capabilities associated with the individual competencies required for each specific or functional situation.

Thus expertise for service/product management may involve the distinctive competencies of motivation, vision and creativity in a given situation.

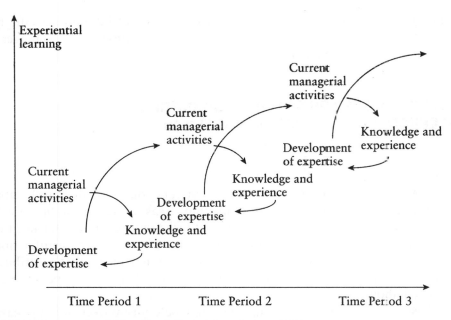

FIGURE 8.2   Experiential learning (adapted from Dewey, 1938)

Pricing management competencies may be developed to include flexibility and creativity; advertising and promotion management may require and include creativity, communication and motivation; customer/ staff interaction management may need co-ordination, communication, motivation and leadership; administration and internal communication management may require motivation, business sense and communication.

Furthermore the development of management specific expertise may involve different approaches and time-scales for each individual. By using an adaptation of Dewey's (1938) model of experiential learning, the evolution of knowledge and experience to become specific expertise is illustrated in Figure 8.2.

To be effective in today's changing world, a manager's expertise must include the capacity for integrative and adaptive learning (Buller, 1992) within the specific context of the manager's work environment. Integrative learning is more concerned with process, with learning how to learn, rather than simple skill acquisition (Kolb, 1984). It is more concerned with executive problem solving about which competence to apply in which circumstance than the execution of the competence. As such, it is more internalized and specifically tailored to each unique individual (Kolb et al., 1987). Thus the development of managerial competencies will also be very specific to the responsibilities and tasks of each individual manager. Learning occurs best through four basic integrated processes: concrete experience, reflective observation, abstract conceptualization and active experimentation (Kolb et al., 1987). This process will be more specific to the current work situation if it occurs within the context of the manager's organizational environment.

COMPETENCIES FOR SERVICES MARKETING DECISION MAKING AND MANAGEMENT

The main focus of any service management function is on their tasks and consequently their specific decision-making areas of responsibility. Each management function's responsibilities and tasks will strongly influence the nature of management competency requirement in terms of the identification of distinctive expertise. All specific management competencies that contribute to distinctive expertise are built upon existing knowledge and experience as discussed above.

Distinctive expertise or competence may be built up over time by managers who take the initiative to try out new ideas, have commitment and involvement, learn from their mistakes, and adapt accordingly. Continual development in expanding the depth and width of expertise will ensure that the organization develops and changes to suit the external environmental changes. The depth of expertise contributes to the suitability of managers' actions, decisions and responses to particular situations in determining how well they can actually do the job. The breadth of expertise manifests itself in the transfer of expertise to different situations and the ability to manage each issue within the perspective and context of the organizational purpose, that is, demonstrating expertise to do other jobs and understanding the wider job dimensions.

Expertise is required in relation to both technical issues such as possessing the specific skills or ability to do a job; and managerial issues, which calls for the ability to manage a situation, facilitate the process and create the environment for the service to happen.

To encourage effective management performance, specific competencies for service marketing management can be identified and defined. To do this, the tasks, roles and issues of particular concern to service marketing functional managers need to be examined and considered. These roles and issues evolve from the nature and characteristics of marketing decision making in a service situation. Of course, marketing decision making evolves around all aspects of marketing activity and performance. That is, as service product and pricing-related issues, communication activities such as advertising, image, PR, and customer/staff interface and marketing administration. These generic areas of marketing decision making can be translated to a service situation by taking account of the specific roles and issues of concern to services marketing managers.

Therefore typical decision-making areas for service managers will include:

1 Service product decision making involving new service development and service differentiation;
2 Pricing decision making involving considerations of price in relation to service differentiation and managing demand for services. For example, prices for peak and off-peak times;
3 Communication decisions revolving around the creation of an advertising message which manages the intangible nature of the service product and highlights the features of service differentiation;
4 Customer–staff interaction management decision making concerning the management of service operations, integration of service activities and processes, managing people, accessibility and timing;
5 Service administration management involving the provision of management information and gathering relevant information about customers in relation to all the marketing activities carried out by the service management functions.

These areas of services marketing decision making provide a framework for identifying specific roles and issues of concern to service managers. The characteristics of service marketing management and the nature of customer relationships in service contexts mean that the issues for services marketing managers need to be addressed in a different way than in a traditional manufacturing or goods marketing context. For example, service marketing situations depend more heavily on managing the 'process' or 'act' of the service product than does marketing in other situation. As people are usually involved in performing services and are not always consistent in their performance, standardization and quality are extremely difficult to control. Therefore the effectiveness of a services marketing operation will depend on the quality of the management of people and personal encounters such as the customer–staff interactions in all areas of marketing activity.

The following examples illustrate the competencies required by different management teams in a travel service context. The roles and tasks of managers were observed to help understand the specific nature of competencies required by each of the five different functions in the service company.

Example 1: Competencies for service product management

Service product development and differentiation is vital in a service organization because of the ease with which services can be copied by competitors. Therefore managerial decision making often tries to:

- carve out new niches or markets
- actively seek new ideas for products, and
- avoid becoming too predictable in marketing activities.

Thus service product managers need to proactively seek new ideas, learn from experience, and have the ability to carefully consider options and select an appropriate one in a timely way. Decisions should allow for changes in the marketing place with managers keeping an open-minded, flexible approach to solving problems, ready to adapt to market conditions and customer expectations. And of course decisions should take account of maintaining a profit in order to stay in business.

Service product managers will require *knowledge* about the markets and overall environment in which the company operates. *Experience* will include involvement in all aspects of service product-related decision making and subsequent learning from experience. *Expertise* may be built upon knowledge of the job and experience in the industry. More specifically, distinctive expertise is required in order to take account of the different options and ideas in developing new products and improving existing core products. It involves *motivation* in evaluating the different options in relation to product development, and *creativity* in assessing priorities, eliminating irrelevant or incompatible ideas, refining concepts and selecting a suitable option to follow through to implementation stage. *Vision* is important in considering new product ideas in relation to competitive actions and reactions and the overall trends and changes in the marketplace. This is particularly important when screening new ideas for product development (or considering when to update or drop existing products) in order to achieve product differentiation. These specific components of distinctive expertise competency for service product management are elaborated upon below.

Motivation

Service product management decision making needs the 'distinctive' job-related expertise or competence of exhibiting motivation and initiative where managers proactively search for solutions to current problems or issues to be addressed, rather than waiting for someone else to intervene or for the problem to go away. Therefore, timely or prompt decision making is important. The motivation competence also requires recognition of the need to adapt the service product for different customers. It requires managers taking responsibility for specific tasks, being proactive in the search for better ways of doing the job, having a positive outlook, and possessing the ability to adapt the service product.

Creativity

Creativity is required for distinctive expertise in service product management decision making to ensure innovative competitive service products are designed and thereby achieve differentiation from competitors' products and activities. Creativity through managerial innovation is required in order to carve out new markets or niches. This calls for managers to have the ability to think laterally and creatively, while always proactively seeking new opportunities and ideas.

Vision

Service product management decision making is about maintaining a service product portfolio which involves careful monitoring of present service products, deciding when to delete old services and planning for new services in order to maximize opportunities. Strategic thinking and forward planning is important in the consideration of a product portfolio. Long-term improvement in the quality of marketing effectiveness depends upon analysing future demand for all products and services. Product managers need to look ahead to prepare for external opportunities and threats so that they can differentiate their activities from their competitors and be aware of changes in the marketplace so that their activity can be adapted sooner rather than later. Therefore, core service development and new service development require consideration of how products can be differentiated from those of competitors. Also, that managers think beyond competitor activity, objectively consider new ideas and all possible options, and/or foresee new markets or niches.

Example 2: Competencies for service pricing management

Pricing management decision making will be concerned with:

- choosing the right price ranges for various service products
- adaptability in pricing structure decisions to allow for different levels of demand, and
- creativity in pricing products in order to maintain uniqueness and competitiveness.

Pricing management's decision making will require *knowledge* and *experience* in relation to: awareness of options within the industry's pricing structure, knowledge of the market and the marketing environment and suitability of pricing options to local agents and customers. Knowledge and experience will involve exercising objective consideration of all options available and having the ability to select an appropriate choice. Distinctive expertise will involve *adaptability* and *creativity* in pricing decision making. These are discussed in further depth below.

Adaptability

Adaptability in service pricing decision making requires liaison with other service functions to consider ways of creating flexible pricing structures and maintaining the company's overall image in relation to the total service delivery. Additionally this competency calls for an awareness of changes in the marketplace, particularly in relation to competitor activity and consumers' perception of price. Price flexibility should help create product differentiation in the form of adapting ideas and procedures to suit customers, for example, different types of credit facilities or terms. This type of distinctive competency will contribute to a flexible, open-minded approach to solving problems or queries, and the ability to adapt ideas and procedures to suit customers.

Creativity

Creativity for pricing services may include developing innovative approaches to the pricing structure in order to carve out new market niches and differentiate the service product. Pricing managers should be actively seeking new ideas and have the ability to think creatively. Overall pricing decisions need to be:

- considered in relation to value for money
- consistent with all other marketing activity, the company's image and commitment to service quality
- suitably differentiated from competitors' pricing policies.

Example 3: Competencies for communication management

Service communications managers' responsibilities will involve integrating all advertising and promotional activity in the context of the company's other marketing activity. These decisions require the development of knowledge and experience to achieve distinctive expertise and the specific demonstration of motivation, creativity and communication in management roles and responsibilities.

When selecting which agency to use, managers need to take account of the different advertising agencies' strengths and weaknesses, have the ability to be objective in their consideration of these options and eventually select the best match for company requirements. It is also important to select a suitable advertising message to promote the service in a competitive and innovative manner rather than appearing to offer the same message each year or season. Service managers with this responsibility need to be able to think objectively about promotional messages, and learn from previous experience. Distinctive expertise will involve motivation, creativity and communication.

Motivation

Managers responsible for service communications need to be motivated and proactive, particularly in dealing with and monitoring agencies' activity. This will involve having the ability to recognize what needs to be done in order to get specific advertising plans implemented. Managers need to illustrate long-term commitment through activities such as participation in tasks, maintaining close liaison with agencies, feeding them appropriate information and obtaining feedback, having the ability to implement ideas, taking responsibility for action-related tasks, inspiring and encouraging staff, and communicating activities to other functional managers.

Creativity

Maintaining competitiveness and being innovative rather than doing the same thing in each campaign or promotional situation is very important. Advertising and public relation management decisions need to exhibit creativity in order to differentiate a service product through innovative communication messages and/or mediums.

Communication

Of course this is self-evidently vital for managers in all aspects of the advertising functional role. Managers will need to take account of other management functions and their activities in the development of suitable messages for each new product or concept. The most visible content of an advertising manager's job is in the brochure and literature design, and in media handling. The quality of this will depend upon the degree of activity in which he or she is involved in cross participation with other functions, especially in relation to the integration across functional departments, interaction between and amongst staff and customers and the co-ordination of all communication activity and messages. All communication of the advertising and promotional management team needs to be proactive in order to get appropriate messages across to different groups.

Example 4: Competencies for customer–staff interface management

These managers have primary responsibility for the operational aspects of service delivery. On a day-to-day basis customer–staff interface managers need to manage and guide the movement of customers through the during-purchase and some aspects of the pre-purchase and post-purchase experience. The activities inherent in this role are:

- managing all operational activities
- providing information and guidance to customers
- proactive communication with customers and staff
- accessibility to customers and willingness to help.

Built upon previous knowledge and experience, the development of distinctive expertise for customer–staff interface managers will entail the ability to exhibit motivation, communication, co-ordination and leadership.

Motivation

Given the nature of front-line service activities, some decision making by customer–staff interaction managers will entail dealing with each situation as it arises and knowing when to be adaptable – for example, recognizing the need for adapting or changing some aspect of the service to suit different customers. Therefore managers need to be motivated, prompt decision makers and their actions should demonstrate responsibility for their tasks through their proactive behaviour. They should have a positive outlook in searching for better ways to carry out operational tasks and service delivery.

Communication

Managing the customer–staff interface involves both verbal and non-verbal communication and interaction with people. It is a prerequisite for successful direction and implementation in ensuring everyone knows what is involved and each individual's role in the whole activity. For example, it is particularly important for a hotel manager or restaurant manager to be a good persuader and have the ability to make good presentations to staff and win over their allegiance and commitment. Also two-way communication in a timely way is vital so that managers receive feedback about specific initiatives and activity.

Different means of communication with customers is beneficial so that they understand what the service product entails and how to use it. For example, communicating with the customers at all stages of their experience with the company in different ways, from pre-purchase, during purchase, through to the post-purchase stage, will provide very rich insights in terms of how the entire service is perceived. Thus communication at all levels in a service operation, from customers, front-line staff and management decision makers, should be proactive and integrative so that a composite knowledge of customers' expectations and perceptions is developed. This allows managers to acquire insights and the ability to eliminate any perceived 'gaps' in the service delivery. Additionally, managers need to maintain dialogue with each other and with customers in order to eliminate misunderstanding and ensure customers have relevant and necessary information for using the service.

Co-ordination

Because of the physical operational aspect of service delivery at the customer–staff interface, co-ordination of individuals and teams, planning actions and sequence of activities, and supervising both material and human resources are vital. Therefore the activities of front-line managers require co-ordinated communication, interaction, integration and participation and the involvement of all staff. Indeed, all customer–staff related decision making needs to be co-ordinated very carefully to achieve the fundamental goal of providing a timely, reliable service with regularly updated physical facilities and efficient service delivery.

Leadership

Front-line service managers are very involved in the entire service delivery, and are clearly evident to both customers and staff; therefore they need to lead by example. By demonstrating motivated involvement and leadership in the implementation process and being available, managers are more likely to inspire the staff by their actions as much as by their directions. This should contribute to the delivery of intangible aspects of service delivery such as responsiveness, willingness to help customers, and refining the service product to suit customers by obtaining feedback and maintaining relationships with customers.

Example 5: Competencies for services marketing administration management

Service administration will involve managing and taking responsibility for facilitating and maintaining all marketing activity by providing the necessary support for all management functions. Management decision making will incorporate the provision of up-to-date management information, facilitating and maintaining communication between functions, facilitating and maintaining a feedback of information from customers and handling customer complaints. This involves gathering relevant information from each function, assimilating and providing useful, timely and relevant management information and maintaining contact with customers through the management of the marketing research activity. In this way the administration and internal communication managers can and should have an impact on all aspects of marketing activity.

For this function knowledge and experience will contribute to the identification of management needs, establish what new information is available or can be compiled and recognize requirements for internal activity. Thus the development of distinctive expertise will entail appropriate use of motivation, business sense or analytical skills and communication.

Motivation

This competence is required for administrative management so that each function's management information needs is proactively identified and requirements for internal activity are sought. For example managers need to be actively motivated and behave proactively in order to continually identify and use new technology and services to improve their efficiency in creating useful information. Similarly, management activities should be participative (recognizing and having the ability to implement ideas) and take responsibility for their tasks and act upon it.

Business sense/analytical skills

These competencies are required for the analysis of data so that managers recognize and compile useful information and that they have the ability to interpret and draw useful and timely conclusions from it. Also an objective and realistic approach to business decisions and the ability to progressively learn from mistakes is important in the development of these competencies.

Communication

Service administration managers' activities need to be communicative both in relation to internal managers and staff but also in relation to external customers by responding to customer complaints and queries. Often they need to be involved in integrative activity across functional departments and interact between and among different levels of staff so that they can co-ordinate all communicative activity and messages across the company. A successful output from such communication would contribute to gathering information about customers regularly and communicating this to the relevant functions. A communication competency is also important in relation to external customers when responding to customer complaints and queries.

Together the key decision makers in the organization need to possess a combination of different types of distinctive expertise and competence. As an overall management team they need to possess these competencies in order to effectively deal with the whole spectrum of service marketing management decision making and achieve an integrative and effective approach to service delivery.

SUMMARY

Given the nature of service delivery and management, service staff and managers often require specific training and development in the context of their roles and responsibilities. Job conditions and incentives are used to motivate staff but often the provision of an appropriate working environment for staff to develop their ability to do their job effectively and efficiently enhances individual job fulfilment.

Given that change is a constant feature in any manager's career, there is continual need to update managerial competencies. Service managers need to possess or be able to develop competencies for the specific role they play in the overall service management and delivery. Through the use of knowledge and experience gathered in a particular industry and company, managers can build and develop some distinctive competencies for relevant service contexts. Distinctive expertise and competence may be developed over time through taking initiatives to try out new ideas, demonstrating commitment and involvement, learning from mistakes and adapting accordingly. Continual development in expanding the depth and width of decision-making competencies will ensure that an organization develops and changes to suit the external environmental changes. Depth of expertise will contribute to the suitability of managerial actions, decisions and responses to particular situations and how well managers can actually do the job. Width of expertise will contribute to the transfer of knowledge and experience to different situations and the ability to manage each issue within the perspective and context of the organizational purpose – that is, distinctive expertise will enable managers to make suitable decisions and ensure all specific tasks are carried out in the context of wider job dimensions. As the customer is involved in the whole service delivery each member of staff should be encouraged to develop distinctive expertise in line with the role they play.

The evolution and development of the managerial competencies in any management situation will illustrate how managers have changed, adapted and progressed to fit with the continuing change within a specific company and in the context of a changing industry. Therefore competency development must take account of both internal and external changes in circumstances, and in the growth and development of management responsibility as managers progress up the organization or through different positions with specific roles and responsibilities.

DISCUSSION QUESTIONS

What personal characteristics do you think are important to look for when selecting service delivery staff?

What are the limitations of formal standards in ensuring good service marketing performance?

How would you define service marketing competencies?

What are the differences in the functional roles of and the competencies required for a customer–staff interaction manager and a service administration manager?

NOTE

Much of this chapter is taken from: Gilmore, A. (1995) 'Quality in services marketing', unpublished PhD thesis, University of Ulster; and Gilmore, A. and Carson, D. (1996) 'Management competencies for services marketing', *Journal of Services Marketing*, 10(3): 39–57.

REFERENCES

Buller, P. (1992) 'Reconceptualising the small business consulting course: a response to the Porter and McKibbin criticisms', *Journal of Management Education*, 16(1): 56–75.

Dewey, J. (1938) *Experience and Education*. San Franciso, CA Kappa Delta Pi.

Jackson, T. (1991) *Measuring Management Performance. A Developmental Approach for Trainers and Consultants*. London: Kogan Page.

Kolb, D.A. (1984) *Experiential Learning. Experience as the Source of Learning and Development*. Englewood Cliffs, NJ: Prentice-Hall.

Kolb, D., Lublin, S., Spoth, J. and Baker, R. (1987) 'Strategic management development: using experiential learning theory to assess and develop managerial competencies', *Journal of Management Development*, 5(3): 13–24.

Levitt, T. (1976) 'The industrialisation of service', *Harvard Business Review*, 54(5): 54–63.

Lewin, K. (1951) *Field Theory in Social Sciences*. New York: Harper & Row.

Normann, R. (1991) *Service Management. Strategy and Leadership in Service Business*. Chichester: John Wiley and Sons.

Paiget, J. (1970) *Genetic Epistemology*. New York: Columbia University Press.

Smith, S.D., Pell, C., Jones, P., Sloman, M. and Blacknell, A. (1989) *Management Challenge for the 1990s: The Current Education, Training and Development Debate*. Sheffield: Sheffield Training Agency.

PART THREE

SERVICE MANAGEMENT ISSUES

9

Contemporary Issues in Services Marketing

There is a variety of contemporary issues in marketing today which pose differing dilemmas for service managers. Some issues concern service managers in any situation, others are more pertinent in particular contexts. Four important contemporary issues for services marketers are discussed and illustrated in this chapter.

First, whether developing relationship marketing approaches with customers, or transaction marketing, is most suitable is an issue pondered by many service managers. Relationship marketing has been advocated as a long-term means of doing business in many fields but this chapter discusses the dilemma this poses in practice.

Secondly, the implementation of service delivery in practice is a perpetual contemporary issue for managers because of the intangible and people-intensive nature of service delivery. So everything involved in the attention to detail required for managing customer expectations in the context of company interactions at each point of service delivery is always important for service managers. Recognizing that there are many different interactive service points in any service delivery illustrates the complexity and the many facets and activities involved in the service process.

Managing or developing sustainable services is a very important issue today, particularly in the context of preserving natural environments and ensuring that future generations will be able to enjoy these as well as the current generation. This issue is particularly relevant in the case of heritage and tourism services.

Finally, in a not-for-profit context, one of the most pressing issues today is maintaining a constant supply of funding and public support. For many non-profit organizations this entails taking a longer-term view of marketing and management activities. Such longer-term management perspectives are particularly useful in terms of changing the focus of managers, from one of preserving or maintaining traditional practices to becoming more market-oriented and reaching relevant customer groups for both general support and funding. For many non-profit organizations, such as charities, future success depends on their ability to develop alliances with profit-making companies and view the entire business in terms of how they can deliver a holistic package of benefits to all users and clients.

TRANSACTION AND RELATIONSHIP MARKETING CONCEPTS

There has been considerable debate in the literature relating to the concepts of transaction and relationship marketing and how both can be managed effectively and efficiently. However in both theory and practice it appears to be difficult to bring these two perspectives together in order to consider the conceptual and practical issues involved. Given that many service organizations aim to reach all types of customers, this issue is worthy of investigation.

Often, in the academic literature, transaction customers are treated as one customer segment and relationship-type customers are considered to be a different segment. In particular, relationship marketing theorists have separated these two approaches with claims that relationship marketing is inherently different from transaction marketing (Gummesson, 1998) and that relationship marketing represents a paradigm shift where relational approaches replace more traditional marketing activities (Gronroos, 1994).

Indeed, relationship marketing has been called a new approach to marketing management and marketing thinking (Gronroos, 1994). Others say that relationship marketing is a new term representing an old phenomenon (Gummesson, 1994; Piercy, 1997). Many believe that relationship marketing is primarily relevant in the context of an organization and its customers (Gordon et al., 1998). Others expand the domain to encompass horizontal and vertical stakeholder relationships in a collaborative effort to improve customer value (such themes originate in the work of the Industrial Management and Purchasing Group in Scandinavia). Relationship marketing has been viewed as a means of implementing efficient marketing practices such as customer retention, customer responsiveness and organization-wide cross-functional involvement. These practices are believed to result in increased profitability for the firm and increased value and satisfaction for the consumer (Peck et al., 1999).

Many consider relationship marketing to be an academic concept and believe that practitioners as a matter of course carry out relation-focused marketing. It is argued that in practice, business managers know the importance of focusing on the customer, the importance of retention and the significance of developing customer-oriented marketing offers. The underpinning themes of relationship marketing are an essential part of the marketing concept. Thus a more generic definition of relationship marketing that takes account of marketing in practice may include collaborative relationships, networks and processes involving the customer, the firm and all stakeholders (Anderson and Narus, 1991; Gummesson, 1994; Piercy, 1997).

Transaction marketing has been defined in terms of discrete transactions and repeated transactions (Webster, 1992). Discrete transactions are where both parties receive and give benefit or value, which in a commercial venture is related to some form of profit achievement. Hence, the organization's primary focus is on achieving profitability through successful exchange of a product or service. In this case, the most important service dimensions are related to product activities, distribution activities, pricing activities and achieving competitiveness by managing costs efficiently.

Most marketing transactions happen within the context of repeated transactions where the customer repeatedly buys a product or service. In repeated transactions there is a recognition of the economic, but also the non- economic motivations, preferences and patterns of behaviour of the potential exchange party, in so far as understanding these can yield additional profitability and justify higher prices (Baker et al., 1993). Hence, while the price is still important, other activities that facilitate demand stimulation such as brand loyalty, differentiation and preference (Webster, 1992) may also be significant. Therefore transaction marketing incorporates mass marketing but may also include more personalized, direct interaction between the two parties to an exchange, such as the personalized interaction that may happen between the buyer and the firm's salesperson. In moving beyond the discrete transaction, repeat purchases, brand loyalty, satisfaction with the product and repeated personal interactions mean that relationships may be established.

Example: relationship and transaction marketing in retail banking practice

Many organizations such as retail banks aim to reach both transaction-type and relationship-type customers in their service marketing delivery. However the question is how both of these segments can be reached in practice? Can one company's marketing activity integrate both transaction and relationship service marketing delivery? This is an area that needs careful consideration before attempting to reach both markets as overemphasis on one market may lead to customer alienation in the other. Indeed any imbalance in marketing activity and focus may result in overall failure.

How transaction and relationship marketing impact on each other in practice will be influenced by the way a service such as a retail bank allocates resources to all service dimensions inherent in both transaction and relationship marketing activity. So retail banks aiming to adopt both transaction and relationship marketing activity will need to ensure that these perspectives are integrated effectively. Consequently the integration of transaction and relationship marketing both conceptually and in practice is vitally important to both transaction-type and relation-type customers and to the overall service delivery.

To help develop an understanding of these concepts, transaction and relationship marketing can be illustrated in terms of a continuum of marketing activities built upon the service dimension frameworks explored in Chapter 1. Application of the service dimension continuum model to highlight the scope of customer recruitment and retention dimensions for retail banks was illustrated in Figure 3.1. Transaction marketing activity, which is more appropriate for achieving ongoing customer recruitment objectives in a competitive and dynamic environment, can be placed at one end of the continuum. Relationship marketing activity, which is aimed at retaining and penetrating the most profitable customers in a competitive and dynamic environment, can be located at the other end.

The service dimensions range from generating product profitability by meeting the needs of customers through the core product dimensions, such as product, distribution and pricing activities, to the activities that generate individual customer profitability through additional service-led activities including people, process and physical presentation activities. All of these service marketing dimensions need to be delivered in order to achieve a balanced service offering. The key marketing dimensions relevant at each point of the continuum are linked to core transaction marketing and relationship marketing activities respectively. However delivering both transaction and relationship marketing in practice is difficult as illustrated in the box below.

This is a specific area of services marketing that requires further investigation. The integration of both types of marketing to suit different groups of

Balancing transaction and relationship service dimensions

In a recent study of a typical high street bank many of the difficulties in trying to reach both transactional and relationship customers efficiently and effectively in practice were observed. Overall, managing both types of customer proved to be a difficult balancing act for the retail bank. To serve both of these markets, specific investment was needed in appropriate measures for both transaction- and relationship-type customers. The findings indicated that resource investment in marketing activities in the retail bank studied was unbalanced. This assessment was based on evidence that resources were not apportioned to marketing activities in relation to their importance to either transaction or relationship marketing customers. Indeed the study found that inadequate resources were invested in the service marketing dimensions most relevant for transaction marketing customers *and* those most relevant to relationship customers. That is, resources were not apportioned to product, distribution and pricing activities on the basis of their importance to the transaction marketing circumstances. Instead insufficient resources were allocated to these activities with the result that they were not delivered to the level required for appropriate transaction marketing. For example because many products were distributed through the labour intensive branch network, management found it difficult to effectively allocate costs to particular products, services and individual customers, which resulted in situations where some products and customers were unprofitable.

Similarly resource investment in the dimensions of key importance in relationship marketing were inadequate. Resources were not apportioned to physical facilities, process and people activities on the basis of their importance in the relationship marketing circumstances. Rather insufficient resources were allocated to these activities with the result that they were not performed to the level required for appropriate relationship marketing. For example insufficient systems meant that it was difficult to identify individually profitable customers. In many cases, the top 20 per cent of customers were not identified on the basis of their net worth but on their potential to purchase additional products.

Conversely excessive resources were invested in dimensions that were not particularly important to either relationship or transaction marketing but were predominantly back-up activities for service delivery. As illustrated in Figure 9.1 (middle section) the retail bank studied invested resources excessively on the service support and activities of moderate importance in both transaction and relationship marketing. These included activities such as mass communication, sales promotion, publicity/sponsorship and personal communication/sales. These activities were over-resourced and were receiving more emphasis than the dimensions required for both the transaction and relationship marketing activities. For example, excessive amounts of time were spent on personal communication with customers who did not have the potential to become relationship-type customers (adapted from Walsh, 2001 and Carson et al., 2003).

customers is an important aspect of marketing in this sector, particularly as it becomes more competitive. It is an area that requires further study and is

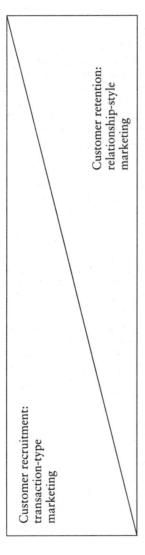

Customer recruitment:
transaction-type
marketing

Customer retention:
relationship-style
marketing

Activities receiving limited attention:

Product-related activities

Distribution-related activities

Price-related activities

Activities receiving excessive attention:

Mass communication activities

Sales promotion activities

Publicity/sponsorship activities

Personal communication/sales activities

Activities receiving limited attention:

Physical presentation activities

Process-related activities

People-related activities

FIGURE 9.1   Retail bank transaction and relationship service activity imbalance

especially relevant to services marketing and management. Understanding the precise impact that relationship marketing has on transaction marketing (and vice versa) would be very relevant for today's competitive retail services and indeed would be appropriate for many service contexts in practice. Many organizations have been myopic in the treatment of the problems and issues facing managers trying to integrate these two perspectives from a service delivery viewpoint by focusing on one or the other, but not both. More investigation of how to fully integrate transaction and relationship marketing service dimensions in practice and within diverse contexts and changing market conditions is currently an area of research interest for services marketers.

However, in pursuit of increased marketing activities, marketers need to be aware that often customers are unimpressed with their efforts to build relationships with them. Indeed the use of marketing techniques employed in developing and maintaining customer relationships, particularly in the use of direct mail and telephone can be deemed to be intrusive and unacceptable in some cases.

IMPLEMENTING SERVICE DELIVERY IN PRACTICE

In practice the implementation of service delivery is fraught with problems. To be successful it entails careful attention to every detail in the service delivery process and the careful management of competent staff. Taking account of the entire process of the customer's experience and how this experience is impacted upon by every interaction the customer has with the company requires good management.

Consumer perspectives are based on generally recognized good service expectations, that is the expectation that normal 'hygiene' factors will be present during a service delivery. For example, when a normal level or good level of service is provided customers accept it without a second thought. However when the service package does not contain what the customer has been led to expect by previous experience or by promises and advertising messages then he or she will be dissatisfied and complain. Customers notice the lack of good service, or service that falls below what they have come to expect, more than they will notice normal, satisfactory service. Also in many competitive situations customers like being treated to higher standards than they have come to expect.

Therefore the overall service package needs to be appropriate for the needs, habits, expectations and value for money of customers for the specific service situation. For example the service package at McDonald's restaurant will be different from a top-class restaurant where customers will have different expectations. Equally a businessperson taking a charter flight on holiday with their family will accept more cramped space, longer waiting times and less personal service than they would expect on business trips when they would fly business or club class.

So a good service company needs to find a way to keep its customers satisfied. It can do this by listening to and handling customers' expressed opinions without accepting at face value everything customers say and think. It is important to recognize that it may not always be appropriate or relevant to meet customers' expectations or give the customers what they want. Sometimes customers can be unreasonable or do not know what to expect in specific situations. Indeed in some service situations, customers do not know what they need or what would be best for them, for example, people receiving surgery or those caught up in an emergency service situation. Thus delivering an appropriate service package for different groups of customers and managing both the core and ancillary or secondary service is vitally important for services companies. Managing the different stages of the customer's experience from a service manager's perspective is vital.

Taking account of the complete customer's experience in terms of their pre-, during and post-service experience can help managers plan and implement all aspects of service delivery in a co-ordinated and balanced way. Thus a company's marketing offerings can be identified by careful and detailed consideration of the fully extended services product, that is, the company's total offer to the customer. This can be conceptualized by considering the pre-purchase, during purchase and post-purchase experience of customers. The fully extended service product concept is illustrated in Figure 9.2.

The purchase experience is comprised of everything that happens during the transaction or use of a service. Aspects or dimensions of the service during purchase delivery will vary according to the particular situation. However it is likely that some of these will include the availability of product, staff, information and advice, physical facilities, choice and range of products, accessibility, special promotions or offers, value for money and complaint handling. Pre-purchase experience encompasses all those aspects that lead the customer towards a decision of choosing and using the service. This may include his/her exposure to advertising and promotional activity, the quality of brochures and information and ease of booking. Post-experience involves all post-purchase motivation and company contact to which the customer may be subjected. Direct customer contact such as the use of mail-shots and customer loyalty schemes may be included at this stage.

Clearly service managers need to consider all three stages of the customers' experience in designing and operationalizing service delivery. At each stage the objective of the marketing effort and the nature of marketing will be different. It is the service manager's role to determine how these fully extended service product dimensions may be co-ordinated and integrated to make a complete whole. This requires commitment to thorough decision-making processes and careful consideration and allocation of duties for the implementation of effective service delivery.

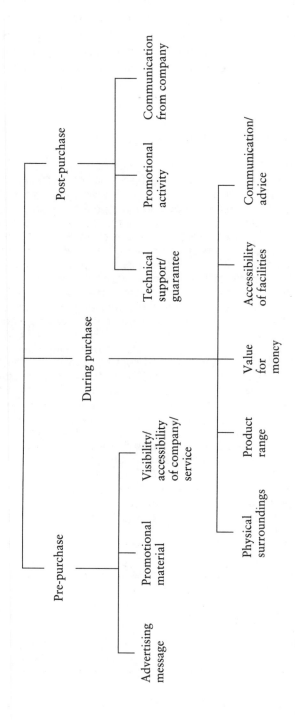

FIGURE 9.2 Fully extended service product

The design and implementation of the service delivery should reflect the strengths and weaknesses of the service company in the context of the competitive environment in which it is operating. If relevant aspects of the service package are delivered at appropriate stages of the service process this will ensure that customers receive a complete service delivery. The implementation of services needs to take account of the identification of managerial issues at each stage of the process.

The extended product of a tour operator

A tour operator's service illustrates the different aspects of the tourism product and how the whole package may be experienced by the customer even though the tour operator may only be the co-ordinator of the range of services included. A tourism package entails many different services including tour operators, airline companies and hotels for example. Given the involvement of so many people in delivering the service there are plenty of opportunities for the service to appear fragmented. Indeed, due to the many components of a tour package, it is difficult to control the quality of service. Each of the different components, such as an airline or a hotel may have quite different interpretations of service quality. One solution is to vertically integrate the whole production chain and control the quality of service as in the case of Club Med. However this limits the choice and range of tourism product available to customers and many will prefer to choose the different components of the tourism package themselves to suit their own preferences and requirements.

There are a number of factors that influence and determine service quality in the tour package industry. First is the initial contact between the customer/client and the travel company. This may entail interaction and communication with the tour operator's representative, using a travel agency or using the Internet. When all the arrangements have been made the customer will experience the holiday and many different service providers will be involved in influencing this service. Finally the customer/client's evaluation of the whole service process occurs. In order to manage this process successfully the tour operator will need to ensure that service quality is implemented through:

1   Integration of the various components of the tour package from travel agency, the airline carrier to the resort hotel(s). In doing this, the company can build upon its corporate image and enhance its supremacy over competitors.
2   Attention to the intangible dimensions of managing people – throughout the entire service planning and implementation involving top management through to contact personnel. This is difficult to achieve as many different organizations are involved and often many are large world-wide organizations so the management, co-ordination and implementation of service delivery details will be important.
3   The tour operator will need to manage, control and lobby for improved tangible elements in the service delivery process, for example, from the physical facilities and technological abilities of the travel agency, to the space/leg room available in the plane, to the facilities at the resort hotel.

To compete effectively tour operators need to place a long-term emphasis on developing the entire service experience for customers with a continual focus on implementing all service dimensions.

The customer–company perspective on service offering and delivery

Giving some consideration to the company's perspective on the operational aspect of each stage of the service delivery helps to emphasize the implementation aspects of service marketing activity and the points of interaction at each stage of the customer's experience.

Because of the importance of each stage of the customer's experience, operational managers need to take account of all marketing aspects and related activity in relation to the customer's experience of service quality. Realizing the influence of all employees, whether part-time or full-time marketers, is important in the consistent management of all customer–company interactions (Gummesson, 1991). So it is vital for service marketing managers to establish, strengthen and develop customer relations at the customer–company interface.

Service organizations need to take account of where the customer will come into contact with the company at the pre-purchase, during purchase and post-purchase stage of their experience; and the specific type of information, interaction and service delivery they will require at each stage. This can be conceptualized by building on the framework of the fully extended product experience of the customer and considering these stages in the context of a service company's operations. The key operational interaction points of contact for a service situation are shown in relation to the three stages of the customers' experience in Figure 9.3, the customer–company interactions model. These operational functions may include telephone and administrative communication at the pre- or post-purchase stage; service entrance, process and exit areas at the during purchase stage and all of the customers' pre-purchase and during purchase experience will have an impact on their post-purchase experience. These operational points of contact can be subdivided and extended according to the type of business activity in which a company operates and its company structure.

Although each operational function will have some impact on the quality of service delivery at every stage of the customer's experience, some operations would have more impact than others at different stages. For example the advertising and direct communication operational activity would be of primary importance in influencing the product choice and repeat purchase motivations; physical operations involved in the service entrance, process and exit areas would have more importance at the during purchase stage. However, all company operational activity will combine to have a direct impact on repeat purchase behaviour. Figure 9.3 illustrates the need for managers to focus their attention on the quality of all marketing activity at each stage of customers' interactions with the operationally related functions.

Example: implementation of a hotel's service delivery

Hotel management entails effective and efficient service implementation and positive people management. However there are some vital aspects of service

Fully extended service experience	Operational points of contact				
	Telephone/ administrative contact	Advertising/ promotions	Service entrance area(s)	Service process area(s)	Service exit area(s)
Pre-purchase	X	X			
During purchase		X	X	X	X
Post-purchase	X	X	X	X	X

FIGURE 9.3   Customer–company interactions model

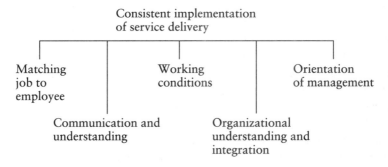

FIGURE 9.4   Managerial focus for hotel service delivery

management in this context, managing the whole package of services and products and the consistent implementation of service delivery as illustrated in Figure 9.4. These are considered below and some of the typical barriers to providing consistent and effective service implementation are illustrated.

It is often difficult to implement marketing or to make considerable improvement in marketing activity for a number of reasons. First, there is a wide range of services provided by a hotel, requiring a wide range of skills, expertise and personnel. This has implications for integrative and communicative behaviour. The implementation of consistent service activity is also impeded by the high level of staff turnover and wide use of part-time staff in the hotel industry. These issues impact upon the following practical issues that often impede good service implementation and consistent delivery. To overcome these issues constant attention to detail, well-motivated staff and efficient systems are required.

Matching job to employee

Employees are either intrinsically motivated to look for job satisfaction in itself or are extrinsically motivated by salary, benefits or other external rewards. Different things may motivate staff in different departments within a hotel. For example motivators may include: good wages, security, opportunity, good working conditions, interesting work, appreciation, loyalty to fellow employees, feeling of being 'in on things', tactful discipline, sympathetic personal help. The nature of the job and the nature of the employee will indicate the most appropriate way to manage front-line service staff. At an extreme, the choice could be between production-line management and empowerment-style management.

Communication, knowledge and understanding

Because of the strong reliance on people in all aspects of the service delivery the hospitality industry needs to provide both formal and informal means of communication with all levels of staff. Service management and staff need to be sure of the nature of their job and be clear about the duties, role and responsibilities involved. If this is not the case they will not have a full understanding of the job and so will be unable to perform it well or will lack confidence to do it well. This may occur where staff feel that they lack the authority to make meaningful decisions or to rectify situations. Therefore staff need to have some responsibility and empowerment to satisfy customers in specific circumstances when things go wrong. When service staff are not happy, they will either go elsewhere or perform their jobs badly.

Working conditions

Traditionally in the hospitality industry, pay and remuneration are poor compared to other industries. In addition, long hours of work, lack of training and no appraisal procedures can de-motivate hotel employees. Because of seasonality, busy and quiet times during each day and week, irregular patterns of work are characteristic in this industry. In response most hotels have a large contingent of part-time staff. These staff are often paid by the hour and have little commitment to the organization. Studies of hotel employees have ranked lack of wages, job security and promotional opportunity as the most frequent frustrations.

Organizational/departmental understanding and integration

Marketing orientation needs to be understood and practised by all organizational functions of the hotel industry. Communication and understanding between all functions will reduce the incidence of inter- and intra-functional conflict. Transparency and communication will also reduce resistance to change and acceptance of role responsibility.

Sometimes little or no thought is given to how each person will contribute to and fit into the culture of an establishment when recruiting, inducting and training staff. Jobs should be marketed from the staff perspective, their importance emphasized in relation to how they contribute to the overall service organization. Due care needs to be given to employing the 'right' people at the recruitment stage as this will help reduce the high turnover problem. Once employed, training at all levels should incorporate task-orientation instruction and service-orientated components to encourage and emphasize the focus on understanding, relating to and solving guest problems.

Orientation of management

A people-operated industry needs to consider how customer–staff interactions can best be carried out as well as how to make the whole service operation efficient. Operations-only oriented managers who blindly follow policies and procedures, often instituted without regard to the customer, can undermine the firm's overall marketing efforts by reducing employees' jobs to mechanical functions that offer little in the way of challenge, self esteem or personal gratification to the front-line staff. By making employees adhere rigidly to specific procedures, the manager ties their hands and restricts their ability to satisfy customers. Although it is the manager's role to develop procedures that will keep the hotel running smoothly, it must allow employees some freedom to respond to situations that arise.

Implementing service delivery successfully entails working towards having a consistent level of service delivered by relatively motivated staff and management who focus on satisfying employees and stressing their importance to the success of the establishment. To do this they should respond to their needs and reward their efforts. If this occurs employees will be more motivated towards satisfying guests. Equally employees need to understand how their job contributes to the guest's experience and if they are given the latitude to do their job precisely in the way that will most please the guest, their job performance becomes a matter of personal reward.

MANAGING SUSTAINABLE SERVICES

The issue of managing sustainable services is very important in the context of heritage sites, natural attractions and the tourism industry. The tourism industry is increasingly concerned by the realization that natural and physical attractions need to be cared for in the short and long term. This has repercussions for the difficult task of ensuring that current and future tourism marketing management encompasses sustainable tourism practices and emphasis.

Tourism by its very nature is often attracted to unique and often fragile environments and societies. In recent years there have been many examples of the achievement of economic benefits being offset by counterproductive environmental and sociocultural consequences. Thus many tourism organizations today have been encouraged to maximize the benefits whilst minimizing the costs of tourism development. This balancing act is a very difficult one to achieve in practice.

Historically it has been difficult to achieve because often the industry focus was on short-term economic benefits and continually attracting more tourists. However today there is more awareness of how previous mistakes have impacted upon the long-term social and environmental consequences of badly planned tourist expansion.

The vision for the future points to providing a good tourism service quality rather than quantity, under the auspices of sustainable tourism. However sustainable tourism requires a very careful balance of attracting visitors, managing the marketing activities and maintaining a sustainable service product. In practice sustainable tourism requires:

- public and private sector synergy,
- seasonal and geographical spread,
- ensuring the continued quality of the service product to encourage satisfaction and repeat business, and
- marketing plans and product developments that are aimed at encouraging geographical and seasonal spread.

The more detailed and specific actions needed to activate the plans for sustainable tourism are not always evident and are difficult for participants in the industry to agree upon. Indeed companies within the tourism sector often need to be informed and educated in relation to how they can all work together to achieve sustainability.

In many growing or developing areas, the importance of true sustainable tourism is hardly recognized by the industry, especially in poorer regions, where the main focus of attention is still on attracting the tourist in the first place. Until recently, many regions around the world have been untouched sites or unspoilt places. Now with modern technology and economic prosperity, many of the world's people can compress time and space and travel to remote destinations that before were inaccessible to all but a few explorers. Thus many relatively unspoilt places may be inundated with tourists in the not too distant future.

Effective management of tourism marketing is vital for achieving a successful balance between tourism development and the preservation of heritage resources. However for many tourism destinations effective management of tourism marketing remains problematic. Sustainable tourism needs to occur within the context of the development of tourism while still managing to preserve heritage resources, such as cultural and natural phenomena and attractions. Therefore this creates a substantial challenge for marketing management.

Cultural and natural attractions are often considered to be honey-pots that attract thousands of visitors because of their uniqueness. The overwhelming assumption is that tourism in the developing world is likely to continue to expand in the future. Some of this growth may be linked to increased tourist arrivals facilitated by faster mobility and competitive travel fares. This large growth could lead to erosion and other degradation on-site and overcrowding of surrounding areas and support services. While it is important to understand the potential cost of the tremendous tourism boom to the cultural and natural areas, it is also important to attract large numbers of visitors to provide economic support for the sustainability of special areas.

Cultural and natural phenomenon attractions are inextricably linked with tourism infrastructure, which can be loosely defined as the tangible and intangible facilities that support tourism activity. These infrastructures are not only a prerequisite for the development of a tourism attraction, they are also essential for its successful marketing.

Many of the cultural and natural phenomenon attractions are world heritage sites protected by the United Nations Educational, Scientific and Cultural Organization (UNESCO) (WTO, 2000). Today these sites are in great demand due to their cultural and natural uniqueness. For example, the Great Barrier Reef, the Grand Canyon, rain-forest regions and many other places.

The Giant's Causeway heritage site in Northern Ireland

The short-term effect of an increasing flow of visitors is now in evidence at this world heritage site. Increasing numbers of visitors to the Giant's Causeway and the Causeway Coast in Northern Ireland have been attracted by excellent opportunities for walking, enjoying a natural environment and seeing one of the world's unique attractions. This in turn has increased pressure on footpath routes and other on-site physical facilities (Scott and Annett, 1998). The growth of visitor numbers will have an impact on the site and therefore needs to be managed carefully if sustainable tourism is to be achieved. The area surrounding the Giant's Causeway and the Causeway Coast in the north-east of Northern Ireland, and similar areas in different regions around the world, are extremely important to local and national economies. Thus there is an increasing challenge for local management groups and both the private and public companies involved in the operation and maintenance of the site. They need to ensure that the site is available, accessible and visitor-friendly while maintaining the sustainability of the site. This entails careful management of the paths, the natural flora and fauna and how people interact with the environment.

DEVELOPING LONG-TERM RELATIONSHIPS WITH OTHER BUSINESSES

Developing long-term relationships with other businesses is important for many not-for-profit companies. In particular charities are increasingly becoming aware of the advantages of building alliances with commercial businesses. The service dimensions and delivery a charitable organization needs to achieve to build meaningful long-term relationships with the commercial sector or business customers are considered here. Charities' service marketing delivery to the commercial business in terms of their respective attitudes to corporate donations is central to effective and efficient management in this context.

The key dimensions that can be tailored by charities to help them build alliances with commercial firms are management communication relationships, perceived value of company's image and levels of social responsibility enhancing service accessibility through professionalism.

Communication relationships

Communication relationships, with an emphasis on the proactive development of close ties, may be the key to success for charities and their donor customers. The need to develop ongoing, meaningful relationships with corporate organizations lies at the heart of successful marketing for charities. Larger charities in particular are becoming increasingly aware of the benefits of relationship fundraising and cause-related marketing. In recent years, there is a growing perception that close association with a charity or charities is more effective than advertising for improving the image of a company, both with employees and the general public. Undoubtedly commercial organizations are increasingly aware of the added value of being linked with charities.

Perceived value of company image and social responsibility

Given the argument in the previous section, charities in their marketing communications to commercial organizations need to be aware that commercial organizations' primary reason for donating to charities may be to enhance their company image they may need to develop marketing strategies with this in mind. Charities should explicitly recognize that their relationship with commercial organizations is a partnership of equals, where both parties stand to gain, with the proviso that there may be a difference of emphasis in terms of their agendas (that charities need to be aware of more than commercial organizations). The natural emphasis for charities is of course social responsibility; however, commercial organizations will want to achieve social responsibility objectives associated with an enhanced company image. Thus company image is of primary importance and social responsibility is implicitly, if not explicitly, of secondary importance to commercial organizations.

Commercial organizations are becoming more aware of the perceived value of social responsibility issues and how they impact upon their relationship with their customers, employees within their organization, and society at large. They are keen to use this to enhance their company image. In this context social responsibility has an impact on the commercial organization internally as well as externally, and organizations are often judged by

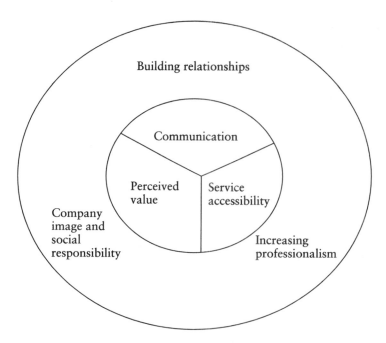

FIGURE 9.5   Developing long-term relationships between charities and businesses

the way they care for the people around them, both inside and outside the organization.

Enhancing service accessibility through professionalism

It is generally recognized that there is an increasing professionalism on the part of charities in terms of their approaches to commercial organizations, reflected in the fact that most charities now employ someone who actively seeks donations. A greater professionalism can help charitable organizations make their service more tangible and enhance their service accessibility. It will be particularly welcome if combined with a demonstration on the part of the charity that it can understand the requirements of the commercial organization. Commercial organizations appreciate professionalism.

Charities increasingly approach organizations' marketing budget rather than their 'charity budget'. This is symptomatic of charities recognizing the value, in marketing terms, to commercial organizations of supporting them. It also points to a potential conflict that may exist in charities marketing: although greater professionalism is approved by commercial organizations, too much professionalism on the part of charities can be problematic (Burnett, 1992). Burnett argues that certain marketing approaches, such as direct mail, for example, are considered to be inappropriate and inadvisable for charities, largely because there is a lack of targeting and no personal contact, and this approach is too easily dismissed by commercial organizations. Also, there may be a conflict between the use of expensive promotional material and a charity's credibility. Clearly, a more personal approach aimed at building relationships is a preferred and more professional approach.

To conclude, charities, by being more committed to developing meaningful relationships with commercial organizations, that is, more versed in the benefits of communication relationships, and more professional in how they approach commercial organizations, are likely to have much stronger appeal. This is illustrated in Figure 9.5., which also highlights the importance of an appropriate focal emphasis on the key benefit to commercial organizations – company image. But, most importantly, it also highlights the need to correctly 'balance' this emphasis with the benefits accruing from social responsibility. It might be speculated that charities could perceive their 'product' as 'enhancing company image' and market the 'benefits' of such a product to enable a commercial organization to be socially responsible. The charity that can get this balance correct is indeed performing enhanced and efficient service quality management.

SUMMARY

This chapter discussed four contemporary issues for service managers today. First, the discussion illustrated the relatively diverse concepts underpinning transaction and relationship marketing. To effectively integrate transaction and relationship marketing activity resource investment should be allocated on the basis of the importance of the activity in the transaction and relationship marketing circumstances. This requires adequate resource investment in the activities of specific importance in transaction marketing and of specific importance in relationship marketing, with less focus on activities that are not important to either. In practice it is difficult for services companies such as retail banks to balance both transaction and relationship marketing activities, as illustrated in the boxed example. Indeed many companies may not fully recognize the situations where discrepancies can exist when trying to deliver both transactional and relationship marketing in practice.

The second contemporary issue focused on the implementation of service activity and illustrated these issues in the context of a tour operator service and a hotel service. The discussion recognized the high reliance on people and the implications this has for the implementation of service delivery. The implementation of service activity inherently involves repetitive and physically tiring aspects of service performance at the front-line for the majority of service delivery staff. Therefore managers often need to balance the management style between a directive and a participative one to take account of the need to deliver a consistent service and also to aim to motivate staff at all times.

Then the chapter discussed the contemporary issue impacting upon marketing and management in the complex area of tourism services. It outlined the ever-growing problem of how to manage sustainable tourism for the long-term survival of key natural attractions and heritage areas while still encouraging tourists to visit them.

Finally, developing and maintaining support and donations in the long term is a particularly important challenge for the managers of charities. The example of working with one donor market, the commercial sector, was used to highlight the specific managerial challenges of developing appropriate service dimensions to build useful and sustainable relationships with relevant commercial organizations.

DISCUSSION QUESTIONS

What is the difference between transaction- and relationship-type customers? Why are these differences important to a service manager?

How can the overall hotel service delivery be implemented effectively?

How can service staff be encouraged and motivated in delivering excellent service to customers?

What is meant by a sustainable service? How can it be managed along with mass marketing demands?

What are the managerial implications for trying to build long-term relationships with commercial organizations?

NOTE

Parts of the section on 'transaction and relationship marketing concepts' are based an the following article: Carson, D., Gilmore, A. and Walsh, S. (2003) 'Integrating transaction and relationship marketing activity in retail banking', under review for the *Journal of Marketing Management*.

REFERENCES

Anderson, E.W. and Narus, J.A. (1991) 'Partnering as a focused market strategy', *California Management Review*, 33, Spring: 95–113.

Baker, M.J., Brown, A.J., Brownlee, D. and Crozier, K. (1993) *Marketing. Theory and Practice*, 2nd edn. London: Macmillan Press.

Burnett, K. (1992) *Relationship fundraising*. London: White Lion Press Ltd.

Gordon, M.E., McKeage, K. and Fox, M.A. (1998) 'Relationship marketing effectiveness: the role of involvement', *Psychology and Marketing*, 15(5), August: 443–59.

Gronroos, C. (1994) 'From marketing mix to relationship marketing: towards a paradigm shift in marketing', *Asia-Australia Marketing Journal*, 2(1): 9–29.

Gummesson, E. (1991) 'Marketing-orientation revisited: the crucial role of the part-time marketer', *European Journal of Marketing*, 25(2): 60–75.

Gummesson, E. (1994) 'Making relationship marketing operational', *International Journal of Service Industry Management*, 5(5): 5–20.

Gummesson, E. (1998) 'Implementation requires a relationship marketing paradigm', *Academy of Marketing Science*, 26(3): Summer: 242–9.

Peck, H., Payne, A., Christopher, M. and Clark, M. (1999) *Relationship Marketing: Strategy and Implementation*. London: Butterworth-Heinemann.

Piercy, N. (1997) *Market Led Strategic Change*, 2nd edn. London: Chartered Institute of Marketing, Butterworth-Heinemann.

Scott, P. and Annett, J. (1998) 'Strategic framework for the Causeway coast'. Belfast: Northern Ireland Tourist Board.

Walsh, S. (2001) 'The adoption and integration of transaction and relationship marketing activity, marketing management decision making/implementation and marketing management competencies in a retail bank circumstance', unpublished DPhil thesis, Faculty of Business and Management, University of Ulster.

Webster, F. (1992) 'The changing role of marketing in the corporation', *Journal of Marketing*, 56, October: 1–17.

WTO (2000) *Sustainable Development of Tourism: A Compilation of Good Practices*. Madrid: World Tourism Organization.

Additional useful reference lists in Chapters 3 and 4.

10

Services Marketing Management – What does the Future Hold?

The final chapter builds on the core concepts covered throughout the book and tries to speculate on what the future holds for services marketing. Speculation and looking to the future is always a risky or 'dangerous' activity so most of the discussion here is based on how current phenomena seem to be shaping up.

SOME SPECULATIONS ON THE FUTURE OF SERVICES MARKETING

Like all dynamic concepts, services marketing is continuously evolving and changing. Although the fundamental concepts are well established, there is progression in both the existing domain and in new developmental areas. Throughout the past decade there has been considerable development in particular areas of services marketing. One area is the increasing sophistication of services in specific contexts, for example in areas such as financial services and not-for-profit circumstances. Another is the way in which services are delivered, particularly in terms of how customers interact with companies. This has implications for how staff are managed and the skills and competencies they require.

Currently, there is debate about the impact of technology in services marketing, for example the Internet. The Internet-driven information revolution is widely seen to be transforming the way both businesses and consumers operate (Docherty et al., 1999). This is particularly relevant in service contexts, such as financial and travel services where transactions do not require interpersonal interaction. In such cases the Internet becomes a new distribution channel. However in other contexts the Internet is widely used as an information source or a promotional tool. For example, the impact of the information revolution will potentially be great for professional services where a significant component of the service product is information and expertise, despite the fact that such services have been, characterized by high levels of interpersonal interaction. For these services the Internet may be used primarily as an information source. However it is used by companies, the Internet will have the potential to fundamentally change the way in which consumers interact with service providers.

Combining hi-tech with high-touch in service delivery

Traditionally high-touch has meant that human interaction forms a large and important part of a total service where the service includes specific, customized or individually provided elements. This was true in the delivery of many financial service products. More recently, elements of hi-touch have been applied to mass-customized services where they are produced with the aid of technology and also include some elements of individual touch.

Today many service industries are using technology to create more synergy for service providers and their stakeholders and customers. This involves a move from low-tech to high-tech operations in many services and is clearly evident in services such as banking and travel. Many service providers have developed their customer database systems to allow them to communicate with customers in a more sophisticated manner and have built 'an electronic service bridge towards new market segments' (Gordon and Fisk, 1987).

Indeed many researchers advocate that services should move away from the low-tech tradition to become more inclusive of high-tech and high-touch dimensions. The increase in sophistication in technological developments, especially the worldwide web and wide use of personal e-mail has created a vehicle for this to happen more rapidly.

For services managers to develop their offerings in this way, they first need to understand the service well enough to know which elements lend themselves to high-tech and to understand the market well enough to know which service elements require personal touch. Then some consideration should be given to identifying and implementing the best mix of both technology and individual touch. This can create a strategic opportunity for many service providers in a competitive environment.

In services, high-tech can be applied at the production and/or the delivery stage. Because of the inseparability of service production and consumption these two stages are often interwoven. However to move from low-tech to high-tech requires some careful planning and integration of the entire service process from both the deliverer and consumer point of view. In particular, service production needs to be largely automated before service providers can take advantage of electronic channels, as it is futile to deliver services through electronic channels if they have to be handled manually at the other end (Lehtinen and Jarvinen, 1996).

Information technology has changed the daily operations in many service operations, especially in the financial sector, where it has been used to enable managers to plan, execute, and evaluate results with greater precision and speed, and therefore improve effectiveness in co-ordinating, measuring and controlling service processes.

However the use of technological advancements in service delivery needs to be promoted to and made simple for customers. They need to be ready to accept the different mode of service delivery. For example, automated teller machines (ATMs) were among the first visible vehicles of service technology to reach the marketplace, but in the beginning they were perceived almost as punishments by customers. Customers need time to adjust to a new service delivery mechanism and often need to be 'trained' to use new automated services and so experience the advantages offered by that mode of delivery. Today banks are moving towards home and virtual reality banking with new activities, like financial assistant services. Similarly, many customers are becoming confident and increasingly proactive about carrying out personal transactions such as financial and travel business either by telephone or using the Internet.

Services organizations can benefit from the use of technology in many ways. First, they can overcome the problem of standardization and consistency of service delivery and so make service operations more profitable and efficient. To achieve this the back office functions need to be streamlined and reorganized to provide an efficient and effective support to the automated function. However, it has also been argued that technology brings disadvantages, where machines replace human faces, and may also reduce the perceived service quality in the eyes of customers. Today some services offer technological alternatives in the guise of combinations of picture, voice and text. Electronic channels through the use of the Internet and worldwide web serve this trend in an innovative and currently acceptable way. All channel members, stakeholders and customers can use these channels. So the commercial revolution in accordance with the Internet could be applied to all kinds of electronic channels.

The use of internet services

To date, studies have indicated that Internet banking is more acceptable to customers with prior computer experience, personal banking experience and a computer-friendly attitude. Also consumer characteristics such as gender, age and occupation and income level have been linked to the nature of the typical Internet banking user. For example, some studies have indicated that the typical user is relatively young, well-educated, family-oriented and has a good job (Daniel, 1999; Jarverpaa and Todd, 1997; Jayawardhena and Foley, 2000). However over time, with growing familiarity and increased availability and use of the Internet combined with further developments in improving security, Internet banking will undoubtedly become more widely acceptable to other customer segments.

Balance of power between professional service providers and service users

Dominance and power in the service encounter has conventionally been based on the existence of an imbalance in knowledge and expertise between the professional and service user. The Internet and its potential for providing information, and scope for interaction between consumers, can provide virtual discussion forums and facilitate on-line consumer 'communities', and which could redress any informational imbalances and empower consumers to challenge the established legitimacy of service professionals (for example, doctors' advice).

There is also some speculation about the implications of the constant provision of more information about existing customers and the existence and provision of new sources of information to help identify new customers. Indeed, many experts (Brown et al., 1996) consider that services are moving from 'people processing' to 'information processing'. This, of course, will have an impact on how services are delivered in the future. In particular, the level of service required and changing customer expectations will have an impact on service design and delivery. For example, a trade-off between the convenience of automated (contactless) services and the psychological need for face-to-face contact is inevitable. Careful managerial consideration will be required to ensure that some balance is achieved. Customers' familiarity and 'comfort level' with the technology used to deliver services and the cost of the service – especially the non-monetary costs in terms of customers' time and effort – may become a serious consideration.

In turn, this will have implications for market segmentation in some service industries. For example, segmentation of customers for Internet/ technical communication can be based on:

- customers who want service delivery face-to-face
- customers who want service delivery without face-to-face contact

- customers who only want service at very specific times, and
- customers who want service delivery with added dimensions such as some refinement of standard service, advice, information, or special needs adjustments.

For example, professional services such as health care services have developed many applications to service the needs of patients. Some illustrations are given here.

1 Use of web sites to build and maintain relationships with patients and their families. Also used to provide in-depth and illness-specific content through the Internet. (For example, a large clinic recently launched a programme to provide specialist consultations and second opinions using the Internet for patients with life-threatening conditions and life-altering diagnoses (Carpenter, 2002).)

2 Video-conferencing is being used to conduct staff meetings on-line and this saves time and travel expenses (Mitchell, 2001).

3 Use of technology for administrative purposes can shorten the time involved in updating patient's records and provide more time for patient contact.

4 The Internet can deliver information about health and illness in electronic form in patient's homes. This can help improve services for people in remote areas. It can provide interactive communication and consist of video, sound, text and graphics. In addition to providing general information, lifestyle advice will be personalised and linked to the individual patient's records. This service can include an e-mail and newsgroup facility so the patients can communicate with each other (Wallace, 1997).

The question is – in practice, is marketing services to different customers as simple as this? Clearly, a challenge for managers will be to identify the typology of those customers who are willing to use more remote technological channels and assess how sales and product adoption can be increased through these new channels. Can improved technology be used to resolve the service quality gaps, such as the degree of reliability and heterogeneity of service, that often occur in the prevailing pressurized environments of today? If this is the case, will this allow service staff to focus more on building trust and empathy with important customers?

The increasing investment in technology in the service delivery process, from the introduction of ATMs to on-line medical consultations, has allowed technology to revolutionize many areas of the service sector. Replacement of service staff with technology not only offers a means of addressing variability in the service delivery process but also facilitates cost reduction by increasing the self-service component of the service delivery process. On the other hand, by removing the personal interaction and the basic social building block of service relationships, such developments may be viewed as undermining the development of closer customer–supplier relationships. Service companies will need to give some consideration to the service quality dimensions required for different delivery channels.

Will these far-reaching changes in technology and management perspectives lead to new definitions of service marketing? There may be a wide variety of new kinds of services, given the opportunities and developments in technology and customer sophistication. A more fundamental debate might focus on what impact this will have on the characteristics of services. Will these change? Or will the importance of these characteristics change? And will this have an impact on how services should or could be managed?

People management

The management of the traditional 'people processing' in services, that is, the operational aspects, also has the potential to change. For example increasingly sophisticated technology can be used as an empowering tool during service *recovery* and for inter-company co-operation, as in the effective adoption and use of hi-tech services such as electronic cash.

The trend towards relationship marketing approaches accompanied by the general movement away from functional marketing departments will also have an impact on the future of services marketing. Although the marketing departments in service organizations carry out useful activities, they cannot carry out all activities that will have an impact on customers (Gronroos, 1989; Gummesson, 1991). In many large services organizations the marketing department does not have the authority to link and co-ordinate all interactive activity between the company and the customer. Indeed any functional department may have a positive or an adverse effect on effective customer interaction. So effective and co-ordinated marketing depends upon good communication and co-operation between and within different functions. This leads to the importance of recognizing that many employees outside of the marketing departments are part-time marketers even though they may not be aware of it. They contribute to the activities of the marketing function and should be recognized and managed accordingly. To improve the effectiveness of service delivery, managers and staff in service organizations should be encouraged to develop and improve their competencies in proactive networking and communication. This should by encouraged by service managers.

There is little doubt that service marketing, both conceptually and in practice, has reached a degree of sophistication. However significant change is in the air: functional and relationship ethos, face-to-face choices have to be made between electronic interactions and interaction. The influx of new service concepts, for example, means that service marketing's parameters and frameworks may have to be rethought. What can provide the 'anchor' in this sea of turbulence?

In this 'knowledge' society it may be that the recognition and development of services management competencies is the constant. Managers' knowledge and experience of a particular industry and company circumstances provide a useful and important platform from which to build and develop their competencies for specific roles. Competence in these two attributes, 'knowledge' and 'experience' will provide a starting point for a manager in a specific marketing decision-making situation to develop effectiveness in his/her managerial performance. Service-specific competencies need to be identified in the context of any new tasks, roles and issues of particular concern to services marketing managers. Although the typical decision-making areas for services managers revolve around managing the marketing activity, taking account of the particular characteristics of services' additional role will involve creating and adapting new ways of designing, developing and delivering services. For example, new service development, service differentiation, managing the demand for services, using different channels and communicating with existing and potential customers will be important activities in reaching the marketplace. Managerial activities such as integrating service activities and managing people, and encouraging improvement in services development and delivery are important tasks within the organization. Constantly trying to develop 'experiential knowledge' in the specific aspects of services will lead to distinctive managerial expertise and encourage an organizational ethos of experiential learning.

SUMMARY

Whatever the implications, the future of service marketing development and improvement will depend on the management of all activity by continuously focusing on the quality of management decision making and attention to detail in all service implementation activities. This will entail keeping abreast of new technological developments, continuously assessing how these may help improve service delivery, and monitoring customer needs. The development of managerial abilities and competencies to match these managers' challenges is vital. Service managers need competencies to give them the ability to harness the benefits of advancing technologies to ensure competitive service quality. Equally service managers need to be effective and proactive communicators with both employees and customers, in relation to all aspects of the business.

REFERENCES

Brown, S., Parasuraman, A., Gronroos, C., Bitner, M.J. and Fisk, R. (1996) discussion at the special session sponsored by the Services Marketing Special Interest Group, AMA Summer Marketing Educators Conference, San Diego, August.

Carpenter, D. (2002) 'Treatment on the Net', *Hospitals and Health Networks*, 76(2): 26–8.

Daniel, E. (1999) 'Provision of electronic banking in the UK and the Republic of Ireland', *International Journal of Bank Marketing*, 17(2): 72–82.

Docherty, N.F., Ellis-Chadwick, F. and Hart, C. (1999) 'Cyber retailing in the UK: the potential of the Internet as a retail channel', *International Journal of Retail and Distribution Management*, 27(1): 22–36.

Gordon, A.S. and Fisk, R.P. (1987) 'Electronic service delivery: design issues', in C.F. Surprenant, *Add Value to Your Service*, Chicago: AMA, pp. 137–41.

Gronroos, C. (1989) 'Defining marketing: a market-oriented approach', *European Journal of Marketing*, 23(1): 52–60.

Gummesson, E. (1991) 'Marketing-orientation revisited: the crucial role of the part-time marketer', *European Journal of Marketing*, 25(2): 60–75.

Jarvenpaa, S.L. and Todd, P.A. (1997) 'Consumer reactions to electronic shopping on the World Wide Web', *International Journal of Electronic Commerce*, 1(2): 59–88.

Jayawardhena, C. and Foley, P. (2000) 'Changes in the banking sector – the case of Internet banking in the UK', *Internet Research: Electronic Networking Application and Policy*, 10(1): 19–30.

Lehtinen, U. and Jarvinen, R. (1996) 'Electronizing distribution channels. The change process of industrialisation, electronizing channels and renewing organisations in service sector', in A. Ropo, P. Eriksson and J. Hunt, *Global Perspectives on Processual Research in Management and Organisation*. Tampere: University of Tampere, Series C6, pp. 95–115.

Mitchell, R.L. (2001) 'Better care – lower cost', *Computerworld*, 35(31): 48–9.

Wallace, S. (1997) 'Health information in the new millennium and beyond: the role of computers and the Internet', *Health Education*, 97(3): 88–95.

ADDITIONAL USEFUL REFERENCES

Laing, A., Lewis, B., Foxall, G. and Hogg, G. (2002) 'Predicting a diverse future: directions and issues in the marketing of services', *European Journal of Marketing*, 36(4): 479–94.

Mathe, H. and Dagi, T.F. (1996) 'Harnessing technology in global service businesses', *Long Range Planning*, 29(4): 449–61.

Author Index

Subject Index